The Gift
of Past Lives

The Gift of Past Lives with Mother, Isabella, God & Elizabeth
Copyright © 2019 by migebooks/MIGE-LLC. All Rights Reserved.

For information about this title or to order other books
and/or electronic media, contact the publisher:
Website: thegiftofpastlives.com

ISBN: 978-1-7343378-0-8 (print)
978-1-7343378-1-5 (eBook)

Printed in the United States of America

Author photos courtesy of Pahl Photography
Ring design by Jodi Bear
Sketches by Janealla Smalley Killebrew
Book configuration by 1106 Design

David Bettenhausen and Carla Bogni-Kidd

The Gift
of Past Lives

with
Mother,
Isabella,
God &
Elizabeth

DAVID BETTENHAUSEN
& CARLA BOGNI-KIDD

Dedications

First … to **Paula** still on Earth
Our constant, loyal, reliable witness,
who gave up so much, to support us.
We love you.

Second … to **TK** still on Earth
Our father, son, brother, husband, owner,
king and murderer and most importantly, friend.
You spent a lot of time watching television in our absence.
You are always in our hearts.

Third but always first …
God
You are a loving God, not *conceited, selfish or jealous and always, forgiving.*

Isabella
Six thousand years is not long enough. What a gift, that I am
never alone. Thank you for teaching me what true love is.

Elizabeth
I am teachable but perhaps a slow learner. I hope you succeeded this time!
Hopefully, I'm in the coffee club soon. Save
me a seat next to you, always!

Mother
I honor you with all your imperfections, although invisible to me.
Your laughter is a joy, your consistency remarkable, and I thank you
for being visible when I needed you most.

Thank you to Carolyn Flynn, Editor and KN Literary Agency
and Maureen Michelson, NewSage Press for getting us started.

PART I: **I**nitiation: The admitting of someone into an obscure group, typically with a ritual.

PART II: **I**ntroduction: The formal presentation of one person to another.

PART III: **I**nscribe: To fix or impress deeply or lastingly in the mind, memory, etc.

PART IV: **A**tonement: The reconciliation of God and Humankind.

PART V: **M**etamorphosis: When a person develops and changes into something different.

I AM

Table of Contents

Part I

I

Initiation

We are never alone.
Isabella

Chapter 1

The Revelation

It all started with a simple question.
Would you like to try meditation?

I could see we were in trouble. With each day, Dave became more and more depressed. This cheerful man who was my boss, a doctor heading up a medical office in Ohio, was gloomy. His spirit seemed to have vanished. His Fred Flintstone-like laugh was heard no more in the office, where I was the manager. I suspected the culprit could have been electronic medical records, which we'd implemented three years before. I could see the tedium was taking a toll on Mr. Simplicity. Some days, he was uncharacteristically irritable.

In the twenty years since we'd met, Dave had become like a brother to me. Dave and I had met in the winter of 1998 when Dave purchased the practice from my husband. I was employed there, and stayed on. Both of us were married. A friendship grew from there and by the time our story opens in 2014, we had become family. It is a strong bond that does not involve romance. I never thought that was possible between a man and a woman, but it is in this situation. I have Dave's back and he has mine. He is a rare friend who would help me at two in the morning, if necessary, and I would extend the same courtesy. Dave is a kind, forgiving man. He doesn't require much out of life, other than the need to help people, make people laugh and, of course, golf. He doesn't need sports cars; he doesn't spend money frivolously on himself, nor does he whine about what he does not have. He is content with simplicity. However, he has spent many an hour analyzing life and any decision that he is about to make. I guess it's not a bad thing, though, and that really is about as complicated as he gets.

Before this all started to happen, Dave had done what society expected from him. He went to college, married, visited his parents, went to church and reported to an occupation every day. He had been completing all the daily routines prescribed to him. As a physician, his vocation had satisfied the need to help others and allowed him to interact with people daily, providing him an outlet for laughter and storytelling.

But by May 2014, I saw Dave had become a shell of himself, going through the motions. I did not realize at the time, but he was extremely unhappy at home with his wife.

Many days, Dave and I had conversation after conversation about his demeanor. I offered to call a counselor to help him bounce back. I am known to read self-help books. I am the kind of person who wants to learn new ways to make a better version of myself whenever possible. I'd certainly bought a lot of meditation books, but many of them had sat on my shelves and not been opened for years.

A long time ago, I had meditated religiously. But I had been raised a God-fearing Catholic, much as Dave had been. My Catholic upbringing roared back up, and I got warning message after warning message that meditation opens you up to bad spirits, or demons and such. Soon after, I halted meditation.

Years went by without meditation. One day I read an article about meditation in a very unlikely publication. It caught my eye because I found it strange that this particular magazine would publish such an open-minded article. The article mentioned the benefits of regular meditation including but not limited to:

- Finding peace and contentment in daily life

- Defeating depression

- Accepting people in general with all their faults and quirks

- Improving health

- Succeeding in any endeavor

I laid the magazine on the bench in my morning library, thinking I would ponder the idea of meditating again. Meanwhile, Dave became more like a zombie than ever.

One morning, as I tried to have a conversation with him, this man who had been my longtime friend was too preoccupied to listen. It really bothered me that I could no longer have a simple discussion on any subject. Then, I remembered the article about meditation. I asked him if he was willing and suggested that we meditate each morning as an office, to help us kick-start the office routine and hopefully ease our stresses and irritations. I also asked him, again, if he wanted me to contact a counselor. He declined the counselor but said that he was willing to try just about anything else if it would help him sleep, get through the day, and stay focused and happy.

The first day of meditation included all the employees: Brenda, Paula, Dave and myself. We relaxed, played calming music, lit a candle and had peace and quiet for about twenty minutes. After trying it, we all had the same complaint: It was very hard to shut down our thoughts and just relax.

That lasted only two days. The second day, we all saw colors floating around and each commented on the different colors we had seen. One of us saw purple, one saw white, one saw many colors and another saw yellow and white.

We had to begin meditating at least half an hour before patients arrived, and the other employees were not willing to come in a half an hour earlier every day. That was understandable. So, the third day of meditation included Dave and me only. The session probably lasted about thirty minutes. When we finished, we mentioned how hard it was to quiet our minds. We also discussed how we both saw balls of light again, in different colors. We guessed this was typical, because all four of us had experienced it that week.

It is amazing how your body responds to peace and quiet. I remember discussing how relaxed we were and how we no longer felt our limbs and were able to block out everything including when the others entered the office, phones ringing, doors closing and so forth.

So, it became the ritual and upon completion of meditation, we would start the day normally, which involved us going into our adjoining offices to begin tasks.

Spending any amount of time with Dave would convince you that he is legitimately real and not the type to have a breakdown. He is a kind individual and rare breed of physician who really cares for his patients and humankind. He is extremely intelligent and open-minded.

I must interject before I go further. Through the years, I have learned all about Dave's life stories, including childhood, divorce, remarriage, death of a parent as well as other relatives and all of the typical ups and downs of raising a family and traveling through on our paths. My husband and I stood up for him and his second wife at their wedding. I truly believe that I know and understand Dave as well as anyone could.

So, having said that, I want you to know I would never disbelieve him. On the third day of meditation, Dave came up behind me and spoke almost a whisper. "I know you will find this strange, but I think I just saw your mother and was talking to her," he said.

All those years of being a God-fearing Catholic did not mean I hadn't kept exploring. I had never believed that religion had completely explained everything. I had spent years questioning it and reading and researching the truth and non-truth about religion. I am very open-minded. I was raised Catholic-Mormon. Then, as a married adult, I attended the Methodist church. None of these three religions had satisfied my quest for knowledge. I certainly did not believe their suggestions that we must all "just believe." My theory has always been that if God did not want me to think, I would not have the ability to question.

So, I wasn't surprised that my mother, who had passed away before I ever met Dave, had appeared. My real question was why she had come through to Dave and not me.

"It's hard to explain," he said. "She looked like you from a side view. She had the same eyelashes."

That caught my attention because Mother and I had once conversed about our likeness in lashes and how without mascara they were barely visible.

"She was jolly," Dave said. "She showed me a shoe."

"A shoe?" I said.

"Like a high-heeled sandal."

Dave confessed that the only two things he really knew about my mother was that she was a ballroom dancer and that she died from a brain tumor. He also said that he saw a purple cloud in her head. He did not know the significance of the purple cloud at that point but would later understand it.

Turning to the computer, I googled an image search on "ballroom shoes." I remembered exactly the type of shoes Mother wore her entire life until she was too old to be comfortable in them. As the array of shoes popped up, Dave picked the exact type shoe my mother always wore. The image search called up fifty or more shoe types to choose from. This was not just a good guess.

Later, Dave looked at a picture that my sister Paula had of Mother in her wallet, to confirm his suspicions. Paula is also Dave's assistant at the office. The picture was taken of my mother when she was younger. It was taken just after her remarriage, which would have made her in her late forties. His eyes welled up with tears. He shook his head up and down. He confirmed that this was the woman he spoke with during meditation.

"Why are you crying?" I asked.

"A feeling came over me, a confirmation," he said. "It felt … religious, overwhelming and spiritual."

My questions didn't stop all day. I wanted answers. I needed to meditate again and again and talk to my mother. I asked Dave all day long, jokingly, if he was on crack. Dave had a hard time focusing. He kept asking himself out loud as well as to all of us, "Am I crazy?" We all knew him enough to know that he was not crazy or on drugs and that his experience had to be a reality.

All Dave and I wanted to do was meditate and get back to my mother. If she was there on the other side to talk with, whom else could we talk to?

Then Isabella showed up. In the next day of meditation, Dave was introduced to his spirit guide, Isabella. She consistently appeared daily and continues to appear to him to this date, seemingly at his beck and call. She scolds him when necessary, advises him constantly like a best friend and appears immediately when he needs her. I love this being, yet I have never met her in this lifetime. She is dependable, which is a rarity. She is funny, nurturing, practical and all-loving.

"Dave, you have many guides, but I will be with you forever," she told him. "I've been with you since your original birth, six thousand years ago."

Isabella is always there for Dave. So is my mother. If my mother seems like she's not apparent, we ask for her, and she comes. I could only marvel at the thought of having someone with you all day, every day, who understands everything about you, loves you completely, judges you not and is simply with you to guide your life.

To create a visual that was easy for us to understand, I asked Dave to describe exactly what he saw in meditation. He drew pictures, and we started to keep a journal of what he was seeing and feeling. Besides the "seeing part" of the experience at that point, Dave was feeling what Isabella and Mother were telling him, not hearing it. "It is hard to explain, but I don't hear them like we do when someone speaks to us out loud," he said.

If I turn to the encyclopedia to try to find the most appropriate definition of what Dave's ability is called, I cannot find one. He is not channeling, not prophesizing the future but, rather, speaking with his spirit guide and angels. He has the ability to speak with passed-over souls but is discouraged in doing so. Isabella refers to Dave as a mystic.

A mystic is someone who "claims to attain, or believes in the possibility of attaining, insight into mysteries transcending ordinary human knowledge, as by direct communication with the divine or immediate intuition in a state of spiritual ecstasy; a person initiated into religious mysteries."

The first few times that we meditated after that, Dave saw symbols and eyes and strange views of cities and buildings. He saw religious signs like crosses and chalices. Each time that we meditated, the pictures were becoming more vivid and as explained by Dave, the images were in 3D. It was as if he could travel around the pictures and see through them. One day my mother and Isabella started to show him pictures and experiences that he apparently had gone through in his past lives.

And that has been our most startling revelation: Yes, there are past lives. The experiences you are about to read about have most definitely confirmed this for us. We all have many lives and are many different types of people before we reach our final destination. More about that, as our story unfolds.

One morning we asked my mother, through meditation, why she was coming to Dave.

He was under the impression that on the days he meditated with me versus the days he meditated at home, the experience was much stronger, more vivid and detailed. He felt that meditation at home was simply relaxation and a peaceful, warm experience. We were trying to figure out the connection or if there was one, or if it was just coincidence that more was happening during our office meditations, including the two of us.

One day Dave experienced going through pools of blood, feeling tightness, then darkness. My mother had led him through a miscarriage that she had before she gave birth to her daughters. She explained to him that she had had, actually, two miscarriages. Dave had been both of them.

That was our connection. Finally, we knew. Dave and I really were brother and sister.

My mother had always wanted a son. After the miscarriages, she successfully gave birth to six daughters, one of whom died before I was born.

Dave was shown this experience yet again on another day, but this time he was made to feel by our mother and Isabella that the different miscarriages were by his present birth mother. His birth mother, who just recently passed, miscarried two times before finally, successfully delivering Dave. I was, indeed her miscarriages. Now we had another connection.

We were blown away by these experiences. These events were making us question everything we knew and had ever known in this existence.

Something wonderful started to happen with Dave and all of us in the office. The other two office employees were meditating at home, and Dave and I continued each day and sometimes even at night while at home. Our old Dave was returning to us. The laughter and happy demeanor were resurfacing. He was going through the same daily rigor but his chi—his energy life force—was undisturbed.

The drudgery was dissipating for all of us, and the daily routine was more than bearable. The article had been accurate. Meditation did produce wonderful effects on everyone. I couldn't wait to get to the office each day, and neither could Dave. It was the first time I had that feeling in many years. I was on my thirty-fifth year of working in the office. Little at that point was new, interesting or enjoyable.

Each evening, I went home and shared all the details with my husband, Tom, a free thinker who was eager to hear about the unfolding saga. A few weeks into meditation, I asked Dave what his wife thought of his gift.

"I haven't told her," he said.

"Why?"

"I'm not sure, but I feel the need to keep it from her," he said. "She would never understand it. She would think I had gone over the edge."

He further said that something inside told him not to give her the details. He had attempted to discuss it with her at one point, and she asked why he needed to meditate. He had confided in her that he was stressed and it helped. She apparently advised him to just get over it. Often, as he attempted at home to meditate, she would interfere and keep him from his quiet.

Somewhere, in those first few months of meditating, Dave confessed his unhappiness in his marriage. He felt they were not on the same page and never had been. His wife had been looking for someone to help raise her children and help pay the bills. She had no interest in a close, loving relationship, and she had no interest in him, mentally or physically. I suggested that he ask his wife to try counseling. Paula and I both did.

Dave was changing. He was becoming happier and more content than I had ever seen him. "You should be sharing your enlightenment," I said. "It's too much to keep from a relationship."

Shortly after this, Mother gave a message to Dave for me. "Carla has a gift as well, and she just needs to practice at it." Needless to say, we were curious.

One morning, Isabella shared with us that our goals here on Earth are personal growth, spirituality and love. That's pretty darn simple. Why didn't we think of that? We exist by grace alone. We grow through good intentions, not through our works, Isabella said.

In other words, if what you do is to gain something for yourself, rather than for someone else, it's lost. If you donate your time to your church because it makes you appear important, it has no meaning or value. If you donate your time to the church because it truly is to help the church and others, then all is gained. You should live what you preach, Isabella told us.

Many times, when we meditated, Dave would see unfamiliar pictures and symbols—hieroglyphics, farms, cities from an aerial view. None of it made any sense. Sometimes when he saw a city, he would recognize something, clueing him in to where the city was but he would not recall ever being there. This got to be normal meditation for a while.

One day, he mentioned seeing a gold dome on a large building. I brought up images from the internet, and he identified the one he had seen. It was a gold dome on a building in Boston.

Another time he saw a picture of what seemed to be an old Roman city. None of this made sense but I just made notes after he relayed it.

Dave's grandmother appeared to him in meditation. He was so happy that tears streamed down his cheeks and he was without words for quite some time.

Then on May 14, 2014, Dave went into meditation, and Isabella took him to a calm place. That is when another guide appeared, and together Isabella and the guide took him "over the horizon," as Dave described it. The place was warm, surrounding him with specks of light that turned out to be thousands of souls. The message he received, "These are the souls that do not have to reincarnate. They have completed their paths."

It always bothered Dave that since his father had passed away about a year before, he never had signs from him or a visit. He mentioned this to me after a meditation session. Within a few weeks, by July 1, it was clear Dave's father must have heard his request.

"It started like a religious experience," Dave said. "This one was different than our usual meditation sessions. There was so much energy."

Isabella had appeared. She showed Dave a God symbol. This was a symbol that Dave saw on occasion, ones he recognized throughout life as representation of God or Christ. He would mention seeing them from time to time. They were never anything definitive but we had acknowledged them just the same. They reminded him of something from his church upbringing.

Dave had a feeling about the birth of Jesus and that he was enlightened, gifted and here for a special purpose. He was told that Jesus was the very first soul that did not have to be reincarnated. We were not surprised.

Then, with an unexplainable amount of emotion, Dave felt his father's arms around him with the love and familiarity for which he had longed. Next, he showed Dave a horizon with extreme bright light. His father explained to Dave that this is the place we all want to go. Needless to say, there was much sobbing. Happy emotion it was, but also stunned, confused and doubtful feelings were surfacing. Dave was so overcome with feelings and hardly able to mutter a word. None of us could.

"That was the most wonderful, warm, loving feeling I have ever felt," Dave said. His father had explained he had taken Dave to the place where they are with God. Dave was overwhelmed because he walked with his father. For years, his father had been unable to walk and had passed away from Parkinson's disease. At the sight of his father walking, Dave cried with happiness.

Our meditation practices were changing from just simple relaxation and requests for our loved ones. We were moving now to questions about our lives as God would have us live. Each day, we jotted down questions. Sometimes Dave would ask our questions before bedtime and through the night he would be visited and counseled as to the answers. Often, he would barely close his eyes at meditation time or at bedtime, and Isabella would be there by herself or with counsel already with the answers before Dave asked the question. It was unbelievably comforting to feel that they were hearing our requests.

When Dave meditates, he goes to a place where he sees energy and lights, then usually Isabella appears. He realized one day that when I was in the room versus him meditating at bedtime, he saw a stronger light, meaning more energy. On days when our entire office staff was in the room meditating, the energy he saw was bigger and more intense. We are all connected, and we are all energy—connecting energy, constantly. Our enemies and our neighbors and foreigners and political rivals are all connected. We are not separate. We need to consider this. We are all one. We need to act as one and treat each other as we treat ourselves. We are selfish, which means we think about ourselves. We need to think about those long extensions of ourselves—which are our enemies, neighbors, foreigners, rivals.

What a difference meditation was proving to make. We had so many questions. What was happening? Who are we? Why us and why now? What we learned was who God is, who we are, and if we follow Five Simple Rules for Living, who we are meant to be.

Chapter 2

The Precipice:
Standing on the Edge

CARLA

One day, Dave mentioned the gold dome again, the one in Boston. When Paula and I conferred, we quickly remembered the dome on the capitol building in Boston, where we were born. That's when Dave said, "I was really young when my parents lived in Boston. I don't remember a lot."

That yanked our heads! We had not known Dave lived there, too.

"When did you live in Boston?" Paula and I said, nearly simultaneously.

Dave nonchalantly said, "Oh, when my father did his master's degree in 1962."

We were stunned. Dave had lived in Boston when we did? Wasn't it fascinating that he had never brought it up until now? For just a few moments, we discussed Dave's time in Boston and what he remembered. It wasn't much, but what he did remember changed our lives forever. His memory suddenly became completely vivid.

DAVE

In 1962, my father was about to leave Nebraska and start graduate school in Boston. I remember the day we were loading the dark blue sedan. It was my mom and dad's first new car, a dark blue sedan. Dad was proud of that car. I had watched the day before as he washed and buffed the car until it shined. My grandma and grandpa, my mother's parents, were there. My grandfather kept talking about the value of a good education. He hoped Dad would learn something in Boston.

Where was Boston? I was three years old. I only knew with every mention of Boston, my grandmother cried. As Grandma stood with a bright white apron over a flower-covered pink-and-blue dress, she again had a tear in her eye but still a smile on her face. I stood in the middle of the front seat between Mom and Dad. My six-week old sister fussed on Mom's lap. Grandma had packed us a small basket with peanut butter sandwiches and one dozen chocolate-chip cookies. The peanut butter sandwiches still had the crusts on them. That was the way my grandmother made them. My grandpa said, "David, keep an eye on your dad." I leaned over and put my eye on my dad's shoulder. Everybody laughed. I didn't really understand why at the time.

We drove long hours through flat land. I hadn't really understood this was going to be an endless drive. We had left Grandma and Grandpa's house before. The back seat always had a crib, blankets and diapers. We always had those green suitcases when we visited. But my sister cried a lot, woke up often and made my parents cranky. We ate the peanut butter sandwiches. It got dark and yet my dad drove on. The road started to wind up into the mountains, making my ears hurt and pop. My dad pulled off and slept about two hours, then we ate breakfast at a road stop. Still, we drove on, into the big city. The buildings were older and larger than I had seen before. So, this was Boston.

We finally arrived at a large group of buildings that all looked the same. They surrounded a playground with swings, a slide and a small patch of grass. My parents carried their things into a small, three-room apartment with cinder block walls. It was hot, and my parents grabbed sheets and pillows. We all lay down on the only bed, my sister and I between our parents. Soon we were sound asleep.

The sun shone through the window in the morning. Mom was unpacking. And I went to play. This started a ritual that continued most of the summer. I went out to play and when I got tired, I turned around and every building looked the same. They were all square dark brick buildings with glass doors. I was scared and lost. I gathered myself and took a breath and headed into the closest building. I knocked on the door and the same lady, whom I would bother every day, answered the door. She was clothed plainly but neatly in a dress with little white socks. She was nice the first day. She gave me cookies and walked me home. I suppose by the thirtieth time, she was a little perturbed.

That summer, I learned that earthworms were not snakes even if they looked large enough to be, that the ocean was bigger than a lake because I had never seen an ocean in Nebraska, that some people cut the crusts off their peanut butter sandwiches. Education was somehow important and a bright, shiny, new sedan made one feel good. I also learned that if you make a little girl upset she might just push you down.

One summer day our family packed the sedan for a trip to the beach. Mom, my little sister and I all wore swimming suits. Dad wore a pair of white athletic shorts and a checkered, short-sleeve shirt with white, high-top Converse All-Stars. Dad was not going near the water: He had never learned to swim. I, however, was not afraid of the water. I had already dived into the baby pool in Lincoln and landed on my head. It did not kill me. So, I guess I was still not afraid of the water.

The sand was warm in between my toes. In the distance, I could see the curved lines of the roller coaster turning around and in on itself. Next to it was a large wheel with blue, yellow and green bucket seats. I now understand it to be a Ferris wheel. Small heads and feet hung from the baskets. It turned in the distance. The beach bustled with families.

I had never seen a beach. I had to run! I had to scream!

Suddenly, behind me, I heard a girl's voice, yelling. "Stop running! You are bothering my family." I turned to see a little girl standing in a two-piece, blue bathing suit. Her face was slightly rounded, her eyes were warm and they were almost laughing and squinting. She stood with both hands on her hips. Her belly was rounded above the ruffled bathing suit bottom.

Like many three-year old kids, I simply said, "Why?"

Suddenly, I felt a shove on each shoulder. I fell back into the sand. The little girl had pushed me down and was sitting on my chest.

Behind her a man, woman and four other little girls of various sizes were seated on a blanket. "Carla!" The woman yelled. "I don't know what came over her." Carla bent over and planted a kiss on my forehead.

Then she jumped up, laughing. The woman said, "Carla, apologize! That is not how a lady behaves."

The woman handed her daughter a small peanut butter and butter sandwich with the crusts cut off. "Share," she directed her.

Carla brought it to me. Half quietly, she said, "Sorry," not very believably.

My father and the dark-haired shirtless man stood and talked. His hair was as dark as my father's was light. He had a tan and dark hair on his arms and legs. My father shook his hand and they laughed. "Kids will be kids," they said. We all soon packed up and headed for our homes.

CARLA

After Dave finished relating this memory, Paula and I just looked at him, startled beyond belief. I also had a vivid memory of that day in Boston, on Revere Beach.

During the summer of 1962, my parents had tried to reconcile, though they had been separated since I was eighteen months old. Many times, they had tried to get back together because they had both been born and raised Catholic. Because our family was so large, my parents got two cabs to take us to the beach although we really could not afford it. We had no car and the beach was too far to walk. My mother packed peanut butter sandwiches with the crusts cut off and split into four sections, as she always did. We arrived at Revere Beach with everything we needed—except a bathing suit for me.

I can't recall why I had no bathing suit. Normally, I would have inherited one from an older sister. I really never got my own clothing just hand-me-downs. Perhaps my bathing suit no longer fit or someone had forgotten it. But we needed to get me a bathing suit, so we walked across the road, all seven of us, to a souvenir shop where my parents purchased my first brand-new bathing suit, a blue two-piece with ruffles.

My sister Joan was angry that she was not receiving a new suit of her own. After crossing the street to the beach, I asked Mommy, what was wrong with Cleo. She explained, "Cleo was sulking."

The next thing I heard was an ear-piercing "AHHHHHHHHHHHH!!"

I jabbed my hands to my hips as I whirled to face this loud, obnoxious little boy. "Stop yelling! You are bothering my family."

I stomped over to him, shoved him into the sand and sat on his chest. Then I planted a kiss on his forehead. I allowed a mischievous smile to spread across my lips.

"Carla, that is not how young ladies behave!"

The only other detail I remember from that day: jumping the waves as they crashed the beach and sandwiches that tasted like sand.

This had always been one of my most vivid memories. I still cry every time I re-read this section. That summer day in 1962, my family was together. I got a new swimsuit. I never thought that day would mean so much more to me later in my life.

Interesting, the things we remember. What was this connection between Dave and me? Why had both Dave's and my mother miscarried us, twice? We were nearly brother and sister, two times. Later, how did a girl born in Boston and a boy born in Nebraska meet in Boston and then again, thirty-five years later, meet in Ohio? And, why, in the middle of all of our meditation, did we recall these memories? Why did we have the same memory from fifty-two years ago on Revere Beach? Dare I mention destiny, or is it all by chance?

The day we each recalled the Revere Beach story had been an emotional day. It was July 30, 2014. On that same day, I had already decided to have my elderly schnauzer put to sleep the next day. Muzette had been suffering off and on for months with pancreatitis. The veterinarian had informed me of the progress that the illness would take and suggested at some point in the near future that it would be kind to euthanize her. The day had come. My husband and I held her until her last breath and left the doctor's office in tears.

I am an animal lover and believe that we have an obligation to be kind to animals because they are not as complicated as humans. For one of the last birthdays we celebrated with Muzette, I made her a fringed, purple pillow. She was inactive in her later years, and there really wasn't much in the way of a present we could offer her. She could not eat much and was on a strict diet. That meant no doggie birthday cake either. She did nap a lot, so, the pillow was her size and an appropriate gift. She slept on it every night on her bed in our room. The evening after her death, I picked up the pillow and told my husband, sadly, that we would have to get rid of the pillow. There was sadness in both of us.

Two days later, on Aug. 1, 2014, Dave texted me when I was at home and said that during the night, he had been contacted by our mother, who had Muzette with her. He went further to say that he saw her prancing with her head high and carrying something under her arm. "It looked like a pillow with embroidery around it," he said. I was speechless. I asked him what color the pillow was and he responded that it was purple. I cried. "I made that light purple pillow with dark purple fringe around the edges, looking like embroidery, for her last birthday," I said. This again verified that animals are important and have an afterlife with us. My husband was so happy when I told him the story later. Muzette was special to him.

After the Boston story and the Muzette story, Dave and I continued to meditate daily and often more than once a day. Dave was at a precipice of life. Unhappiness in work, health and marriage had pushed Dave to the brink.

Why did we learn all of this now? Why this life and this time? The answer is simple. Dave was praying for peace in his soul and happiness in his heart. I now know that Dave was praying for me as well, that I could also find peace and happiness. Little did he know that I was praying for him, too. He saw my unhappiness and despair but really didn't understand where it came from. He had no idea and I had no idea what was really going on in our private lives. He hoped I would find some form of joy, just as I hoped he would. God answers and hears our prayers, when we need it the most, it seems.

Chapter 3

The Insinuation: Entrance Through a Narrow Way

What Makes Us Open?
Who are our Angels and Spirit Guides?

DAVE

Who are our angels and spirit guides, then? And what makes us open to them? This was the question I was asking myself. What I finally came to is that being open means allowing access, passage or a view through an empty space. When we are open, we are not closed or blocked. Our minds are not cluttered with the things keeping us from being reached spiritually. This is what happens when we meditate.

For me, it is letting go of the current. How can I explain it? I see nothing, hear nothing of my surroundings and completely lose track of what is going on around me. I place myself in a relaxed position, although after years now of doing so, I no longer need to follow a routine to connect. I simply close off the outside world and focus on my mind.

The meditation music that I sometimes use to calm myself starts to disappear. I focus and it feels as if my eye muscles contract. I carry my mind backward to find the place that is not here. This is what it feels like.

Energy fills my field of vision. It is bright light, warm and comforting. I see, I feel and then I hear. The voice I hear is familiar but not mine. She seems female and she told me I could call her Isabella. She is distant but present. She confesses to be my spirit guide.

She says she is trying to learn to be human. She wishes to master human emotion. Human emotion fascinates her. Emotion is like art and expression in one, she says. Because the more she understands human emotions, the more she can guide and help me. This brings more joy and happiness to her because it fulfills her purpose.

Human love is beautiful. Her experience as a spirit guide is very different from ours. God is ever present and the thought of not being in God's presence cannot be imagined. She is bathed in joy—no fear or worry, only happiness. She speaks because God has inspired her to reach out to me. Does she laugh and cry? I will say, yes. It is, however for me, that she laughs and she cries. She learns from me, and I from her. She is my guide, teacher and friend. She tells me she has been present with me for six thousand years over my forty-two lifetimes. In some of my lives, I was open and could hear her. Sometimes, she was but a small voice or thought in my head. She does not make my decisions or choices. Yet, she rejoices in my good decisions. She is disappointed by my poor choices. She has learned of pure sadness because she has felt mine. She revels in my love.

At my lowest point, in this present life, she facilitated an answer to my prayers. She saw my mind opening, while I meditated and reached out. It was such a gift.

When I meditate, the energy is visible. The tightening of my eye muscles and mind to look backward brings focus. The energy divides. There is a bright light from the center. There is an eye to the left and an eye to the right.

In the beginning, when I meditated, I saw an eye to the right that reminded me of my dear friend Carla. It belonged to her mother who had passed away years before and whom I had never met.

The eye to the left was Isabella. The light in the center of the energy was from God. How do I know that? It felt warm, loving, familiar and peaceful.

In those first few days of meditation, we also learned of Carla's spirit guide, Elizabeth. Elizabeth told us that she has been with Carla for six thousand years. She is sweet and yet quiet and ever present. She is in some way Isabella's sister and best friend. Which is coincidental because Carla is like a sister and best friend to me, and our spirit guides are best friends. Elizabeth continues to watch over and guide Carla through her lives. Carla has had thirty-four lives. I have been in twenty-nine of them. Apparently, from our first life together until this present one, we had like minds.

God's careful joining of souls with their spirit guides started in the beginning. Each soul was matched to a spirit guide who complements his or her already-present qualities. For example, a soul with a strong personality may be matched with a spirit guide who is rather quiet and easy-going. Having the best of both qualities is representative of God who holds all qualities both strong and soft, male and female, to name a few.

Not so ironically, my spirit guide Isabella is strong and challenging, much like those qualities in Carla's personality. Elizabeth, Carla's guide, is soft, ever so supportive and comforting, much like my own qualities. This was always God's intention.

Everyone on the earth has a spirit guide. We may have been convinced through our religions and upbringing to believe in guardian angels only. Some might say our spirit guides are called guardian angels when, in fact, we each have separate angels in addition to our guides. They also are assigned to us at our birth. It is God's intention. God does not send us to live on Earth without guidance and help.

An angel is a liaison from God. By that, I mean the angel brings us God's messages. Angels were created to serve God, although, we are assigned specific angels throughout our lives.

Spirit guides are assigned to a soul individually. But, sometimes they are assigned more than one soul. They feel privileged to accompany us through our lives. Because during those lives, they learn to understand our emotions and choices. That is their purpose to fulfill for God.

I feel passionate to explain to you about the feelings Carla and I have for our spirit guides and angels.

The early days of meditation brought a bevy of feelings about our guides and angels. They went from fear, nervousness, apprehension and sheer fright to peace, calm, comfort and love.

The fear came from our unknown. Just like any true friendship, you learn to appreciate with understanding and form a bond that lasts forever.

Carla and I, although we had no knowledge of it, have had a relationship with our guides and angels for over six thousand years. It came to the surface in this life.

I speak with Isabella all day, every day. It begins, as I awaken, although they tell me that we have conversation all through the night, during our sleep.

Isabella has introduced me to my angel. His name is, indeed, Gabriel. He seldom speaks with me but sometimes delivers a message to me from God. I am not the only soul on Earth to hear from Gabriel. You have heard about Gabriel speaking in the Bible, over and over again. The angel Gabriel is the speaker for God in the Bible. He speaks with Zachariah in the Bible telling of the birth of John the Baptist, also to the Virgin Mary about her birthing Jesus and in the Book of Daniel he tells Daniel he has come to give him insight and understanding about sinning and atoning.

When Gabriel comes to me, I see him as a bright white light on my left field of vision and sometimes an extremely large eye. I experience a sense of awe taking over my entire being as I feel the hand of God reaching to me through Gabriel. It overwhelms my field of vision. It completely takes over what I see. It is larger than what I can possibly imagine.

Imagine the arms of the person you love the most, wrapping around you completely. The warmth, like from the sun, is intense and welcoming. All of my senses become electrified. My heart begins to race and literally my breathing shallows, as I become aware of everything. Then, a sense of pure comfort and love emanate throughout my body. The voice I hear is authoritative and true, making me undeniably believe this is God. There is no room for disbelief in my mind, heart and soul.

Carla sometimes sees Elizabeth in the transition from sleep to consciousness or in meditation.

She has appeared as a middle-aged, black woman with short dreadlocks, dark sunglasses and attitude but also as a very young girl with long, dark curls, bow in hair, head bowed and hand holding a staff. These are representative of the tough and the innocent.

Isabella explains to me that Carla needs to be dealt with on both levels. Sometimes Elizabeth can appeal to her hard, strong-willed side and sometimes her soft, innocent side. That is the way to approach her.

Carla does not have my gift of "hearing" the spiritual world, also known as clairaudience. In my deepest state, I have clairvoyance and Clair tangency. Her gift is called feel, or Clair empathy. Isabella explains it as an overwhelming sense of an emotion or the ability to sense a feeling involved in an experience. For instance, Carla can feel other people's emotions, be it pain, jealousy, happiness or joy, to name a few. She feels tremendously the feelings of the world, animals and others. Her feelings are related to her passion about everything in life. She can hear differently than my gift allows. She feels it and, therefore, hears it. Her gift has intensified and continues to do so as time passes.

Carla sees her angels, Estes and Mariel, during the transition from sleep to wake or during meditation, as is the case with Elizabeth. Estes appears as a violet purple. Carla sometimes sees his eye. Estes also appears as a large, beautiful, white stallion with wings, sometimes carrying small animals on those wings, which we have learned are our past pets in this life or others. Estes has soft and strong sides, as do all of God's angels. Estes's specialty is in writing. He is God's personal scribe. He assisted Moses in writing the Ten Commandments. He has assisted Carla in the writing of our book. It is God's intention.

Mariel is seen as yellow with a hint of green. Carla sees him when meditating or transitioning from sleep to consciousness. Mariel was connected to Carla as the angel of spiritual healing, which is "feeling" and is also very present when Carla is physically ill or upset.

Carla speaks to Elizabeth, Estes and Mariel as I do, daily, constantly and during sleep to consciousness and meditation. They are our constant friends, loved ones and helpers. Remember, everyone on Earth is given a spirit guide and an angel. We are not alone. Angels and spirit guides are neither male nor female. Our guides take on gender-related names that we feel most comfortable with. God named the angels. Spirit guides name themselves with your choice.

We now know we've had many lives. We also know there's a place that is not of this world where our family and friends go when they pass over. And, we know that we want to go there.

So, we couldn't help but ask ourselves, why do we live life after life? How many more times would we be coming back? Would Isabella and Elizabeth be with us again?

And, the next most important question: Who are we now? Why do we keep coming back? And who were we?

I had the most important question of all for Isabella: Who is God? And what does God expect from us?

Because we are not special.

Part II

I

Introduction

We are here to help you.
Isabella

Chapter 4

In the Beginning, Dave and Carla

For as far back as I can recall, I felt different. I was always on the outside looking in. I carried responsibility for everyone and everything. I had one therapist during my first marriage who asked me, point blank, why I felt responsible for everything. I couldn't answer her. I am a Fixer, by nature.

I spent my life paralyzed with fear—fear of failure, fear of disappointment, fear that I wasn't smart enough, fear that I was not like everyone else. I thought too much, analyzed too much, cared too much and considered too much. I assumed everyone else could function without consideration. I was the only one paralyzed.

The last of six daughters, my entrance into this world was hardly noticed. My mother waited until the last possible moment to go to the hospital, knowing full well the routine of delivering a baby. The problem was, we had no automobile, so she had no other recourse than to enlist the help of the police and their paddy wagon.

Interestingly enough, even with my dramatic entrance only one photo of me as an infant exists. My father was an avid amateur photographer, our home filled with cameras, negatives and snapshots, and still, he forgot about me from the beginning. That set the stage for our relationship.

The mantle in my parents' home while they were married, and afterward in my father's home, sported studio portraits of their five daughters (one died before I was born). Every one of their daughters sat in their prettiest poses while a professional photographer captured them for posterity. Wait, except for one. They forgot me again.

My mother and father separated when I was eighteen months old. Quite honestly, I am surprised she lasted that long. She was high-strung, driven and damaged by her father's sexual abuse. Daddy was a spoiled Italian boy used to getting his way and having everyone wait on him. Did I say that although we were poor and our Christmas presents were donated from the fire department, Daddy always had records and a stereo and whatever he required for his hobbies.

My mother just couldn't handle the Catholic-related stress of bearing six children, taking care of absolutely everything in the household, having a nonexistent husband and father to her children. She bailed. I really never blamed her.

The doctors advised her to leave before she had a complete nervous breakdown. She was well on her way when she moved out, took a job, rented a tiny apartment and turned the gas on her stove to die. Luckily, her landlady came up to check on her and called an ambulance. That wasn't the only time she attempted to leave the world and rid herself of the pain.

That set the stage for our happy home life.

I remember vividly lying in my crib one night at the age of four—yes, I was still in the crib as there was no money for another bed. Two of my sisters shared the room and the other two sisters were down the hall. Daddy slept in the makeshift dining room/bedroom. Sharyn, my oldest sister, had already passed away, and Mother had moved out a couple of years prior. You won't be surprised when I confess to wetting the bed until I was about the age of eight or sucking my thumb with a blanket until I was in fifth grade.

That night, I was lying in bed, it was late, and I decided that my bladder was full. I also had fear of going to the bathroom unaccompanied. If you stood at our bedroom door and looked left, down the hall, there was a big, scary freezer behind a curtain that hummed, reflecting red light from the top like something out of a space aliens movie.

I called to my sisters, Paula, then Joan. No answer. I called their names over and over, hoping one would wake up and take me to the bathroom.

My crib was situated near a closet door to my left. After calling out over and over, growing nervous I would wet the bed, I heard from my left a loud woman's voice. "Carla, go to sleep!"

Who was this woman in my closet, scaring me into sleep?

I recently confirmed with Elizabeth, my spirit guide through Dave that it was, indeed, she, advising me that night. Elizabeth was speaking to me then and continues to speak with me now.

She was not in my closet but did speak to me from where our guides always speak to us, in our left ear. I fell back asleep, too afraid to get up.

I hold sad memories of a little girl who, by the way, is not still that way, needing her mother and father, no one around. On the weekend, however, Mother normally came to visit us or take us back to her apartment for the night. This was not an every weekend event but it was enough for me to remember her making the attempt to spend time with us and use what salary she made to buy pretty dresses and toys for us.

She was also financially responsible for my brief dancing career. My long legs and knock-knees were not conducive to the daintiness of ballet. Mother tried to give us what we needed, including herself.

Once, when I was five, I was standing in the school playground in first grade, listening to a classmate's incessant bragging about her mother taking her for ice cream at the end of the day. I listened and listened and then casually strolled over and punched the girl in the face.

I hid under my disdain for bragging, when, in fact, it was more about her spending time with her mother. It wasn't about the ice cream, either. I missed my mother. I wanted someone to notice I was alive.

I vividly remember a day when I told myself, or rather heard someone tell me, I was the only one looking out for me. It was Elizabeth, my guide.

I needed to adapt to this way of thinking and act accordingly. No one really understood. I was out here on my own. My sisters were all as "messed up," for lack of another word, as I was.

Skip ahead to age eight: Mother and Daddy finally got divorced. It was quite the ordeal in Massachusetts in the 1960s. (Daddy and Mary, his second wife, actually had to wait six months to legally marry.) They were Catholic, as I mentioned, and tried over and over again to reconcile. Mother would move back in with us, but Daddy refused to relinquish the territory to his girlfriend, Mary.

We were living close to Cambridge, in Watertown.

Saturday mornings, while Patrice and Cleo were still asleep, Daddy and his girlfriend demanded an audience with Paula, Joan and me, the youngest three, where they would pose the question, "Who will you choose to live with, your mother or Mary and me?" Of course, we would give Daddy the answer he desired: "You, Daddy."

Mother had fallen in love with the one we called the Breadman. During those days, our milk and bread were delivered to our home.

Mother had been twenty-one years old when she had chosen Daddy over Johnny Allingham because Johnny confessed to not wanting children.

After they married, it took my parents nearly five years to give birth to their first daughter, Sharyn. Previously, they had conceived and lost two children. Mother knew with certainty that one was a boy. We know now that both of her miscarriages were our Dave. He would have been my big brother in this life. Isabella confirmed it was Dave.

Sharyn died suddenly at nearly six years of age from probably what was Reyes syndrome. She had a cold, ear infection and aspirin, apparently, a lethal combination for some children. When she passed, my parents must have died on the inside. Their relationship was never the same. They gave birth to three more daughters, but with each birth, the marriage died a bit more.

Sometime after my birth, Mother discovered the Breadman. Apparently, Daddy had long before discovered Mary. Paul was actually more than a Breadman. He had been my mother's confidant. During his deliveries, he and my mother became friends. He listened when my father would not.

Isabella confirmed that my father stepped out of the marriage once it became too complicated and laden with responsibility. He somehow managed to cope with marital sex but couldn't handle being a husband or father.

After the Breadman decided he could not leave his socialite wife for business reasons, Mother left the state. Paul owned his bread company but his wife threatened to ruin his business if he left her. The Breadman did not have a happy marriage. Their children, a son and a daughter, were long since raised and the marriage was in name only. He loved my mother, but he couldn't be sure, either, if this time was the last time Mother would leave Daddy. She had gone back to Daddy too many times. She left town.

Mother brought three of us out to Michigan to visit the first summer after she remarried, to a man named Gerard. Paula, Joan and I flew from Boston. Patrice and Cleo stayed because they were working.

The second summer, she brought four of us—Paula, Joan, Patrice and me—to live permanently. Cleo was still in nursing school. Cleo moved with us about a year later.

We finally had a complete family again with a participating father. I would not figure out for many years that my stepfather's agenda was to purify himself in our eyes and turn us against our mother. My experience of him was that he was verbally abusive but I wouldn't have the language for this until much later in life.

My sister Cleo hated Gerard from her first introduction to him in Boston when he plunged his tongue in her mouth. She said she told Mother but Mother did not believe it. They were newlyweds, after all. Who would want to believe such a thing?

We were younger and much more impressionable, needing a father figure and someone on whom to depend. Patrice, the second oldest, was in her own world and not critical of either parent. But Paula, Joan and I were duped. We worshipped the ground Gerard walked on. He started early, giving us an allowance, buying us things we hadn't had. He purchased my first bicycle when I was ten years old. So, maybe he wasn't a total beast, but turning children against their mother is always wrong.

The first year we lived in Michigan with Mother and our stepfather, Daddy sent a birthday present with a card that read: Karla. I was hurt. I was named after Daddy's father, Carlo. How could he not remember the spelling of my name? Shortly thereafter, Mother stopped the presents from coming. She said if he could not send support, he wasn't getting off that easy just sending presents. I felt abandoned again. He never remembered our birthdays or Christmas after that. I was angry with Mother. I blamed her for Daddy's negligence. It wasn't her doing. It was his. Mother also knew that Daddy's replacement wife was responsible for our gifts, not him.

I felt so confused as an adolescent. I had this new father, now but didn't know whether to trust him. They had huge fights, it seemed, on every holiday. He would write Mother the most hurtful, despicable letters, which caused Mother to stop talking to him, sometimes for weeks on end. We would sit at the dinner table in total silence. Some of the sentences in his loving letters referred to her being just like her abusive father. Gerard would leave them on the kitchen table where, of course, we would find them before Mother. The letters consisted of sheer derogatory accusations and abuse. Yet he expected her to just get over it and feel nothing. After a while, he would go to her and admit he did wrong and somehow justify it because she had hurt him. She'd let him get away with it, over and over again.

Needless to say, by the time I was thirteen, I threw up every time I was under pressure of any kind. The doctors said I was just a nervous child and prescribed Valium. They made me take it for a while and then I began, on my own, taking small doses of partying, drinking, drugs and time away, to rid my mind of my parents' unhappiness and constant fighting.

The summer before my freshman year, my best friend and I went on a shopping spree that turned into an afternoon of shoplifting in department stores. She got away with her theft; I, unfortunately, was apprehended by two undercover policewomen who plopped me into a paddy wagon, my second adventure in such a vehicle, and escorted me to jail. I was locked between bars and kept there for several hours until I heard from my mother. She was demanding from the guard an explanation as to why they had accused me of such actions.

I further heard her say that I would never have done what they were accusing me of. The guard told her she should ask me. They walked down the hall to my jail cell.

My mother said, "Carla, did you do this?"

I answered, "Yes, Mother."

She began to cry and asked me why. I said I didn't know. The fact of the matter was that I had spent hours swiping pierced earrings for my sister Joan. My own ears were not pierced. She took me home where she and my stepfather lectured me for hours as they tried to understand how their child could have done this. I was on probation by the magistrate for six months.

I got attention, didn't I? Maybe this was meant to be a wake-up call for my parents. I believe indirectly I was trying to teach them.

The next year, my mother tried to commit herself into the mental hospital. My stepfather called me while at my friend's house. It was as if he was happy she left. He joked about her coming home and not being able to find the place.

What kind of father figure has a discussion with his children on such a subject? He berated her again and again to us younger girls, while my mother was whipped yet again into submission. I didn't see it, though. I only knew that if she were out of the way, he would let us do as we pleased. He would do anything to be the favored parent.

Every time they argued, I became nervous. I thought assuredly we would be left somewhere alone. I cried to Patrice and asked where we would go and what would happen to us.

We got a dog. Daisy, a Schnoodle, a cross between a schnauzer and poodle. She was a puppy and acted as such. We loved her. She was our "something" to love. She chewed, as puppies will, on a piece of woodwork in the breakfast nook. My stepfather immediately ordered Mother to get rid of her. She did so with anger. The next day, as usual, he saw the error of his ways and agreed to get her back. Daisy had already been put to sleep.

He blamed Mother for taking her so quickly. Again, it was Mother. She got blamed for his actions. We liked her even less. He was off the hook again.

The summer of my sophomore year, Mother decided Joan was getting into too much trouble in a big school. She decided to move us south about an hour away to a country school.

My parents never gave thought to why Joan was getting into things she shouldn't. Perhaps she needed a stable home and parents who realized we needed peace and not constant fighting and upheaval. Every other month, they were planning a divorce. They never knew Joan had cut her wrists or Paula and I had discovered her and stopped it.

My life was over.

Until John. He had been my first love. I was in awe of his chiseled physique, beautiful, long golden hair, crystal blue eyes and his ability to charm the pants off of anyone including me. I carried a torch for John for years. What a waste. He had many girlfriends during our relationship. I allowed him to own me. He did travel to my new home, though, several times to see me.

He had class enough to send me a letter after he was careless enough to put one girlfriend in the motherly-way. He explained that he had to step up and take responsibility and be a father. At least he got something correct. I respected his decision and the fact he didn't just disappear from my life without explanation.

So, back to the moving. To date, I had attended seven schools in my lifetime. I hated being the new kid who had to be at the front of the class, since my name started at the beginning of the alphabet. I had barely gotten by in school, pulling Cs and Ds. No one asked if I had homework. No one asked how I was doing. The only time I remember Mother participating in anything school-related was when I came home with a story about a male teacher yelling at me in front of the class. She marched up to school the next day and set him straight.

In retrospect, I wish she could have had that determination with our stepfather. Then, maybe it would not have taken me so many years to learn how to stand up to men.

So, here we went again. We started in a new school; this would be number eight. It wasn't long before we found the kids who smoked pot at lunchtime and partied on the weekends.

Joan had the luxury of graduating just six months into our first year there. She was very unhappy away from her friends and she acted out accordingly. One evening she did not come home after curfew. Mother woke me up throughout the night asking where she was. It was a Saturday evening. I really had no clue where she was. I did, however, know she was with a boy. Half past seven a.m. she arrived, and I heard Mother open the door to her room in an attempt to catch Joan coming home. Mother asked Joan what she meant by coming home so late. Joan casually looked down at her watch and responded with, "Oh, is it that late? I hadn't noticed." Mother immediately sent her to bed and ordered that I get up and prepare for church.

I couldn't understand. Why was I being punished and not Joan? I had been kept up all night and still had to be the good girl and follow the rules.

I remember thinking again that my parents had no clue about my feelings or that I existed. No wonder I felt responsible for everyone and everything, not to mention my mother stating every so often, "You are smarter than the five of you put together." There was no pressure from that statement, of course.

I had constant thoughts of not being able to wait for the day that I could exit their house and be on my own. I hated Mother most of the time. I hated her rules and insistence on church. The Catholic Church had abandoned her once she divorced and was no longer allowed to take the communion. The Mormons, as they most often do, had convinced a woman in a sorrowful, unhappy state to join their church, being the only true one of God, so they say.

Not only did she constantly preach about us not being alone with boys, because of the potential threat of sex, which I found out much later was due to her abusive childhood, we endured the Mormon views of no Coca-Cola, no alcohol and no cigarettes, all of which I was using as my buffer for life.

I could not wait to graduate and get away from them. I could find peace once I left. My junior and senior years, I finally started to grade higher in my classes. The summer before my senior year, I went with my two best friends to a large, well-known amusement park where we stayed overnight and partied with alcohol, sloe gin fizzes and pot. What the hell were my parents thinking? What were my friend's parents thinking? I was sixteen. They were seventeen.

After drinking and smoking, the rides left me ill. I promised God that if He would help me feel better, I would stop doing drugs and partying. I kept my promise about the drugs. I drank a little, but actually stopped by the time I was nineteen.

My parents never asked what I had planned to do after graduation. No one discussed college with me. Cleo, Patrice and Joan had all attended college by their own doing. Paula and I had fallen through the cracks. Paula moved out and worked in a hospital.

The fall after I graduated, my steady boyfriend moved to Indiana for college. I still worked as a waitress. I had no direction. I moved in with Paula to get away from my parents only because Gerard had gotten fired after his mouth did him in, and he was forced to take a job in Indiana. I had nowhere else to go. I was not moving in with them. Mother did suggest that I could move with them but I needed to free myself. I was a constant nervous wreck with their habitual fighting.

At the restaurant, I waited on a man regularly. He was nice, and I guess you would say flirted with me a bit. I admired him because he always brought his daughters along with him. I remember thinking, "What a good father he is" because he had his girls with him. I believed him to be a family man.

One evening after my shift was over, friends visited me, arriving at the restaurant, where I changed clothes and prepared to leave with them. Before we left, a woman entered, walked straight over to this father with his daughters, screamed at him and swung her purse at his head in outrage. She stormed out.

The scuttlebutt was that she was his wife and had left him. I felt sorry for him. She had embarrassed him and hit him in the head with her purse. How outrageous! I had already broken up with my boyfriend when he left for college. A couple of months later, this father with the two daughters asked me on a date. "Aren't you married?" I said. My wife left me, he said, and we're divorcing. She's moved to New Jersey, he added. I agreed, not really understanding the complexity of marriage at age seventeen.

We dated for several months when one day I saw his wife in the restaurant wearing the sweater I had given him for Christmas. I was appalled. She was back. She never knew that they were getting a divorce. She had been visiting her mother as a cooling-off period. Problem was, I was already pregnant.

Cleo and Patrice were incensed after Joan informed them of my condition. They showed up at my apartment door with intention.

Really, I had no clue or tools at seventeen to understand how marriage worked or even how to avoid getting pregnant. I only knew that this older man, who was thirty, was willing to care for me the way he did for his daughters. He said he loved me.

My sisters took me to Detroit for an abortion. I was thirteen weeks pregnant. My mother never knew because my sisters said I couldn't tell her. After all, she was living a state away and really didn't know for sure what was going on in our lives. She wasn't aware that I was dating anyone. Eventually I did tell her that I was dating. I converted the story to, "a man who was getting a divorce" and not that I was part of the divorce. I am sure she knew but never discussed it with me. No one asked me what the hell I was doing. I now know I wasn't the cause of the divorce, just a symptom.

The man finally got a divorce and we married; I was nineteen, he was nearly thirty-three. Yikes. He did not allow me to work. I, of course, thought he was taking care of me, not that he was controlling me. He was abusive, verbally and sometimes physically and usually blamed me for aggravating his temper. Because of him, I was convinced that I was a selfish person who only wanted my way even though I was raising his children, putting toothpaste on his brush in the morning, laying out his clothing and literally standing at the back door with his slippers after his work day.

The girls, his children from his first wife, and I were not allowed to talk during dinner because he wanted quiet. He was an engineer for an electrical company and a bass fisherman. He spent many weekends away fishing, with me as his daughters' babysitter. I was not allowed to see my friends as they were bad influences and could not go anywhere without him. If I did, he was angered and a fight ensued once he learned of it. We did not eat broccoli because he did not care for it. I did all the housework, cooking and yard work. I was to be seen and not heard. I was not allowed an opinion. I always felt that I was not making him happy and tried so hard to do what he expected, but it was never enough. I puttied the windows, took out the trash, painted every house we lived in and did everything "His Highness" wanted.

He withheld sex. Said he wasn't interested. For a time, I tried to get pregnant. He did not want additional children and was very uncooperative when my doctor advised that my eggs were dropping. He allowed me to feel as though I was disrupting his day, asking for his assistance in creating a baby together.

We did conceive one other time after we married. It was a girl. Unfortunately, I had contracted rubella during the pregnancy, passed along by his youngest daughter. The pregnancy ended with my delivering a baby already in heaven, stillborn.

I was crushed. I eventually gave up. My husband was always unwilling to make love.

They say that when you turn thirty, you know exactly who you are. Well, that may be partially true. I certainly did not. I was starting to speak my mind though this man did not like it one bit. I had managed a few years before to finagle a part-time job to pay for his new bass boat and prom dresses for his girls.

He hated the independence and knowledge I was gaining from my receptionist position for a local doctor. Had I been steered in the proper direction as a senior in high school, I would have kept the secretarial position I had with a well-known oil company at its headquarters.

I joined the YMCA so his daughters could swim there. I asked him to come along but he refused. He had been a boxer and avid exerciser earlier in life but this, however, was not his idea. It was an outlet for me to get away from the house and work out. He hated it. He accused me, with every workout, of "blanking" around with men while I was there.

I was afraid to come home after working out but I kept going. I was becoming defiant in a way, but I thought, "Who do you think you are? I wait on you hand and foot, raise your children, forfeited my own children for you, take care of every duty and responsibility possible in our lives, cook like a gourmet, have sex withheld from me, can't have friends, can't eat the vegetables I choose, you mistreat my dog and I put up with your abuse day after day for what reason?" I started to voice my opinion.

Thirty was turning out to be the age of enlightenment for me. This behavior went on for four years. I wanted a divorce, yet I didn't.

Of course, my reasoning for the inability to decide and stick with it was due to my paralyzing and analytical mind. I felt sorry for him. I thought he was my responsibility. I felt sorry for his daughters, who did not have a stable parent. By this time, the oldest girl had graduated and the youngest was getting ready to. He accused me on many an occasion of being on their side on the issues. I would ask myself how it was possible for a parent to not see their child or their needs? Yet, I did not recognize my own life in theirs. I did start to understand how I chose a husband who was an exact replica of my parents.

I thought this man was a family man. I so desperately needed a family. I thought him to be a great father. I lacked a father completely. I never had a parent to lead me. He had led me, all right. I allowed him to control every breath I took.

One day, an acquaintance from the YMCA said she was sorry I had missed the sermon at church. She knew I was unhappy in my marriage because she and I worked out in the mornings together. She relayed the pastor's message of how God forgives divorce when the marriage is breaking one's spirit. Something resonated with me.

I went to the secretary in the office next to mine, who happened to be an attorney, and filed for divorce. I handed my husband the news on his birthday. I was a nervous wreck. He was not changing my mind but my "Inner Carla" tried to, over and over again. Old habits die hard, I guess.

I had to be on my best behavior for eighty-nine days with him. I had filed for dissolution and knew that it must be completely agree-able or would be thrown out of court. I hated this time period of sheer manipulation on his part. He also understood how that type of divorce worked but was conceited enough to believe I was just going through a stage and would change my mind. He was smug.

I performed the finest acting job for those eighty-nine days until I moved out shortly before. I felt relief coming. I was going to be free. It was much the same feeling I had when I left my parents' home and the disabling conditions.

I purchased a small home and was on my own for the first time in my life. I, of course, took nothing from him but a mere $25,000, which was distributed to me over a five-year period. He did not bother me much for the first year after the divorce. I did hear from one of his co-workers that he joined a dating site and had about four hundred dates. Did I care? Absolutely not. I had no feelings but, "Good riddance."

A year later, he called me from out of the blue. "Are you ready to come home?" he said. I was so angry I wanted to scream, "Blank-off." I ever so calmly explained that it had taken me four years to decide about our marriage but once I had, it was final.

He begged a little, saying that he figured I was going through a stage because I had been so young when we married. I wanted to say, "You stole my youth," but I had learned through counseling that I, and only I alone, could let anyone do anything to me. I had control and did not take it.

I was lonely. I came from a house with five girls. My house was quiet and still. I had alienated most of my girlfriends for this man. I went to work, exercised and came home. My sisters lived an hour or more away, which was not convenient for short visits.

My old ways came back to me. I was stupid. I did not think. I looked for a father again. I never trusted myself to have thoughts as to what I wanted in life or what I deserved in life.

Men at the YMCA flirted with me, but quite honestly, I felt too different from them. The more I aged, the more particular and different I felt. I am not the type of woman who enjoys frivolous liaisons or actions at all. I've never had a one-night stand, nor could I.

I have an extremely serious side. I need to feel necessary and that I am accomplishing good.

A few men asked me out. They were not the caliber of man that my soul required. When I chose my husband, I had not the slightest idea of what my soul desired. I just needed someone to take care of me, I thought. I needed a father.

Anyway, my employer and I had always had a great friendship. He was funny, very complimentary in the proper sort of way, easy going, kind and married. I truly believed that he and his wife were happy. He never complained about his life or his wife. We interacted casually through the years over dinner or holidays but never bonded as couples. He was supportive of my divorce and never judgmental. I considered him a good friend but never anything further until one day when he stepped over the line. He had been in a funny mood as I discussed dating and my life. His wife was in Florida visiting her parents. I knew something was wrong but he left it up in the air.

The day was over and I went home wondering about his mood. I called him and asked what was the matter? Was there something going on? He paused after my question, and then made a statement that changed our lives. "I am sad because I'll never walk in the park with you." I was floored.

My response I believe reflected my usual thinking and behavior. I felt sorry for him and said, "Well, maybe I will."

One thing led to another and before I knew it, I was getting married again. This man was going to take care of me. I trusted him. I should have trusted myself. I again saw everything in this man that was not there. Thank God, this man was a good man. Tom was not like Jaime in the least. He wasn't argumentative, never mean and never grabbed or hit me.

Do you remember falling in love for the first time? Your sweetheart could do no wrong. You smiled and laughed at every word coming from his mouth. You ignored his idiosyncrasies. You saw him through rose-colored glasses.

My second marriage stayed at the rosy stage for many years. I would like to think I learned valuable lessons after my first marriage ended. Those lessons somehow allowed me the luxury of remaining happy and satisfied with my second husband for an extended period of time. However, my second marriage's rosy stage came to a screaming halt once Tom lost his ability to perform as a man. It didn't have to be that way, but unfortunately, he succumbed to his pride and misguided beliefs, after surgery for prostate cancer. He thought making love was just as simple as intercourse.

I chalked this thinking up to his age because I couldn't fathom the thought he might be acting selfishly or that he didn't care for me anymore. He had the option to choose injections, which would help him sustain his abilities. He discarded that option as well.

Time passed and my anger raged. I had conflicting thoughts. I had been a large part of the decision for the surgeon's aggressive removal of the cancer. I loved this man and had given no thoughts to chemotherapy or radiation. A radical choice removed the need for either treatment. I couldn't stand him being sick or having constant pain or discomfort. I thought a wife should be selfless if she loved her husband. I believed a wife should not think about her own needs in such a case but consider only the health of the man she loved.

The error in my consideration was the assumption my husband was as selfless in his thoughts of me and my well-being, as I was of his. The rose-colored glasses faded and became clear, bright, all-seeing windows.

The romance and relationship we had in our thirteen-year marriage dropped dead after Tom's prostatectomy. I felt deeply sad.

Tom's surgery changed him. Our sweet, playful, close, romantic relationship was gone. I felt neglected, ignored and unnecessary.

It's not Tom's nature to feel sorry for himself and really, he never displayed such behavior. Retrospectively, he was feeling sorry for himself after surgery and taking it out on me, his closest friend. That's what I had become, his friend.

My anger turned to sadness, then to depression. Tom never seemed to notice if I had a lot to do or was tired. God forbid, I was sick or needed minor surgery. I relied on my friends to help and after a while I gave up waiting for Tom to notice. If an outsider watched him, he seemed fine. Only my closest friends knew that he had changed and a huge part of him had died. I believe he thought his ticket to flirt or be a man had been cancelled.

My life had changed from happy and fulfilled to barely existing. I was spiraling into sheer Zombie-ism. I went through the motions daily. I planned outings with my friends after work hours and on weekends but my heart was empty. I had lost my love. He no longer existed. Tom loved me as his friend and that was all he was ever going to give me, friendship.

Many years later, I now understand the devastation Tom went through. He had married me despite our twenty-three-year age difference. He had been a happy-go-lucky, charismatic, confident man in his abilities and unaffected by our differences when we married. I am certain he had some pride issues related to his performing with a much younger woman, as most men would, yet he had been extremely capable and was appreciative of his abilities.

I believe he was displeased with himself after the surgery and in fear of his role in our relationship. He had never given thought to our future and his role in his later years, apparently. His father and mother had twenty-three years between them, in age. He had learned well.

That way of thinking angered me. Was there no substance in our relationship minus intercourse? I was continually mad at Tom for the mere insinuation. He wasn't even aware of how he was affecting our relationship. Tom's personality has always been to not address his feelings or others' feelings so not to deal with any potential problems. This type of behavior was the exact opposite of what our relationship needed.

We became roommates. He wouldn't sit next to me on the couch, always using the excuse that he was already comfortable or too hot or some other reason. We didn't snuggle anymore. He literally gave up on the inside. We seldom kissed, hugged or showed any affection. He golfed and worked as normal but stopped doing a lot of the helpful things around the house that he used to. I started going to the store by myself, something we had always done together. I went out with girlfriends on weekend nights, which was always reserved for Tom and me in our past.

Tom is never angry. Tom never yells, swears or shows disapproval in anything. That is one of the attributes I have always loved about him since coming from a screaming, yelling childhood. I tried on many occasions to incite a discussion about his surgery and our lack of affection and changed relationship. He would shut down and say very little. I couldn't release his anger. Eventually, I stopped bringing it up and he seemed perfectly content to never discuss any part of it again.

I think in some way, shape or form, Tom was lashing out at me for what had happened to him. He was thinking, as much as I was, about our age differences and how it was now affecting our life. I told him point blank one day, I was not going to pretend to be his age. I was going to live my life as a woman in her fifties. I believe he was relieved. He could now sit back and be a man approaching eighty and be all right with it. So, we had come to an agreement of sorts. We were housemates.

I still loved Tom and protected him as any wife would. We were just on another level. He liked me a little more, I believe, because all the pressure was off. He could be who he was during this stage in his life and not feel guilty.

I know now that this relationship was supposed to happen and that we have had many lives together before but prior to this knowledge and until this point, I went through a bevy of feelings from disgust with myself for my neediness to anger with Tom for not pushing me away before we married.

Tom and I are friends. We respect each other. I take very good care of him. He ignores me. He lives in his head. He does let me be me, however, and never judges me. He is not a jealous man. He doesn't own me. Until meditation began, I believed him to be my soul mate. I am a very naïve woman at times. What I see is often not what is.

I thought Tom was a family man. He is not, although he does love his grown children.

I thought Tom was strong, confident and an adult. I thought he had the ability to meet my needs and take care of me. What I discovered over twenty-five years and through my animosity and anger is that Tom is carefree, stubborn, oblivious, selfish, yet supportive and somewhat giving, but not of himself. I pray he realizes it.

DAVE

I found a picture of myself at eighteen months old. I wore a navy-blue baseball jacket with white-striped knitted cuffs at the wrist and a navy baseball cap. My cheeks were fat and rounded with ears sticking out from under the cap. I am wearing stretchy, white baseball pants. The jacket reads "Little Slugger." My father bought me this outfit. Baseball was his favorite sport. I was to be his little slugger.

From my beginning, I believed I was special to my parents. My mother had difficulty maintaining a pregnancy. I was to be the answer to their prayers and be their perfect child. I would represent their perfect life. It was important for them to do what was right. In the 1960s, it was "father works, mother works part-time, a three-bedroom house, new car and two children." This also included church on Sunday.

I was born in small town Nebraska just before 7 p.m. I know this because Mom tells me they used forceps to hurry the delivery. The doctor and my father both had bowling league at 7 p.m. I understand at the last minute my father decided he could skip bowling that night. See, I really was special to them.

Early in the summer of 1962, I was a three-year old boy with a buzz cut. My father, in my memory, was a tall, strong, fair-haired man with short hair, already balding on the top. My mother still resembled the cutie she had been when she sent my father a pin-up picture of herself in a swimsuit while he was in the Korean War before they married. She had dark hair, was 5-feet-2 inches and quite petite. Now they had two children, me and my newborn sister, just six weeks old.

My father's parents were not well off financially. They lost every-thing, including the family farm, during the Depression. They were immigrants from Germany. I really never heard much of the story except they came over on a boat together. My grandmother and grandfather's families were close and not surprisingly, they married. My father was the youngest of six boys, the only one to attend college. My only memory of my grandmother is a photo of a short, old, round, gray-haired lady with a scowl. She holds an infant who is me.

My father never spoke about her. Mom says she still spoke German when she didn't want anyone to know what she was saying. After my grandmother died, my memories of my grandfather on my father's side are somewhat sad. He was a thin, depressed old man who lived in an apartment over someone else's house by himself. We would climb a rickety old stairway to visit him. He was quiet and not friendly. His voice was feeble, gruff and cracked when he spoke. He sat alone in a dark room in a broken-down, old, stuffed chair. We visited but never stayed long.

When I was ten, my grandfather died in a nursing home, after suffering from dementia. My father stopped taking us to see him when I was six. My grandfather had stopped bathing and could no longer care for himself. The next time I saw him was his funeral. My father never spoke much about his parents. I always thought he was ashamed. His older brothers all left home and entered the service while he was young.

My father told stories about cold nights and missed meals. Winter mornings, he woke up to notice that the newspaper he had stuffed between the cracks in the windows had fallen out and snow had gathered on his bed covers. One day his older brother Elden bought him a baseball glove, another day, a basketball, which quickly became his prized possessions. He went on to play those sports in high school. His father and mother never watched him play. They never found importance in the activities of their children.

My father worked his way through college as a lineman, repairing and laying tracks for the railroad, then finished college on the GI Bill after the Korean War. He became a staff sergeant during the war. He was responsible for inventory and morale. He used basketball as a major diversion for the men on the Air Force base. When he returned to college, he was an education major. He was a walk-on to the University of Nebraska basketball team, but he only ever played in junior varsity games. After graduation, he taught high school English, math and physical education and coached baseball and basketball. He was, however, unsatisfied with this and continued to work toward his master's degree in school administration. He continued to use the GI Bill. He ended his career as my high school principal.

My mother's parents were quite the opposite. My mother went to Catholic school. The family lived in a beautiful, four-bedroom stone house on a corner lot with a lush green lawn featuring a trellis with red roses and greenery that led to the bright white garage with blue-gray shingles that matched the siding. My grandmother was a homemaker, an affectionate woman who made fudge, cinnamon rolls and fresh bread. She was a teacher in a one-room Nebraska schoolhouse. My grandfather, a mechanic, started a gas station and auto service in a small town in Nebraska at nineteen.

Speed ahead about two years, and my grandmother, then eighteen, remembers a great thunderstorm approaching, the wind howling, the sky black. She feared for the children in the one-room schoolhouse. She tore a piece of fabric from her skirt and tied eight small children together by their wrists. She prayed a "Hail Mary," and they all ran for the neighbor's root cellar. All eight children made it to the cellar before a massive tornado struck, flattening the schoolhouse. My grandmother prayed every day from that day on.

Move ahead again just a few months, to what my grandmother called the "second miracle." One night in the middle of the summer, my grandfather was still working at the station. My grandmother had gone to bed. That night she said she felt her bed shake. A young brunette surrounded by a bright light appeared at the base of her bed.

My grandmother peered over the end of her feet, frightened. She surely believed the apparition to be the Virgin Mary. She heard a voice say, "Catherine, kneel beside your bed and pray." Amazed, my grandmother climbed out of bed and obeyed. Suddenly she heard a loud explosion. The gas station where my grandfather worked had just exploded. He was thrown across the street through the window of the general store. The gas station burned to the ground. My grandfather stood up, brushed the glass off and stepped through the broken window. He stood and watched as flames shot up into the sky. He walked home to his frightened bride. My grandmother hugged him, saying, "Maybe you were meant for something else."

Shortly after this incident, they moved back to Lincoln. My grandfather applied to the University of Nebraska, from which he graduated from law school, and then was appointed as a state Supreme Court Justice. They started a family. My mother attended the University of Nebraska, their only child to pursue college, but she quit college to marry my father. This was something my grandfather never quite forgave. I believe my father worked his whole life to try and make up for this. My mother spent most of her life as a grade school or junior high school secretary. This meant, for most of my childhood, one of my parents was always in the school building with me.

As a child, I went to church every Sunday, whether we were in our town or visited my grandparents. It was just what we did. I went to catechism class every week. At seven, I took First Communion. The anticipation built: This was to be a special day. I would take Baby Jesus into my heart. He was important, and I liked him. The way it felt was that He was so special I could not touch Him. Only the priest could touch Him and put Him on my tongue. I tried it in practice, and the cracker was dry and had no taste. It stuck to the roof of my mouth. I couldn't get it off. I stuck my finger in and scraped it off. I hoped that wouldn't happen again.

My grandparents were coming for my First Communion. I was sure they would not like me sticking my fingers in my mouth in church. I got a little black book that said, "Your First Communion." It had my prayers in it. I memorized the prayers so that they would be proud of me. I also got a suit and tie to wear. I didn't like the tie—it snapped on—but Dad wore a suit. I thought I looked just like him that morning. Everyone took pictures and said they were proud of me. My grandparents gave me rosary beads blessed by the pope, whom I understood to be the big priest in Rome. I never really understood why Jesus and God were the same or why I had to eat Him.

Afterward, we had a big meal with ham and I got cake afterward. It had to be important. I remember praying when I went to bed the Our Father prayer, which I had memorized. Then I told God I hoped it did not hurt today when I chewed Him up and swallowed Him. I thanked Him for the cake. I always thought God could hear me.

As a child, I had many recurrent dreams. I had a dream of being a young king dressed with a crown. I was a warrior in battle in Greek or Roman times. I dreamed of being a soldier in the Civil War. I even decorated my room with the U.S. flags and fake period musket pistols hanging on the wall. I also dreamed of falling and falling. I know many kids have these dreams. I never understood what these meant. I dreamed and remembered almost every night. I dreamed also of owning my own ten-speed bike.

March 9, 1968, I woke up, a nine-year-old boy. I rubbed my tired eyes and looked around the upstairs dormer in our small, rented home. My twin bed sat next to the railing at the top of the stairs. Through the only door is my five-year-old sister. It is chilly. Most of the heat comes from the vent in the floor. I want to jump out of bed, but because of the cold, I pull the blanket up to my chin. The sun is already streaming in the window at the top of the stairs. I am excited because today is my birthday.

It is also Saturday, and there is no school today. Not that I mind school—I am a good student, and third grade is fun. My teacher lets me explore my "flair" for drawing by making posters for every holiday out of Charlie Brown characters. I like math and science. My mother worked as a secretary for the grade school. She just went back to work as my sister entered kindergarten. My father is a teacher and vice principal at the high school. My parents are proud of me.

We live in Mayberry RFD. Okay, so that is how it seems like when I watch Andy Griffith on the thirteen-inch, black-and-white TV in my father's den. Nebraska City is a small town on the Missouri River. There is a capitol square, a new Woolworth store and my favorite place is a little, pink neighborhood building where you can buy candy. I love that red shoelace licorice.

Up until this birthday, I think I had a pretty normal childhood. I had dived head first into the baby pool at age three and did not die. As you know, I had been to Revere Beach in Boston and met a feisty little girl. I had been on the homecoming court as the little prince with a princess, me in a suit, black tie and buzz cut, meeting my mother's expectation of being a perfect boy. Once, when I was five, I ran away from home to my friend's house, for about one hour before I wanted to go home. I took with me two pairs of underwear and a blue stuffed dog. My mother said it broke her heart.

I played tag with neighbors and generally did kid things. I would go to football games at the high school with my father. I visited my grandparents and ate homemade cinnamon rolls my grandmother made. It was an all-American childhood.

So, what makes this birthday so different? I just knew today was going to be big. I was growing up and had asked for a red, ten-speed Schwinn bike. I would be able to go anywhere by myself. So, I gathered up some courage, threw off the blanket and ran down the stairs. Mom and Dad said, "Happy Birthday." I looked around and saw nothing. Dad said, "Go wake up your sister and get dressed. We are going to Grandma and Grandpa's house." I dragged myself back up the stairs and woke my sister. I pulled on a pair of dark blue jeans and some tennis shoes and went back downstairs. I thought, "There will be no bike. Maybe, I will get a cake at Grandma's."

Dad put up the garage door on the single, unattached garage next to our house. In the garage was a dark red Schwinn with chrome fenders and white sidewall tires. I screamed with excitement. Now, it was probably thirty-eight degrees out and we were leaving for my grandparents' house but they let me ride down to the end of the block and back. The cold air hit my face and it stung like ice, yet I smiled and thought, "I am free."

As the weather slowly warmed, I rode my bike everywhere. I rode my bike to the county courthouse in Nebraska City where Bobby Kennedy was campaigning for president. That summer he would die by an assassin's bullet. I rode my bike to baseball practices and games. I could make it to my friend Chris's house in ten minutes. This would be the best summer of my life. School ended, and I was excited for baseball, one of Dad's favorite sports. Baseball was starting tomorrow. I rode my bike to Chris's house.

I left for home a little late. I was in a hurry and also liked the feel of the wind and speed as I went down the big hill from Chris's house. I was flying down the hill as fast as I could. I ran straight through the stop sign and heard the squeal of the brakes as a car slid and stopped just short of hitting me. Much to my surprise I turned and looked straight into the face of the driver, my father, staring through the windshield.

At that moment I thought, "Did he see me? Did he know it was me?" I started to pump the pedals on my bike as fast as I could. I could almost hear the music from *The Wizard of Oz*, as the Wicked Witch pedaled her bike furiously away with Toto, "Dat da da da da dah, dat da da da da dah." I rode home, threw my bike in the garage, ran up the stairs. Jumped on my bed and covered my head with the blanket. I waited.

Hours elapsed, and nothing happened. The sun was setting and I was hungry. Nobody said anything. I fell asleep scared and hungry. Mom came up and tucked my sister in. Still nothing.

I woke up to the sun streaming in my window. I lay there, still in the same clothes I wore the day before. I got up and eased down the stairs. Mom put a bowl of cereal with milk on the table. She asked if I was excited for baseball to start. I meekly said, "Yes." I looked around and saw that Dad had already left for work. I thought, *Did everybody forget? Did Dad not even know it was me?* I looked around for my baseball cap and glove. The ball was tied in the glove, the way my dad had shown me. Mom said I had better hurry or I would be late. I thought I have plenty of time with my bike. I headed out to the garage.

I opened the garage door and at first, I gasped as I saw no bike. Then to my horror, I saw my red, ten-speed Schwinn with chrome fenders and white sidewall tires. It was bolted to the ceiling of our garage. The bike was out of my reach. My freedom was gone.

"Hurry up!" I heard my mom yell.

I shook as I ran toward my first baseball practice. I don't know if it was from anger, confusion, shame or the adrenaline of running. My heart pounded. I was going to be late. My friends would laugh at me. Would they even let me play? I had to play. This was my father's favorite sport. How would I make him proud?

For the next three months, I walked. To my friend's house. To baseball practice. My bike remained bolted to the ceiling. Playing second base, I had one good game that summer with one double that drove home a run and double play. My father didn't even see that game. I probably was not really into it. I never played baseball again.

On the first day of school for fourth grade, I found my bike on the ground. Dad said, "Have a good day at school. Don't be late. You should know the value of a good education."

My fourth-grade teacher died that year. We had a substitute teacher the second half of the year. I missed Mrs. Williamson. She let me make Charlie Brown posters for the bulletin board. She also let me play Linus in our play, "A Charlie Brown Christmas."

She never came back after Christmas break. She was the first person whom I had ever known to die. My dad's father died a year or so later.

While my father was sad, I did not know my grandfather as well as I knew Mrs. Williamson. I knew, however, how my father felt—like the way I felt when I missed Mrs. Williamson.

Soon after that, we moved to Emmetsburg, a nice little town. I hated the move. I missed my friends. My father took the job of principal. I had to ride a bus to middle school. Older kids made fun of me because I was the new principal's kid. I soon discovered the expectations extended to the principal's children. We were expected to be involved and be good students. We had to be good examples to the other kids. I watched my father cry when he had to expel kids from school or suspend them from sports teams. These were the rules. I could not disappoint him. Remember, I was to be their perfect child. I knew about the value of a good education. I studied hard. I was involved in sports. I never did play baseball or basketball. I did, however, letter in football, wrestling and golf. I served on Student Council and sang in the show choir.

I graduated at the top of my class, a model student and son. During that time, I got a job as an aide at the local hospital. Health care would become a big part of the rest of my life. I knew Dad was proud when he handed me my diploma on graduation day. I never really felt the pressure in high school but I was relieved to go to college. Maybe, I could be like everybody else now.

Arriving at the University of Iowa, I still felt the same pressure. I would need to be a good student and son. However, as the semester played out, freedom from constant observation allowed me to develop my own opinions and personality. Was there a small rebellion? I would say yes. I partied like many kids. I became more liberal in my thinking. I had my first real girlfriend.

I rebelled against pharmacy school and soon transferred to nursing school. I was attending the campus Catholic Church. The host for communion was different here. It tasted like banana bread and wouldn't stick to the roof of your mouth. Other free thinkers were everywhere. I took classes on religion; my favorite was the Quest for Human Destiny. A Catholic priest, Jewish rabbi and Lutheran minister taught it. I had Jewish, Muslim and New Age and born-again Christian friends. I always questioned why my newborn friends thought my Jewish, Muslim and yes, even my Catholic friends were all doomed to hell.

I still felt different. I prayed every day. I walked nights alone along the Iowa River and would stop to talk to God. I always stood by the same lamppost. I knew God could hear me.

I had graduated from the University of Iowa College of Nursing and started my career.

My work as a nurse was fulfilling, and I soon became part of an Open Heart team, which entailed carrying a pager and working long hours. I saw life and death frequently. It became a vocation or calling. I spent hours with families going through very difficult times. One night, I realized that the long hours would be difficult as I got older, and I explored being a physician as a possible career move. It was either that or a nursing management position. I could not see how I would give up patient contact.

During this time, I was married. My wife was fun and spontaneous. However, she was not as stable as I would have liked. She attempted suicide, and I believe she had bipolar disorder. In her defense, she had an abusive childhood and was just trying to survive. I hold no animosity toward her.

I entered medical school and she soon left, had an affair, became pregnant by another man and then had an abortion. I offered to raise the child as my own. She made the decision to abort her baby, telling me about it after the fact. She returned and left again during residency.

I was raised Catholic, and divorce was foreign, as my parents remained married for over sixty years. I was sure that I would disappoint my parents, even though my parents knew the marriage had been turbulent. The hospital chaplain helped me the most during this difficult time. He told me one day, "God only expects you to do all you can. It is okay, if you already have."

I finished my medical residency and filed for divorce at about the same time. I moved to a small town in Ohio and bought a practice. However, my insecurity and loneliness had taken over. Because my divorce took over two-and-a-half years, I was soon engaged to my second wife and married within four months. I was overweight and alone. I did not want to live companionless.

So, it was thirteen years later, I was married, and still alone. I had stepchildren and step-grandchildren whom I loved, but I felt as if I was married in name only. They belonged to her, and she made that quite obvious.

I worked fourteen hours a day, working on the Electronic Medical Records and when home, I felt alone. I don't hold this against my ex-wife. We were different people. She married for someone to take care of her and her children. I was but a shell of who I should have been. I forgot that taking care of patients was of the utmost importance. My happiness was gone. I was depressed. My office family, especially Carla, noticed. I never stopped praying. I still believed that God answered prayers.

This brings me back to the summer of 1962. If that makes you think "summer of 1942," then … the so-called older woman was four years old at that time. Her name was Carla. Thirty-five years later, I walked into the home of Dr. Tom, who was contemplating selling his practice. I was just finishing my residency. I was introduced to his wife, Carla, with whom I immediately felt comfortable. At that time, she was thirty-nine years old.

Later I did purchase his medical practice, where his wife would become my office manager. Eighteen years would pass before we would figure out, we had actually been introduced ages before, on Revere Beach near Boston. What Carla remembers most vividly is that on that day, she proudly wore a brand new, blue, ruffled swimsuit.

Interesting, the things we remember. How was it that thirty-five years elapsed between the first and second meeting between Carla and me? Was there some connection? How did a boy born in Nebraska and a girl born in Boston meet in Ohio?

And, why, in the middle of all of our meditation, did we recall these memories? Why did we have the same memory from fifty-two years ago on Revere Beach?

How had our choices brought us together again? Was it possible that the Virgin Mary or some other spirit guide somehow intervened from the other side for my grandmother and grandfather? If not for a miracle, my grandfather would have died in the gas station explosion. My mother would not have been born. I would not even exist. Interesting how everything falls into place.

Chapter 5
In the Beginning, God

Dave and I were each raised God-fearing Catholics. That did not stop our overactive minds from wondering how it all began, whether it could be explained with evolution theory or the Big Bang theory. We were questioning everything we had learned and thought we knew up until this point what was real, what was invented and how had we come to exist? Where did angels and spirit guides come from? How did it all begin?

DAVE

One night while meditating, Isabella shared with me the following. These are Isabella's words, verbatim:

In the beginning, there was One. Complete in every way, God's male side was love, God's female side was inspiration. The love was like vital energy and the inspiration was like creation. One God in wholeness, completed by unity with a male side and female side. The joining of love and inspiration equaled one. That is God's wisdom. The wisdom is from completeness.

Then, an explosion started it all.

All of creation occurred.

Isabella continued to share that God shared love with the angels when they were created, never to be separated. They honor God's presence, are bathed in love and are in awe of God's presence. There is no choice. They cannot fathom God's absence, ever.

The infinite spread of God's reach is an ever-expanding universe and Heaven.

Creation from nothing.
Light from nothing.
Then, there was darkness.
The heat was immense. Too hot for light.
Then the heat cooled. Thirteen billion years had passed.
The energy slowed and then again there was light from vibration. God matched the vibration and created all souls.

From one-fourth of the vibration he created Spirit Guides. The vibration of the Spirit Guides matching the vibration of the souls.

Matter formed, then the pull of matter called gravity.

Then there were stars.

The earth was a speck in the solar system, the solar system a speck in the galaxy, the galaxy but a speck in the ever-expanding universe and surrounded by God and Heaven.

The earth was unique, warm and cold, wet and dry and rotating about the sun. The oceans and the land formed.

There was combining of atoms, and then cells.

Evolution occurred in the sea, air and on the land.

The human was evolving, with the vibration in the human mind matching the vibration of the light.

The vibration could be present in heaven and on earth. This being could now understand choice, different from the animals.

God placed the first souls, six thousand years ago, when the human was ready. The human was placed in stewardship of Earth.

God first placed a soul in woman and said, "You will be inspiration, creation, the Tree of Life, strength and beauty, both. You will bear the future."

God then placed a soul in man and said, "You will be her love, vitality, partner and equal; complete, only together." Together the two will possess wisdom they do not have apart.

God's commandment was to love one another and choose the path back home to "I AM."

Thus, they will be the example for their offspring to love one another, create with one another, grow with one another and learn from one another, each one important, separately.

God's commandment to love one another is meant for all forms.

So, what does God expect?

Human choices are not always wise, Isabella told us. Yet, like a loving parent, you are given life after life and chance after chance. God is not angry, just disappointed. The lessons must be learned. You must learn what love is with acceptance of who you are and who others are. *Love* shared makes you whole. You must learn what *love* is not; not *conceit,* not *selfishness,* not *jealousy.* You must *forgive* those who act this way. They still have lessons to learn.

Love and inspiration, vitality and creation, human enlightenment or wisdom; meditation and prayer will help you.

Choose the correct path, which is *LOVE.* That is the struggle of the human soul. It may take many lives but you are never alone. We are here to help you.

What was God's plan for humankind? God created us with the intention for us to grow with both masculine and feminine qualities. Our needs, wants, fulfillment and happiness are equal to our growth for self-preservation, awareness of others, awareness of self and self-actualization, which leads to enlightenment. We were all created with the intention to grow through these phases, all the while with free choice. This was God's plan: Create a being who could grow, help one another to grow, love and share. Let me confirm. God used wisdom to create each of us with a male and female side. Together we would be complete, partnering to grow. Our strengths would complement each other. Choosing a path back to God was the design from the beginning.

Just like any parents, in the beginning, God provided for our basic needs, as we were infants. We evolved from human-like creatures to be in sync with God and be able to understand the consequences of our choices. God placed souls in the early women and men. We were above the animals but only through our mental abilities. *We could all hear God, in the beginning.* We were born to those with instincts just like other animals. We needed food, shelter and each other. All animals start this way, in need of protection and guidance. But God made us creatures with lessons to learn. That was the difference.

The instinct for self-preservation is basic to our survival. Without this, we and the animals would not flourish, but die off.

We grow through stages. It starts with the basic needs of food, survival and belonging, like an infant. We start to become aware of others. The human being then learns to compete to survive and belong.

It is our choices that must be nurtured. When we are aware of others, we become aware of what they have. Do they have more than we have? Do we have more than them? Are they better than us? Are we better than them? These are questions that halt our growth. Killing another is possibly the greatest form of ***conceit, jealousy*** and ***selfishness***. Placing ourselves before another, robbing them of their chance to learn and grow is stealing their chance to ***love*** and complete their path.

Just like children, we must be taught to share and be happy with what we have and who we are. We are taught not to covet or want to be someone else or what they have. We are special just as we are, but not more special than another. ***Differences are our own uniqueness. Differences do not make us better, just different.***

Life after life we come back as someone different. We must learn the other side of the experience.

Jealousy is just a form of wanting. ***Conceit*** is just a form of prejudice tied to awareness of others and believing you are somehow better. ***Selfishness*** is just a form of self-preservation that is no longer necessary. This behavior halts our growth. We must be aware of others and their needs to understand our own needs and self. However, ***love*** and understanding of oneself only promotes more understanding of others.

We learn from loving parents, who are giving of themselves to us. They give to us and nurture us. The good parent gives us chance after chance to learn. God works this way. God is patient and willing to give us chance after chance and life after life to learn our lessons. God wants us to ***love*** each other, ***forgive*** our differences, accept those differences, share and work together and accept ourselves.

Chapter 6

Pieces of the Puzzle

And then things started to change …

CARLA

We continued to have lots of questions. In May 2014, I got it in my head that because some psychics and mediums hold your hands when giving a reading, maybe we should also. My reasoning was that with more energy, we would produce more results.

So, the four of us—Dave, Paula, Brenda and myself—sat at our table in the office and held hands. Dave closed his eyes and then opened them with awe and amazement. Apparently, with holding our hands together, he saw the image of a four-leaf clover. He saw our bodies and hands united, forming a light against a black background. Picture a strand of Christmas lights in the shape of a four-leaf clover on a black sky. That was what Dave drew for us to explain what he saw. We were all connected with energy—bright, lighted, connected energy. What an amazing feeling!

When Dave held Paula's hands, he saw her mother's eye and her father's eye behind her (also my mother and father, because Paula is my older sister as well as Dave's assistant). So, our parents. That made me happy.

Other times, the four-leaf clover would appear, every time we held hands together. One day, Dave's lighted four-leaf clover showed a break in the continual flow of light. It happened to be broken at my energy. I had been experiencing some kidney pain and was getting ready to start a round of antibiotics. Several days later, once my kidney pain had resolved, we held hands again and Dave saw no break in the continual flow of light. Apparently, illness breaks energy. That made sense to us.

It was all so wild and wonderful and interesting and confirming. There really was more to all of this birth, life, death, afterlife than just conjecture. It was unfolding before our eyes.

Dave asked himself and me, on many occasions, "Why me?" I answered that question with, "Why not you?" I was sure that other people had this ability who never came forward or spoke up for whatever reason. After all, in the past, people with such gifts have not been treated favorably. History tells us that Joan of Arc claimed to be receiving inspiration from above. Look how that information was received. The English burned her at the stake. In Salem, Massachusetts, in the seventeenth century, people believed some of the women among them were witches. The colony hanged them. History has countless accounts of people who are tortured or murdered because they brought a message of guidance. The ultimate confirmation that humankind has a hard time with guidance from our spiritual realm is, of course, Jesus Christ. You all know what they did to Him.

We continued to meditate daily and sometimes twice daily. However, my fear-based upbringing came rushing back to me, and I was then worried that my meditation would conjure up something that would horrify me.

Dave told me he was still a little fearful of all the events. He was waiting for someone to tap him on the shoulder and say, "Oops, just kidding." It was hard for him to fathom that he could close his eyes and access the spiritual realm. And still, he asked himself … why, why, why?

One day, during lunch, we decided to meditate with the entire staff again. Every day, I wear my mother's and father's wedding rings. I took them off and put them in Dave's hands. He immediately saw my mother and father. We now know that my parents appearing to Dave had nothing to do with the rings but came only to make Paula, Dave and me happy, but we did not understand it at the time.

Paula pulled out a picture of Aunt Mary and her former husband from her wallet, which produced a visit to Dave from our Aunt Mary as well as Paula's former husband. Both had already passed away.

We did this with Dave for a few days, and it worked over and over again. Many of our relatives surfaced for Dave. I was so happy. It was unbelievably satisfying to know our relatives were reachable and doing all right.

One day when we took turns holding Dave's hands separately, he held Brenda's hands and saw a pinkish/purple aura around her and a crystal on her head. He was flabbergasted and wondered what the heck that meant. He let go of her hands and did it again and still the crystal was on her head. Brenda is much younger than the rest of us in the office. She has only two family members who have passed over and no friends on the other side. Dave was greeted while in meditation mode by Brenda's grandparents. He only knew it was them after asking Brenda about her family members that had passed.

Interestingly enough, they were superimposed over each other and each had a purple cloud on their body. Brenda's grandmother's cloud was on her throat and her grandfather's was on his heart. This cleared up the purple cloud question. Remember, Dave first saw a purple cloud around my mother's head. My mother had died from a brain tumor, Brenda's grandmother died from thyroid cancer and her grandfather died from a heart attack. When Dave saw passed-over souls bearing a purple cloud, it was always in the area that took their lives on Earth.

Both grandparents had a crystal on their heads, just like Brenda's. Dave described their entry into his view as coming from the "over the horizon." Isabella informed him that Brenda's grandparents had completed their path and did not have to be reincarnated. "Over the horizon" is apparently where souls go after completing their lessons, or paths.

Paula was next. When Dave held her hands, he saw a rainbow aura around her. She had brought in a keychain that belonged to her deceased former husband. Dave got the image of a lightning bolt hitting a male's head and then complete purple color everywhere. Paula's former husband was killed when a large, steel beam broke from a chain and struck him in the head, killing him. Dave admitted to knowing Paula's former husband was killed on the job but had not known the details.

That night when Dave started to fall asleep, he said that it felt like someone smacked him in the head, as if to say, "Wake up!"

This was the first time that the spirit world communicated with him when he should have been sleeping, rather than while meditating. Isabella came to Dave first, as always, but was assisted. Many others came with her. None of them stood out in the forefront or were recognizable because they all stood on the left side of his viewing screen where the Spirit Guides, Angels and (for lack of a better word) Counsel were. They call them Counsel because they seem to give lessons and information about the Bible. So, one would refer to them as counselors.

We had been talking about the Bible that day, as we often would. Always we confronted the questions about how much of it was factual and how much was misinterpreted by humans. Dave's lessons from Isabella and Counsel during the wee hours of that morning were as follows:

- God exists. Prayer is like asking for a gift, magical intervention. It's like expecting and asking for something that you are not necessarily supposed to receive. Making a commitment to God is like asking for strength. It means you are trying to find the right path. Counsel and Isabella confirmed that there is, indeed, life after death.

- Some individuals on Earth have the gift to, indeed, communicate with passed-over souls. There are many types of souls. Only two human beings haven't reincarnated for a second life. But, we'll discuss those details later.

- Our goals here on Earth are personal growth, spirituality and love. At the risk of making this sound religious, Isabella told us: We exist by grace alone.

- Isabella reminded us we grow through good intentions, not through our works. In other words, if what you do is to gain something for yourself, rather than for someone else, it's lost. If you donate your time to something because it makes you appear important, it has no meaning or value. If you donate your time to a cause because it truly

is to help the cause of others, then, you have succeeded.
Always remember to live what you preach.

Later that morning, Dave attempted to meditate at the office. Isabella gave no information but rather took him to a warm, relaxing and peaceful place. She must have known that he needed rest after teaching him all night.

A lot of times when we meditated, Dave would see unfamiliar pictures and symbols such as hieroglyphics, farms and cities that he could view from overhead. None of it made any sense. Sometimes in a city, he would recognize something, clueing him in to where the city was, but he could not recall ever being there. This got to be normal meditation for a while. Another time he saw a picture of what seemed to be an old Roman city. Yet he had never been to Italy. Dave just viewed it while in meditation, and I made notes after he relayed it.

It seemed in the beginning that many of the passed-over souls knew Dave was a portal, because many were approaching him and asking about their living loved ones. Dave did not recognize these souls. One day, a soul approached, and our mother immediately got in front of that soul, pushed them away and demanded that Dave "AVOID." Mother explained these souls carried a great amount of negativity as they waited to reincarnate. Further, she did not want to chance them predicting the future to Dave. God does not want that, ever.

Sheila, Dave's other guide, then took over. Isabella seemed to be more distant. Sheila appeared to be in charge of Dave's past life experiences. She showed him a vivid picture of a farm with a white house with a brown roof and a huge tree. Vines covered the house. It appeared to be from an earlier time, about the 1800s.

This meant nothing to us. We would later learn these were areas of past lives for Dave. Sheila was trying to elicit feelings in Dave and stimulate his memory. She showed him the area as it was and as it is now. We now know that what Dave was seeing was New York, where he had previously lived in the 1800s.

I had the idea that maybe I could converse with our mother as if she was still on Earth. I asked her about me writing books. I had dabbled a bit with children's books but never published. She gave no predictions or insight. She responded with a statement that was, "There is value in writing."

This went hand-in-hand with our guides confirming we should never ask for future information. Our paths are to be lived without future knowledge.

Sheila and Isabella did give me ideas on subject matter for my children's books, which were about my cat. They knew that my cat, which my husband and I had found on our porch one night, tipped over a plant in my living room. They described the pot and the specific decoration dangling from it. The precision of the details shocked Dave and me. Dave wasn't even aware of the incident until Mother and Isabella mentioned and described it. I felt joyous, knowing these spirit guides were watching all the time and knew exactly what was going on. I found it rather comforting to know that someone is always with us, watching over us.

Dave was shown the miscarriage experience again about the third week in July 2014, which always made him uneasy. Although he did not actually feel pain and discomfort, he felt the closed-off feeling of coming down the birth canal and then darkness and hopelessness. It was strange and random when this experience would pop up.

The following day, Mother and Isabella had a message for me about my books. They gave me new ideas about what my cat's next experience should be. I found this so funny that there is nothing better to do in heaven, or wherever they are, than come up with subject matter for my books. How absolutely fantastic that there is such contact available to us!

When the strange, unspecified thoughts and pictures came to Dave, we never knew what to do with them. We documented them in the journal but were uncertain as to what they meant. We hoped that someday it would all make sense.

For example, the day of July 22, 2014, Mother came and told Dave she was taking him to my brother's past life. We couldn't be sure what this meant, because I have no brothers. The only brother that I was now aware of was Dave—my mother's miscarriage.

Mother took my brother Dave to what he thought was a farm in the 1860s. He could see a dog on the farm and then they showed him an up-close view of leaves on a tree. He noticed how colorful and visual the entire scene had become. But, he and we, had no idea what this all meant.

He also saw a big, white house with wooden posts, but again, no recollection of this place and time. We found out later, Mother was Dave's sister in this 1860s life, living their summers in New York, in the white house. She was trying to stimulate his memory of a past life as *her* brother.

Every new day brought some other questions to ask or family members to inquire about those who had already passed over.

It was fun, addictive, uncertain and very entertaining. None of us were late for work, unhappy to be there or in crabby moods. What a difference meditation was making!

Another day of meditation, and Sheila transported Dave to another time. Dave knew it had something to do with the Civil War during the 1860s. A man held up a book, and Dave understood the book was meant to be special. Isabella told him someday that book would have more meaning. It was the Bible. The man shaking the Bible at Dave was named Silas. He would learn more about Silas later.

Yet another day of meditation and Dave discussed a great, stone, pyramid-shaped monument structure he saw. Steps led up all sides of the structure. Tom and I had visited Chechen Itza in the Mayan Rivera several years before. I brought up a picture of the great temple on the computer, and Dave said chills ran up his back. We knew Dave had experienced a life there at this time. We just did not know the extent of that life.

Dave came in one morning with a bruise on his head from falling out of bed during the night. We all laughed and joked about it. Then, he explained why he fell out of bed. We finally had an explanation as to why Dave and I were so close.

Isabella and the Counsel informed Dave, once again, that he had been my mother's two miscarriages prior to the births of her daughters. But then she explained that Dave and I had shared many lives together. In a most recent past life together, she went on to tell him, he and I were children, ages four and six. I was falling from a third-floor staircase, and he stepped in front of me to save me. We both fell to our deaths, breaking our necks. That was why Dave fell out of bed that morning. Dave had relived it.

A couple of nights later, he fell out of bed again. This time, Isabella and the Counsel explained that in two lives previous, Dave and I were older. Dave got into a fight over me, and it ended in his falling on the ground after being shot to his death. He had, again, relived it and fallen out of bed.

That same night, his present-life friend, Willie, surfaced in his meditation. I should give you a bit of a background into their longtime friendship. Dave had known Willie almost as long as Dave and I have known each other. A year before our meditation began, Willie came to Dave's home late one night announcing he needed to have a serious talk. Dave really never had an in-depth conversation with Willie about life, just golf or work. So, he figured something was definitely up, important enough for Willie to call ahead and ask.

"You may think I'm crazy," Willie began. "I'm not sure what you believe about the spirit realm, but I've come to deliver a message to you."

Willie went on to explain that ever since he could remember, he had been able to speak with passed-over souls. "Your grandmother has a message for you," he said.

At this time, Dave's parents were both ailing, and he had seriously considered moving them to his home, a move that would have been across many states and with a lot of complication. Dave's grandmother conveyed to Willie that Dave's father would not be living much longer and she did not want him to proceed with moving them. Dave's father did, indeed, pass away several months later.

Needless to say, Dave was shocked. He had no idea that Willie possessed such gifts, and this revelation opened up an entire other aspect of their relationship. Before this, Willie had only told his wife and children about his gifts.

Willie even admitted to Dave that he drank too much to stop the voices contacting him from the other side. Apparently, drinking too much alcohol or partaking in other mind-altering substances disrupts the connection into the spiritual world. Willie was afraid of his gifts. His religious upbringing had taught him that the spirit realm was dark and he should fear who might contact him. As you'll see as we continue to discuss this, we would learn that Willie should not fear these gifts.

The minute Willie left, Dave called me.

"I had no idea all these years," he said. "Willie could see and talk to dead people. I had to tell someone. I knew you would be open-minded."

Isn't it a shame that some people possess wonderful, God-given gifts such as Willie's or Dave's, and in this life, other people and church beliefs have thwarted them, trying to insinuate a satanic nature? For centuries, kings, queens, churches and normal folk had mediums, mystics and psychics in their family groups to help get them through wars on the battlefield and crucial junctures of life. When did that change? Who started the rumors that these gifted people were the Devil?

This also brings up an integral part of the story line. Dave's wife was a devout Catholic. So, he never told her about Willie for fear of the conclusions she would reach. He certainly did not tell her about his abilities. He was trying to shelter her as well as stop her from thinking that he had completely lost his mind. In the beginning, I asked Dave every day if he had told his wife yet. Every night, I discussed the day's events with Tom, who was open-minded and interested. I kept asking Dave to have that conversation with his wife. He started by tuning in to a television series featuring a medium, which opened the conversation to meditation and the positive stress-reducing effects he was experiencing. His wife didn't ask any questions and showed no interest. So, Dave asked Isabella and the Counsel how he should handle this. They advised him that his wife would not understand it and that he should tread lightly. He said no more.

Even though Willie brought Dave a message from a dead person, Willie was not open to conversations about it, and it is still a rare day when Willie brings up the subject. Dave does not bring it up; he waits for Willie to do so. Still, Dave decided soon after their conversation to confide in his friend about his gift. Willie was not surprised or reactive, yet still did not want to discuss it. He finds the gift disruptive to his life.

Once, Willie explained, he had been to a medium and a channeler who confirmed the two friends shared a past reincarnation in Greece. Willie was an army leader, and Dave was one of his soldiers. Willie was ordered to take his army into an action that would have most probably killed all of his troops. He reluctantly obeyed the order and consequently was killed along with his entire army. That would prove to be only the beginning of the past lives the two friends have shared.

Another night, Dave was shown a past life in which Willie was his commander in a Greek life, and I was in that life. Both men were protecting me. Sheila showed Dave a metal shield with a Roman or

Greek symbol. Dave drew a picture of it but wasn't sure what the symbol meant. We did not know why they were protecting me. This would be the third time Dave was shown a part of a life with me where he was trying to protect me.

Chapter 7

Who is God?

Over Labor Day weekend, I had been to a party with Brenda, and the hostess had brought in a medium. We had showered her with questions. Brenda's questions focused on her future life with a husband and children. Because Dave had seen a crystal over Brenda's head, she mentioned it to the medium, who advised her to purchase a quartz crystal to keep with her always through life. We learned later this meant nothing. It was clear this medium had no clue. She was suggesting something, not giving an answer. Besides, we would soon learn, mediums, psychics and others with those gifts of connection should never predict the future. It affects our paths, the actions we are to choose and take on our own without insight.

But that weekend I asked the medium about Dave's gift and ways I could more effectively meditate. Remember, in the beginning, our mother had informed Dave that I had a gift and needed to practice it. I was having so much difficulty just quieting my mind. The medium advised me to purchase a pyramid stone to use in meditation. She said that Dave seemed to have dynamic gifts because of what he was able to achieve. She insinuated it was not common. Of course, Isabella later said, the pyramid was not necessary. Stones and objects are not necessary. All we need to meditate, find peace and reach God is: ourselves, quiet and a comfortable position.

But before Isabella could explain this to us, the third week of September 2014, Brenda and I decided to shop at a holistic store that sold crystals in a town about forty minutes away. At that point, I had hoped it would help me. When that Friday came, we double-checked the hours of operation, but when we arrived, a note on the front door announced the store was closed.

Needless to say, Brenda and I were not pleased. I called the telephone number on the door and got the shop owner. She explained that she was at a college nearby mixing essential oils with students in a class. "It's just about over," she said. "Stay there." She offered to open the shop for us, so we waited. We purchased crystals and a pyramid stone, but the best part was the conversation with the storeowner.

I noticed her store pamphlets on the counter. I picked one up out of curiosity and to spread the word. The name of her shop included the name, "Asherah." I knew from her business card that her name was not Asherah.

"Who is Asherah?" I asked, and she lit up.

"Asherah is God's wife," she said, which launched us into a religious discussion that riveted Brenda and me for at least an hour or more. I was so focused on God having a wife, my mind didn't absorb much else. We also touched on the world's views of men and women and the inequality between them. This led into the owner's story of deceit and divorce from her husband. We had not intended to take up all her time, knowing that she had somewhere to go, but it was obvious that she needed to get a few things off her chest.

This would open up an entire new topic with our meditation and contact with the spiritual world. Nothing happens by coincidence. Everything has a purpose. Later, Dave would discuss with Isabella the truth of Asherah, and her role with God. We were starting to connect the dots. Things were happening in our lives, causing us to ask particular questions. With each question, new subjects arose. Answers were given to common questions. Life was thrilling and exciting. They were answers that questioning minds would seek.

A few days later, Dave rushed into the office and started babbling about the previous night's meditation. "Listen to this!" he said. "You need to journal this immediately."

He continued, "I talked to Isabella all night. I asked her about Asherah, and if she was God's wife. She said, 'In a way. She is part of God.' This caused me to ask her, 'Who *is* God?'"

Dave was speaking loudly, talking fast and exuberantly. I waited for whatever it was he was about to tell me with bated breath. Something big was coming. I was excited for him without even knowing what he was about to say.

"I asked Isabella who God was."

His voice still raised and tears streamed down his cheeks. "After I asked Isabella who God was, I heard a loud, deep voice answer.

"I AM."

"The voice sounded nothing like anything I had ever heard before, or, should I say felt before? It was warmer, softer, comforting and yet electrifying. I was aware of everything inside of me changing. I literally felt as if my heart jumped in me. My body calmed to the point that nothing else mattered but the joy that was pulsating in my body at that exact moment. What I was feeling was all encompassing. I have to admit that I felt it, saw it, smelled it and experienced it all at once. I seemed to be vibrating from head to toe yet nothing was moving. I knew who I was experiencing, and it was not Isabella. It was God."

As I listened, I tried to imagine what I would have felt to hear this voice. I looked at Dave. I could feel his awe, elation, complete joy, unworthiness but mostly warmth in his heart, all because God had spoken with him. He was so emotional for a few minutes, just relaying the story. Dave's tears were tears of happiness.

"It was really like having a normal conversation, as you would with anyone," Dave said.

God told Dave that the name He calls Himself is YWH, pronounced like Yahweh. Yes, I had heard this before, and it is mentioned in the Bible but not spelled exactly as it was given to Dave that night. God further went on to say that it is what God calls Himself, and we are not to refer to Him by this name. In this book, we respect and honor that wish.

But Dave's conversation with God did not end at that. Now it got even better. I personally loved this part because I already knew this part my entire life and felt it with every inch of my being.

God told Dave, "He is also *She*." The name She gives her female side is SHR. That is pronounced Asherah, but as you guessed it, we are not to use that name. It is what She calls Herself. As with YWH, we shall read these names with reverence and not speak them out loud.

Dave continued. "God explained, 'It is essential for each person to harness the yin and yang of the soul. The male needs to nurture the female side of himself, and the female needs to nurture the male side of herself.'"

God's intention is that all, male and female, evolve to become one, Dave said. She further said, "How can a husband fully love and understand his wife (partner) if he never taps into his female side? How can a wife (partner) understand and fully love her husband if she never uses her male side?"

So, Dave and I were thinking, it is simple really. Society has instructed us over the years as to how we should and should not behave. Someone decided that males and females should act specific ways many years ago, and for whatever reason, we went along with it.

This gave us much to think about. We talked about how some of the best marriages work because no one is keeping score on who acts feminine or masculine. The couple work as one. It can work. Many unhappy marriages are unhappy because of just that. The partners are trying to be who they are not, instead of who they are. Nobody wants that. So, why shouldn't we be who we are, be proud of it and be happy? If the man is better at staying home and nurturing, then by all means, he should stay home. If the woman is a better mechanic, then she should repair their cars. Why do people put labels on everyone? A person is a person.

Remember when Brenda's grandparents appeared to Dave super-imposed over each other as one in the last chapter? This is God's real wish. The love that a couple shares, whether married to each other or not, is intended to make them as one. The ultimate in that connection would be what we call a soul mate. (That discussion would come later in our lessons with Isabella and the Counsel.)

Here is the bottom line, our goal in each life, per Isabella. "Just know, our goal in each life is being in touch with God spiritually, spiritual growth and love. We all have a never-ending stream of spirit guides, angels and passed-over loved ones who watch over us. God watches over us constantly. Dave was given a gift. A gift, allowing him to speak with his guides and yes, at times with God. He is not special.

He is blessed. We are all blessed in different ways. He was chosen to deliver messages to others. He has chosen to do so. Just because you are not hearing them doesn't mean they are not there."

Hopefully, after reading this story, you will be able to meditate and connect with your guides. The reason we kept a journal in the beginning of our meditation was because Isabella and our mother advised us it would be important to do that. We did what we were told because, obviously, we believed that we were and are receiving divine messages. We hoped we would always be able to connect. We had learned so much and wanted to continue to learn.

Chapter 8

Questions for God

CARLA

I figured if Dave was given an opportunity to ask God questions, I would ask Dave to relay some questions that were always puzzling to me. I am an animal lover. I always wondered if we should eat animals. I do, but I often ask myself if it is right. So, I asked Dave to ask God, and God responded with this answer through Isabella:

We should not eat anything that eats any other living being.

That makes it quite simple. So, if you know that the animal you are planning on eating has eaten another animal, do not eat it. That includes meat, fish and poultry. We asked Isabella again to ask God for clarification.

Do not eat scavengers or carnivores. God said so. If you are unclear, read Leviticus 11.

My next question was, "Is the Bible completely factual?" Isabella relayed God's answers to Dave:

The Bible is somewhat true and somewhat made up by humankind. Most of the Bible was written many years after the events occurred. It was inspired. However, humankind has made mistakes in translation. The stories and words were changed to suit the times and needs of the authors. The part of the Bible that is absolutely true, without any hesitation, is the Ten Commandments. There is no way around them and no exceptions.

Love *one another as you would have someone* ***love*** *you.*

Isabella relayed that this really is the sentence that sums up the Ten Commandments. Everything is about *love.* Think about it, if you loved your neighbor, you certainly wouldn't steal from them and if you loved your God, you certainly wouldn't use God's name to curse, since there are a hundred other words that would suffice. If you loved your parents, you would hold them in the highest regard and if you loved humankind in general, you certainly wouldn't kill someone, just to name a few. You wouldn't lie or cheat.

Then I had another question, "What about adultery?" Because marriage is human-made and not necessary, how can you commit adultery? Isabella responded:

*A relationship and bonding of a couple where there is **love** should not be broken by another. You should honor their commitment until they deem it ready to be ended.*

Two persons can be married and have no **love,** for whatever reason. God would call that a waste. God expects and wants you to have **love** and not stay in a loveless relationship for money or laziness. That is **selfish** and **conceited.**

So far, we were on a roll. I decided to ask a big one. "What about abortion?"

Abortion is murder. Thou shalt not commit murder. Only God should decide which soul lives and dies. You have choice but only God can justify.

Dave had questions, too, so he asked God through Isabella, one day at the end of September 2014, "Who was Jesus?" God confirmed through Isabella again.

Jesus was, indeed, one hundred percent man, created by God. His soul was created to be in full connection with God. Jesus felt pain, sorrow, heartache and all the emotions that a man would feel. He was a man. A beautiful, kind, loving soul of God. Because he felt all human emotion, and because he was in full communication with God, he has become the link between God and all Spirit Guides, seated at the right hand of his God.

Proof is in the Experience

The end of September brought visitors to my home. My stepson and his wife came from several states away. They visit quite a bit. They are both professed atheists and are not afraid to tell you. They like to believe that they are scientists and have the need for everything to be proven to them. This really is the case in regard to any subject. I have tried over the years to have discussions about belief and offer possible scenarios that would change their minds. Nothing has worked.

I apprehensively gave Tom's son and his wife insight into Dave's and my meditation sessions, hoping this could provide a change in their thinking and thus belief in God or something.

Immediately, my stepson required proof. He has a longtime friend in South Dakota whom he met in the Air Force. They had a pact that if one of them died, there was a word each one of them would recognize. So, if the dead one tried to contact the other one from the spiritual world, this "pact word" would be the only true confirmation that there is something else beyond life here. My stepson said that his friend's wife, who had died from cancer, should be able to tell us the word. Her name was Deena.

Naturally, I turned to Dave and asked for this word—anything to provide proof to these two scientists. I was living and breathing confirmation daily. They needed "proof." Isabella said, "Your stepson needs to learn to grow on his path. We won't give him 'proof.' His path will lead him to realization. If he chooses, he will find realization and with that, 'proof.'"

All of those of us at the office had been reading the Bible—Paula, Brenda, Dave and me. I had given Brenda a Bible as a gift because she had no religious upbringing or background. My thoughts have always been that everyone needs a basis from which they can make their own decisions about religion. Not everyone seeks answers once they reach adulthood. Therefore, I purchased a Bible for Brenda, a new version, readable and large print, with her name engraved on the cover. I bought one for myself as well and suggested that Paula find one that she found easy to read and understand. I purchased a Bible for Dave as well, for Boss's Day, and it sat on his desk as a reference when we needed it throughout the day.

Many days, when we would discuss something we thought was factual, we would find out through meditation that it was not necessarily so. Keep in mind: None of us attended church anymore. This was all new behavior since meditation had begun. Growing up, Paula, Dave and I had read many Bibles front and back, the child's version, teenage version and, of course, the adult one. It had been many years since any of us picked up a Bible and read it.

Paula asked Dave one day about the Rapture, as mentioned in the Bible. This was an interesting response and actually a comforting one to have. She had been discussing the Rapture with our other sister, Joan, who attends a church that believes Jesus is coming back to us on a big, white horse and taking just four hundred thousand "born-again" Christians to Heaven with him.

On this question, Dave turned to Isabella. She, along with Counsel, informed Dave that the Rapture is nothing more than a human-fabricated event. It has nothing to do with the end of time as we know it. They went on to say that we are living the Rapture as we speak. War, pestilence, greed and selfishness are all taking place right now in a human-made hell. They again said to use the Bible as a guide for daily living and to use it at today's standards.

I used to awake in the morning and remember parts of a dream or dreams. This hasn't happened for a long time. When I meditate at home, I will get pictures, randomly during and afterward. Sometimes I remember them and sometimes I do not. One evening as I was coming out of meditation, I heard a voice say, "We have your Italian grandfather with us." I found that interesting because I was named after my grandfather, and I feel especially close to him for that reason. He passed away when I was about nine or ten. I always think of him fondly. What I do remember of him was that he always gave me quarters before we said goodbye. My mother used to say that he acted more like our father than our grandfather. He provided us with bread and milk and stoked the coal furnace when my own father was too lazy or too selfish to take care of things. I have nice, kind and warm thoughts of my grandfather. It was pleasant to hear he was with my spirit guides.

Often, when I awake in the morning, when my mind is not quite in full gear and I am still in an unthinking mode, between consciousness and sleep, I will hear or see something. The pictures are of random things. They do not make much sense, usually. I always see them with a kind of veil over them. In other words, I see them unclearly. I guess it's a gift, as Isabella says. It is to protect what I see.

Dave always says that what he sees is in 3D and as clear as clear can be and as colorful as possible. Meditation opens you to the spirit world. That world is able to reach you, when your mind isn't clouding your thoughts. Apparently, the space between sleep and full awakening is a great time for their world to reach us. I look forward to it each morning now. Dave interprets through Isabella what I see if I remember to ask him or journal what I see. Often, Elizabeth, my spirit guide, is giving me a message of some kind or reminding me of something of significance in my past lives.

I came home from work and sat in my chair to meditate one day around the beginning of October 2014. My husband was out of town. I picked up my Birthday Book, which is a description of personalities based on astrological signs. There is also a section on love, marriage, friends and coworkers. I read all the areas related to my birthday and found that none of my friends, husband or coworkers got along with my birthday. Silly as this may seem, I found myself very depressed. I had been having difficulties with my best friend. She seemed distant and not her usual self. I felt really bad. Clearly, I was confused. Nevertheless, I was depressed.

I woke up in the morning with the most vivid picture ever!

I could draw it today in its exact entirety. It was that clear, that memorable, that 3D and that colorful. It was an eye. An extremely crystal clear, slightly blue-gray eye with a circle around it. Around the outside of the circle was a white background with black design. I thought to myself, whoa, that was interesting. I went back to sleep as it was only 5 a.m. I woke a second time. Again, the picture was as clear as clear could be. It was in 3D, colorful, clear, precise and interesting. I could draw the picture exactly, yet today. The picture was a cobblestone street. The middle of my viewing screen was the head of a serpent. It looked to my left. There really was no body attached but a slight body behind the head. That was intense, clear and strange. What the heck did that mean?

I went back to sleep, got up with my alarm and the two visions were as clear as ever. I did not forget any part of them.

Later that day, I explained to Dave about my two visions. I asked him if he could find out what they meant. The next day, Dave came in with news of his conversation from the previous night with Isabella. Isabella said I had seen the eye of God. I had been shown God since I could not hear God. I am not open enough to hear God. I was all right with that.

Actually, I was more than all right with that. I just didn't understand why. God went on to explain to Isabella that I was not on the correct path with my thinking. God then showed me a serpent on a path, to insinuate that I was on the incorrect path. I was not afraid when God showed me the serpent. It did not scare me, I was curious. God showed me something that I would recognize from my upbringing. I understood when God told Isabella, God showed a serpent to signify the wrong path. My Catholic upbringing uses the serpent to signify anything wrong.

Dave asked me what I had been doing the day before that God felt the need to come to me? I really did not remember reading the Birthday Book.

My thoughts were on the fact that God came to me and was shown to me. Now, come on, who wouldn't feel a little overwhelmed about that? To know that I had some direct caring from our God above was a bit crazy. But it happened. I was blown away.

We decided to go into meditation mode and ask again exactly what it meant. When we started, I had all kinds of thoughts in my head, trying to rekindle the day before. I went over everything I had done the night before, and when I got to the part where I remembered the Birthday Book, and my getting depressed over it, a wave of feeling, came over me. I knew it was like God was saying to me, "Yup, that was it … you remembered it."

I opened my eyes. Dave opened his. "Your thinking on Monday night was not on the correct path, and God is trying to alert you," he said.

"I remembered exactly what it was," I explained it to Dave. "God said the astrological part of our personalities is correct. It does influence us and our behaviors, but the way we get along in the section about marriage, friendship, love and coworkers was all incorrect." It was good to know and understand. Who wrote that stuff anyway? I was beating myself up over something that wasn't even factual. Luckily, we had an inside track that was keeping us informed.

That night, Dave received more information about the zodiac. The next morning, he conveyed to me how the zodiac signs do affect us. They are responsible for our ups, downs and personality traits. Sometimes you are at your best, and sometimes at your worst. When those around us have ups and downs, it affects how we relate.

Isabella and the Counsel had many lessons to discuss with Dave that night. They confirmed that the Bible is to be used as a guide. It is often correct but also incorrect. Use it as a reference, they advised.

A great example that they gave about the Bible was how we need to use it with today's standards referring to men and women. Women and children are not possessions and are not to be treated as such. Men and women complete each other and become whole. The Bible makes it sound as if women and children are under men's orders. That was then, this is now. Use the guide at today's standards.

The Bible is historic and not always factual. There are many errors in the Bible, as it was inspired but written by men. For example, war and the end of the world cannot be predicted. God is the only one to predict or foretell what is about to happen. God has never told man when the world will end. It has all been conjecture and misinterpretation through languages.

The subject of baptism came up. Baptism means nothing. It is human-made. Only God washes away your sins, not water, not man, not confession to a man.

One morning, Dave decided that he would attempt to go on the right side of his viewing screen. Now, remember, this side has always been a bit scary for Dave, as there are tons of eyes looking at him and soul after soul trying to talk to him and convey messages. He wasn't sure what the outcome would be.

Our mother appeared and gave him permission to travel to that side. He saw our Aunt Mary, an owl and an easel. We already knew that the owl referred to Paula but we were not sure the essence of the easel. Paula and I have another sister; actually, we have two other living sisters. Joan is an artist. She resembles Aunt Mary more than anyone else in the family. I assumed that this easel meant Joan. Aunt Mary also showed us a little cross and told Dave that she is not returning, not reincarnating. Dave's father is not, nor are Brenda's grandparents. She and Mother explained to Dave that when he travels to the side with all the souls, they are waiting to return, reincarnate. They further explained that there is negativity attached to that side, and they urged Dave to not visit if possible.

The souls on the right side, for lack of a better way to explain it, are returning— reincarnating—for lessons to be learned. When they return, they are blinded from their past. This ensures that they learn on their own and not with assistance from past mistakes. Dave figured that he was unable to communicate with many of those souls due to their knowledge, and that it could affect his path here. That made sense, in an absolutely, unbelievable manner. But then this entire episode has been that way to us regularly.

Finally, the second week in October 2014, Dave asked Isabella why he has been given this gift with the spiritual realm. He believes she is trying to protect him from psychic mistakes. She explained to Dave that he is openly innocent and because he did not ask for this gift or want it, they want to ensure he uses it for good only and not for gain or profit. She went further to explain to him that many psychics, mediums, etc., use such a gift for personal gain and for power. The bestowing of this gift on Dave is not for any such thing.

This was truly no surprise for me or the others in the office. We all see and understand Dave enough to know that he would never use this gift other than to help people. He is that caliber of person. If there is such a person who is pure, wholesome and selfless, it would be Dave. It is very apparent, through this entire process, he is becoming even more so.

His transformation from crabby and overwhelmed to free-spirited, contented, giving and kind has been remarkable. I am not surprised this gift was given to Dave. He has the nature to handle it. He lives it.

My dear friend Diane has chosen a tough path in this lifetime. She works hard labor, is divorced, has unsupportive parents and a son who is a heroin addict. Though her life is difficult, the light in her life is her wonderful daughter and her grandchildren.

Ironically, though, Diane is full of sunshine. She is beautiful and smart but held back by her fear. She has stayed in a job where she is comfortable but has no growth and no opportunity to use her gifts. Anyone would expect her to be in fashion or in the beauty field; however, she is stuck in a plant doing manual labor and driving a huge truck. She knows her potential but is stymied by her lack of confidence. This lack comes from her unsupportive parents.

Like so many other women in life, Diane fell in love when she was young, became pregnant and got married. Her cheating/addict husband went on his way and left her to find a job that could support her children and herself. We meditated, and I asked Dave to talk to Counsel about Diane. I wish so much that I could take her pain away and replace it with happiness. She so needed it. Then a lesson came from the Counsel:

We are to follow the rules of the Earth. Give to God, give to man and follow the rules of the Earth while you live on Earth.

Diane is a free spirit. She does tend to do things a little differently than the average person, maybe, but she certainly is not there on her own with these actions. The entire world is full of persons not obeying the rules of the Earth. Apparently, they notice it up there? Anyway, there was a little parable attached to my questions and this was the example given to us. Three farmers each have an incredible harvest, better than any they have ever had.

- The first farmer gives his excess to the poor.

- The second farmer puts his excess in storage for the future.

- The third farmer doesn't harvest anything, and the crop dies in the field.

Which farmer was not following the correct path?

The third farmer, of course. He was given a gift and chose not to do anything with it. The lesson to Diane and to all of us is to take the gifts that are given to us and use them. Do not waste them.

Unfortunately, in the course of Diane's path through this life, she has been a little careless with the gift of her body. She has had many boyfriends on the path to finding Mr. Right, and many of those choices were poor ones. The only example she had to follow of how a man behaves had been her father, not the best one, in her case. Thus, Diane chose men who used her, mistreated her and made her feel like an object rather than the beautiful woman she is. She was on a quest for love and acceptance, which she has never received from her parents.

When Diane shares about her pain with me, I hope and pray that something I offer her touches her at her core. I want her to realize her worth and proceed on a better path.

Isabella and the Counsel emphasized that sex is a gift not to be wasted, that it should be a gift used under appropriate circumstances. I passed that along to Diane. Sex is meant to comfort and to show love. It is not for physical pleasure alone. It is meant to cement a relationship.

God spoke to Dave again during the night of October 14, 2014:

I am your reason for living and your purpose. Having said that, I am not the only purpose.

Our purpose in life is to find our path and figure out our way back to God. We are given path after path in life after life with chances of living the correct way and means to get back to God.

God told Dave:

I gave you Moses, Jesus and Muhammad to guide you back to me.

Then God added:

Your gift was given to you in an attempt to prove to others that reincarnation is real, and it is meant to help others find their way back, either in this life or the next.

The discussion did not end that simply. God's other words of advice were to take heed in regard to the passed-over souls. God said that they are speaking to Dave, like our mother is, for inspiration only. They are not connecting for future predictions.

Remember also that you reap what you sow and as the saying goes, what goes around comes around.

The next time God spoke to Dave, God said:

All souls were created before the Earth was made. When God decided, God wanted to make life, God created all souls. It was before all time.

That said, it means that Jesus's soul was made before the beginning also. However, only Jesus and Muhammad have had just one life.

In mid-October 2014, Isabella and the Counsel told Dave to have me write a book for Dave and to include all of these stories, lessons and past life experiences. That was food for thought. Up until this point, I had been journaling only. So, we continued to journal, hoping that we would know how to create the book in the future. As usual, I had more questions for Dave.

I wondered about some old sayings used by my parents, grandparents and others in my life. Dave asked Isabella for answers. I inquired about "cleanliness being next to godliness" and your body being the temple of God. Dave was told that in order to follow your path in life and stay focused, mind, body and soul must work together. The way to stay on this path is by caring for your body (your temple) and your mind. Keeping your body, mind and soul clean, healthy and whole—that is the correct path.

All his life Dave struggled with weight issues. Over the years, his weight had fluctuated often. At that time, he weighed over three hundred pounds. Most of Dave's eating habits stemmed from self-worth issues—not caring enough about himself to remember that your body is, indeed, your temple. But now the "big guns" from upstairs had told him he'd better get healthy—and that was his path. That had a profound effect. After this, Dave changed his eating habits and shifted his thinking about how important his health was.

I have long been an advocate of eating healthy and gluten-free. My mother was a health fanatic long before it was a fad. She started us in the 1960s with vitamins and healthful eating. I remember getting excited when she made soup if I thought there was a potato in it. But I was always disappointed to bite into a parsnip, disguising itself as a potato.

About ten years ago, a friend was diagnosed with celiac disease. He and I had many similar symptoms. My friend's wife worked for a group of gastroenterology doctors, and she explained that although I didn't have celiac as her husband did, many levels of wheat and gluten allergies existed. "You have allergies," she said, and that sent me into gluten-free eating.

Dave knew about my eating habits. He is plagued with many allergies and has been since birth. I often tried to urge him into eating without gluten because it appeared after he had a sandwich or a bun, the next day there'd be a rash all over his head, face and neck. Years of my nagging, for lack of a better term, finally sunk in and he decided to give this style of eating a try.

Amazingly, his rashes vanished, and he started losing pounds rather easily. He was on a great path. The weight loss, meditation and connection with the spiritual world combination was creating a new Dave. He had a newfound self-confidence and an entire happy, content side, which was trickling down into his practice and everyday life.

We were all ecstatic with his progress. He was funny again and a pleasure to be around. His patients continued to adore him.

Part III

I

Inscribe

Love is a choice and an action.
Elizabeth

# Chapter 9
The Five Simple Rules
of Living

One day during meditation, Isabella gave us *Five Simple Rules* to follow and live by. They correspond with the biblical Ten Commandments and, actually, are easier to remember. Three of five are behaviors you should live without, while two are actions you should carry in your heart and soul forever.

We should:

+ Live without **conceit.**

+ Not harbor **jealousy.**

+ Be without **selfishness.**

+ Let **love** fill our heart and soul.

+ **Forgive** always.

Each choice or action in life needs to begin with asking yourself, "Am I trying my best to not be **conceited, jealous** or **selfish?** And do I choose to **forgive** others their trespasses and **love** others despite them?"

Isabella tells us to live as Jesus did. She reminds us that if we are behaving as He did, we will automatically follow these simple rules. It will be easy to put others before ourselves and if they wrong us, *forgive* them. In the long run, not one part of what they do to us is permanent.

Isabella made things even clearer.

Conceited is believing the color of your skin somehow entitles you to take precedence over another one's soul. How can this be? We have all been dark-skinned and light-skinned during our many reincarnations. I have lived fourteen lives with darker skin. How else can one understand another unless they have walked in their shoes? I have been a slave several times, and I have owned slaves. Dave has had seventeen lives with darker skin. He has been a slave and an owner of slaves.

Remember, no one owns another. It is *conceit* that allows us to find virtue in controlling or owning another human. Whether it is being a slave or being enslaved by an empowered spouse, one who controls has *conceit*, believing their way is the correct way.

Any form of prejudice, be it against skin color, sexual choice, religion, political affiliation or your social position in life, is called being *conceited.*

Are you a Republican who is sure every Democrat on the earth is stupid? Are you a Democrat feeling superior to any Republican who doesn't vote as you do? It is *conceited* to be a bigot. It is terribly *conceited* to believe that either party could ever be absolutely correct in all of their actions.

All forms of bragging are being *conceited,* whether in person or on Facebook.

It's understandable if you defend righteousness. However, is it our place to decide what is morally correct, justifiable or virtuous? Giving an opinion in the right setting is one thing, but do we need to wage an all-out war on each other for a difference of opinion? The correct idea, as with any two people who are gathered together, would be to place yourself in the other one's shoes.

Is war necessary? We engage in war to prove we are more powerful and entitled than another country or person, because let's face it, we also go to war in life with our relatives and friends at some point. If someone disagrees with us, are we going to all lengths to prove our correctness? When it is a country, are there no other means to reach an agreement? Can we walk away from a situation that is not ours, and should we? Did we carefully consider the future outcome before attempting to prove our point? Think about how you would feel if another country invaded our homeland and left us without our everyday niceties, like our warm home, bed, refrigerator or car, not to mention our place of employment, grocery stores or churches. Can you imagine the town where you live being destroyed beyond recognition and food not being readily available to you? We take so much for granted. Our country is very lucky and blessed to not have been attacked. Can we place ourselves in our so-called enemy's shoes and think of the horror that is theirs? Their country is not just composed of fighting soldiers. There are mothers, fathers, children, babies, grandparents, not to mention doctors, lawyers, hairdressers, grocery clerks. These are the persons we take for granted and forget when attacking another nation. It is not just a country of soldiers we attack. We are attacking ourselves. Think about it. And, it's all in the name of who is correct and who is more powerful.

Change in the world has to start with one person—one act of kindness or thoughtfulness—and blossom into a world of kindness, thoughtfulness and unity.

We must respect each other's differences. We must not be so **conceited** to believe we are always right. We are not more special than anyone else. But self-evaluation is always best.

We go to all-out war because we believe our ways are the correct way. We or they want what the other has. It is very **selfish** to believe this way.

Why are we habitually **jealous** of others and what they possess? Can we be satisfied with the blessings we have? And what a horrible excuse it is, to go to war in the name of God. God does not need to be defended. God is almighty.

For instance, Dave and I were Vikings in AD 900, then one of us reincarnated in AD 985 becoming English Royalty, fighting against the Vikings. We lived both sides. We are both sides of the wars at some point. It's karma.

Kings and queens have felt and been entitled, for centuries now. It is silly to believe the blood running through your veins is somehow more special than another's. It's all the same blood. Not money, fame, fortune, your name, sex or the color of your skin gives you the right to feel more special than another. That is **conceit**.

Actors, actresses, singers, musicians, artists of all kinds, have been given gifts from God. They should just be grateful for their gifts, but not feel superior. Whatever their specific gift is, it does not make them somehow special or spokepersons for the entire nation. Who is more special—an actress, a trash collector, a mail carrier, a clergyman, a brain surgeon? None of them. We are all the same but somehow, some people more than others believe they are more special just because they lead better lives, financially, than we do. We should not revere another human being as more special than ourselves. Because, if we do, it leads to our next simple rule to follow: Do not harbor *jealousy.*

Jealousy is not only wasteful—it is laughing in the face of God. Because if God created the other and their situation, it has to be right, just as yours is. Every gift and talent given from God is for a specific outcome. Don't you believe God would be disappointed if you chose not to use whatever the gift was bestowed on you? We need trash collectors, mail carriers, clergy leaders, doctors and entertainers.

Remember, we have all been kings, queens and servants, paupers, wealthy, black, white. We are not better than any other human being!

Imagine you give birth to a child who grows up and comes out as being gay. Are you appalled? How could I produce a gay child? Isabella says:

God says love is love whether between a man and woman or woman and woman or man and man.

Are you so **conceited** that you believe God would bestow upon you a gift you did not want? Are you embarrassed to tell people you have a gay child? Are you so special and so full of yourself you believe this child was an error? Being different than you does not make someone a mistake, wrong, bizarre, a freak, beneath you or not loved or produced by God. God creates perfection; it's our choices that are imperfect.

My husband and I have a new cat. He's rescued, of course, as are our other two pets. It normally takes a couple of months for them to adjust to one another. Basically, our pets need to know they are loved and learn; they are as important as all of our pets. During the adjustment, they are *jealous.*

People are the same but with the reasoning ability, unlike pets (which, by the way, is an advantage). If you know in your heart you are **loved** and feel content with yourself, there's no reason to compete for the center stage. If you are doing your best and being the person God would want you to be, there is no reason to worry or be *jealous*. So, then examine carefully and ask yourself, are you the best you can be? Are you content with who you are? If you need improvement, then improve. It's easy, all doable by you and you only. No one is to blame for your discontent but you. There is no reason for *jealousy.*

Dave and I believe *jealousy* to be the most wasted of all our emotions.

Another huge area of *jealousy* and *conceit* comes with churches. It makes absolutely no sense that the one place that should be holy and sacred holds the most *conceit*, *jealousy* and entitlement. Why do those who attend a church believe those who do not are beneath them? What gives them to right to judge in that manner?

These persons can often quote the Bible front and back, yet they somehow miss the parts about judging and everyone being equal. Isabella quoted, after all, Matthew 18:20, in which God states that anywhere two or three are gathered in my name, there am I with them. It never says in the Bible, anywhere, that persons gathering in a certain kind of building, in their best clothing, on a Sunday morning, so I will be. If a person feels the need to attend a church, great. But if another chooses not to, that's great also. The only true reason for attending a church is for fellowship and connecting with human beings. It is not going to church that gives you the golden ticket to heaven; it is making the correct choices in your daily life.

You can pray to our God anywhere, anytime, inside, outside, in a crowd, by yourself, and you are still special to God. *Conceited* persons would believe they are better than you, for dressing up on Sunday and gathering like sheep to a church building. If you have God in your heart, it does not matter where your heart sits. *Jealousy* makes us strive to be more important in God's eyes than another. Wouldn't you rather help someone find favor in God's eyes with you?

My stepfather, who passed away during the writing of this story, fought in World War II and returned home hating the French and anything to do with them. Up until his last days of clarity, he would criticize anything French, be it food, travel, clothing or art. This is absolutely ridiculous. During his life, my stepfather had chosen to not enjoy coq au vin, Bordeaux or soufflé, all in the name of war. Did the French people, living at this moment in time, cause any harm to this man? No. Shouldn't my stepfather have been angry with the Germans? Or for that matter, the Vikings? Name any other country in the world. We have been to war with everyone through the ages.

Can't we forgive the poor judgment of others along the way and remind ourselves we haven't always made the best choices in life? Hate begets hate. It's a useless waste of our energies.

Holding a grudge is not being *forgiving*. It only hurts you, not the one you're holding the grudge against. It is so **conceited** to think you are always correct and there are not two sides to every story. And what about the *love?* Where is the *love* in all of this?

Is being your best self also loving yourself? How can you *love* another without knowing, understanding and loving yourself? Self-doubt makes you less likely to have the ability to *love* and understand others. And isn't self-doubt a form of envy which is *conceit?* Self-criticism should not be confused with self-evaluation. Self-evaluation is always good and always welcome—that's how we grow. It is about being your best self. Self-acceptance is also growth. Do you really believe that God makes imperfection? Imperfection is a human term, not a God-made one. If you appear to be making **selfish, conceited** or *jealous* choices, it could be traveling with you through karma. Examine those choices.

Love, and *forgiveness* in its many forms, overcomes **selfishness, conceit** and *jealousy.*

Chapter 10

Let Love Fill Your Heart and Soul

*L*ove is patient, *love* is kind. It does not envy, it does not boast, it is not proud. It does not dishonor others, it is not self-seeking, it is not easily angered, and it keeps no records of wrongs.

Love does not delight in the evil but rejoices with the truth. It always protects, always trusts, always hopes, and always perseveres.

Love never fails. Where there are tongues, they will be stilled; where there is knowledge, it will pass away. If you have been bestowed with the greatest gifts from God but do not have *love,* you have nothing.

If I speak in the tongues of men or angels, but do not have *love,* I am only a resounding gong or a clanging cymbal. If I can fathom all mysteries and all knowledge, and if I have a faith that can move mountains, but do not have *love,* I am nothing. If I give all I possess to the poor and give over my body to hardship that I may boast, but do not have *love,* I gain nothing.

1 Corinthians 13:4-12

If you read the above passage from the Bible, you will realize it is, in all actuality, the most complete definition, above all others, per Isabella.

Love does not envy, that is *jealousy.* It does not boast, it is not proud, that is *conceit.*

Love does not dishonor others and is not self-seeking; that is **selfishness.**

Love keep no records of wrong, because *love, **forgives.***

Love rejoices with the truth and is not deceitful which is **selfishness.**

If you have the greatest gifts but have no *love,* material wealth does not bring you *love.*

If I have all knowledge, that does not equal *love.*

Charity and hard work, if not done out of *love,* mean nothing.

Love eliminates **conceit, jealousy, selfishness** and elicits **forgiveness.** *Love* one another. *Love* yourself. *Love* is shared and is given. *Love* is an action, not just a feeling.

Having *love* in your heart doesn't just apply to romantic relationships. There are so many ways to give *love* to those around you.

Love is appreciation for your life, home, friends, family, nature, animals, humankind in general, humankind who are different than ourselves. *Love* is kind, *love* is acceptance, *love* is giving, *love* is nurturing, *love* is unwavering, *love* is all-powerful. ***LOVE IS FROM GOD.***

CARLA

In October 2014 I awoke to a voice saying that in two days something would be revealed to me. I was excited to know what this would be. Dave confirmed it was Elizabeth, my guide, speaking to me.

Another day began with meditation, and Isabella was adamant with Dave about journaling and writing a book about his experiences with her. She said that the time was now, and that the world needed knowledge of the spiritual world and to know that we are not alone. She advised Dave to be careful with interpretation and justification in our journaling and to remember it's all up to God.

On October 30, 2014, Isabella confirmed,

There is indeed no hell.

She explained that each person receives a judgment day after each and every life, with Atonement as well. We are all responsible for our karmic debt. By that, she means that whatever wrongdoing we commit in our lives, we will be responsible for and face the consequences when we pass over and/or during one of our next lives. God does not punish us by sending us to hell.

We reap what we sow. You have all heard the expression and here we are confirming it from the source. If you kill, you will be killed in this lifetime or another. What goes around, comes around. So, be mindful of your actions and remember you are helping plan your own future lives with your karmic debt.

J.J. and the Speakeasy

The next day, October 31, 2014, was a day we won't forget. From this moment on, our lives here would never be the same. During Dave's sleep the night before, Isabella narrated a story while Sheila, his past life guide, transported him to a past life in the 1920s. Since receiving this story, we have researched the events and corroborated them through other sources. We have not changed the names here.

In Dave's past life, Brenda and I were flappers in a speakeasy in Chicago. The scene opens in an alley. It is raining and he spots me, standing in the dark, deserted alley. Dave wears a black suit, white shirt and a pencil tie. I've fled the bar, where my gangster boyfriend has become enraged that I was having "too much conversation," and ordered his thugs to drag us out to the alley. I stand and watch in horror as they shoot Dave through the heart and kill him.

"You died shortly after that," Dave told me. "Brenda lived another sixty or seventy years."

When he told me this past life, Dave was shaken. But pieces were starting to fit together; pictures, faces or objects that he hadn't known what they meant. But now he was gaining clarity.

The day he told me about this past life, he'd had to call me because it was a Friday, my day off. He called early, before patients started arriving. As soon as the day was done, he called again.

"Tell me more," I said.

I wanted to search the internet for facts about Chicago during the speakeasy era. I felt like a detective, but in a strange way, we were investigating ourselves—a life we already had lived. If what Dave was telling me was true, and these lives were lived in the 1920s, we should be able to find record of it. We needed names, dates, places and more information. While I searched, Dave actually meditated while on the phone with me.

At the speakeasy, I see Carla right away, about six feet from me. Now, when I say "me," I mean the person that I was in 1925. And though Carla did not look exactly as she does right now, in this past life, I know it is Carla right away by her eyes. She is familiar, though she is wearing a knee-length, white, fringed skirt with beads and a sleeveless, bright red shirt with a high collar. Her lips are bold, bright red, and I am taken aback to see her taking a drag on a cigarette. With each inhalation, Carla leaves traces of red lipstick on the cigarette holder. Billowing smoke rises from her mouth.

On her right hand, I notice, she wears a red ruby ring. Her hair is slicked back on her head, a lighter color than Carla's hair is now. I hear men calling her Ruby, like the ring on her finger. She seems surrounded by gangsters.

Behind Ruby/Carla sits a woman named Lila, and she is Brenda, the same eyes and mannerisms. Lila/Brenda wears her long, blond hair pulled up in a bun, with heavy makeup and a white dress with silver trim. Beautiful women dressed in furs and fancy jewelry are scattered through the tables in the room, surrounded by attentive men, either their husbands or boyfriends. The scene drips with money.

I look down at my black patent leather shoes.

"J.J.!" I hear Ruby call to me.

I am Jonathon, and J.J. is my nickname. I am a banker at Henry Spingola's bank, and Henry does business with Angelo Genna, manager of the speakeasy. I know this because as I linger into this scene, Isabella and Sheila are feeding me information.

I look around the bar and see a man standing at the door. I recognize him. A woman at the bar is my present-day wife, her heart-shaped face I can recognize. That's true of many of the faces in the room. I recognize them, but I can't say who they are.

It feels like this is my second time in this speakeasy. I have seen Ruby before, when I was working at the bank. Every day at the same time, I would see Ruby walk past in a long, light-colored, wool coat. I see myself wearing a trench coat, not an inexpensive one, either, walking toward Ruby on the street. It's daytime.

The next day, Saturday, November 1, 2014, Dave needed to go to the funeral home after one of our patients passed away two nights ago. As he arrived, Dave went to pay his respects, he wondered if he would feel anything or see anything with his newfound spiritual connections. He felt nothing nor did he have her presence. However, the next night, his guides told him that our deceased patient was still with Counsel.

This was the revelation about what happens after death. Counsel cleared up some of the common misconceptions about death. First, all souls do pass over, despite what television and movies show us. Shortly after passing over, souls go to Counsel, a group that makes each soul relive all of their actions while alive, including the good and bad they have inflicted on others.

My mother has told Dave during their discussions on this matter that no one really wants to go before Counsel. Apparently, it is intense and all-encompassing. It is not just an hour-long ordeal. They are quite thorough, and it is meant to show you the error of your ways so you will not repeat them. This could take hours or years, hundreds in fact. It's called Atonement.

Quite simply, it is all part of a huge learning experience. You must feel complete sorrow for what you did to others. It is our path to learn. The Counsel teaches us and hopes we learn from our mistakes.

Some souls choose to return to another life right away, and it depends on whether they have truly learned from their past mistakes. Other souls have to go to classes, so to speak, for a matter of time until they are ready. Whether they are ready is decided by their Counsel, God and themselves.

There could be a lesson for you to learn with another specific soul, let's say, or a karmic debt you must clear up with another soul. This karmic debt could be something that the two of you caused in a past life and have yet to fix or you have not had a life together yet and will in the future, to learn one of your lessons.

We asked Isabella what lessons we must conquer during our existences. She again outlined the following simple rules on these four subjects:

- ✦ *Jealousy*

- ✦ *Selfishness*

- ✦ *Conceit*

- ✦ *Forgiveness*

She went on to say that although there are many, many lessons that souls must learn while reincarnated, they all stem from these simple four subjects. **Love** supersedes them all. Because, without real **love**, you cannot follow these rules.

Isabella reminded us when we act in the manner of Jesus and the way he lived his life, we are following all of the above rules. We talked about this at length during meditation. Paula wrote down the four words and posted them where we could be reminded daily. We thought about this. The method is so extremely simple. Just put others before ourselves, and if they wrong us, forgive them because, in the long run, nothing they do to us is permanent. If we think about others in that manner, we cannot hold a grudge or not **forgive** them. Truly, most people are not aware when they hurt us. We couldn't possibly know their path or struggles, but the majority of people act out of ignorance rather than malice. Although, yes, there are those individuals who make it their life's mission to lash out at everyone and anyone in their path. Each life consists of learning lessons so we can become Christ-like. It should be easy, but it's not.

Here is the clincher. Our minds are wiped clean of all our memories with each new reincarnation. How simple it would be if they were not wiped clean and we just reincarnated and knew everything. It is not like that at all.

God wants us to learn and to learn the correct way. God wants all of us to be pure of heart, which brings total happiness to us. But, nonetheless, God gives us time after time of **forgiveness** and the chance to get it all correct. It doesn't matter who you are or what you have done, the bottom line is that you are, indeed, given the chance again and again to do it correctly and become like Jesus. Isabella says that few get it correct the first time. Only Jesus and Mohammed have so far.

Let's say that we are born as a rich man, and we take wealth for granted and never help the poor or others in need. Do you suppose that if God sent us back as a poor man in the next life, a lesson would be learned? Hopefully, deep in our soul, a memory would click and we would understand.

This is karmic debt. Remember all the adages from your parents and others in your life such as, "What goes around, comes around" and "You reap what you sow"? It makes perfect sense to us now.

Another scenario would be that you are born and have children in your adult years. You have a sibling who is not able to conceive. Are you kind to that sibling or do you hold it over her head, she is without children, one of the greatest gifts in your life? If you behave in the latter way, chances are, you are, indeed, coming back to a life without children.

You harvest what you plant. So, it's not so hard for us to fathom the concept of reincarnation. God has a plan and makes it really easy for us. It is us who aren't listening and paying attention.

Collecting Past Lives

The next many months were focused on collecting Dave's and my past lives together, of which there were many—twenty-nine, in fact. Every day, we couldn't wait to get to work, and it wasn't just Dave and me. Because entwined in Dave's and my lives were Paula's, Brenda's and my husband's, as well as the many others surrounding us. We all seemed to be in each other's lives over and over. But the one life that Dave and I were endlessly curious about was that life in the speakeasy. So, we waited for the next word from our guides, eager to hear more of the story of Ruby and J.J.

Finally, it came. We didn't have to wait long. On Sunday, November 2, 2014, Isabella bombarded Dave with so much of the story that we added tons of pages to the journal. Meditation the next morning was really just Dave reciting everything that he had been fed the day before. Isabella was trying to provide us with solid information we could investigate and corroborate. She is quite wise, of course, and knew I would attempt to verify anything they conveyed to us. We had researched as much as possible through a well-known genealogy site—names, dates, birth records, places of birth, marriages, deaths, etc. It was all there, the proof we needed.

Ruby Donaldson was born in Bulloch, Georgia, in 1904 to James Donaldson and Anna Donaldson. She was one of ten children. She had one stepsister.

And then it got really interesting. Ruby's father, James, was my present husband, Tom. That is, Tom was Ruby's father in his past life. James was born in 1851 and died in 1934, just in time to turn around and again be born as Tom in 1935. A quick turnaround!

I jumped on the well-known genealogy site, Ancestry.com that afternoon. Ruby Donaldson apparently was a common name in the South, or was at that time. I researched many birth certificates, which led to other trails. But when I found the one, the one that was me, Ruby, in a past life, the strangest feeling came over me. I tried to find a picture but could only find pictures of Ruby's mother and father, James and Anna Donaldson. I confirmed they had 10 children—actually, eleven, one from another marriage. I confirmed my parents' births and deaths. Dave had been given names, dates and places, I could actually confirm. It seemed surreal.

During the download from Isabella to Dave the day before, at one point, he was not only speaking with Isabella but also speaking with my previous mother, Anna, who informed Dave that, as Ruby's parents, their finances were tight and because of that, Ruby and two of her sisters were taken to Chicago to live with a relative. So that was how Ruby got to Chicago. The pieces were connecting.

Anna also said to Dave, "She and Tom, my present husband, had many lives together. And she had other lives with Dave as well."

Isabella and Anna showed Dave a previous life of mine in which I had a wagon accident and died at a young age. He saw Anna at my funeral. But, of course, she was someone other than Anna.

Years ago, at a psychic/medium event, I had been told that I had died at a young age in the seventeen or eighteen-hundreds when I fell out of a wagon and that my "now" husband had been driving. Twice now, I had heard the wagon story with the same young age, death, time frame and husband. Fascinating. Two separate, unknown sources to each other, were divulging information about my past life with the same details.

Still, around the beginning of November 2014, the four of us in the office continued to actively refer to the Bible during meditation and study time before the office opened. One day I was reading in Genesis and thought how God appeared to be harsh and angry early on. God seemed to reward the ones who behaved badly.

I asked Dave to inquire from Isabella as to why it appeared so. She explained that God, in the beginning felt as though people were not listening. Despite the fact many persons had the gift of hearing God, they chose to ignore what God asked of them. God needed to have wishes followed and as with children, often they just would not adhere. God acted accordingly.

Dave had his own story to tell that morning. He had been shown a previous life taking place in England in the early 1600s, 1602 to be exact.

Robert Smith Sails to America

Dave was Robert Smith, and his wife was Sarah—me. We were poor. To purchase our tickets on a ship sailing to America, we had sold all of our belongings. The reason we wanted to leave was the crushing tax load in England.

About the same time this past life was revealed to us, I was interviewing candidates to replace Brenda, who left to attend nursing school. One interviewee stood out, and I gushed about her to Dave. I was drawn to her. In the back of my mind, I figured that it was likely she had shared a previous life with us. As it would happen, Lara was, indeed, in this past life. She had sailed on the same ship from England to America.

Lara had been Sarah and Robert's neighbor in England. She had been a single mother of a son, just as she was in her present life. Sarah had helped, much as I had helped her in this life, hiring her to work in our office.

I felt gratified to realize that in a past life I was a good and kind soul. The story, as Dave conveyed it, was very touching. It caused me to really think hard about how difficult our ancestors' lives had been. I started to feel myself softening. I really felt as though I was becoming a much more understanding and compassionate person. We all were. The stories were touching us, reaching us deep in our souls.

The Story of the Stonecutter

By the middle of 2015, we were still meditating and going strong. Dave's sister invited him to accompany her family on vacation to England. By this time, Dave was going through a divorce, and she thought a change of scenery would help. What she didn't know was that Dave had found a new gift.

DAVE

My sister and brother-in-law had adopted a three-year-old girl years ago from Russia. For many years, they had promised to take her back when she was old enough to understand and enjoy the country of her birth. She was now turning sixteen, so the time had come. Her parents told her she could take a friend of her choice. Because Russia was troubled at this time, her parents suggested their daughter choose another destination, and she chose England. Her parents originally thought she would ask someone from her swim or dive team to go along. She called and asked me, her uncle Dave. I was blown away. I never considered not going with them to England. Carla cleared my schedule and I was on my way.

Boarding the international flight, I was excited as they packed eight hundred of us like sardines into a long tube with wings. I walked through first class, where early-boarded passengers sipped wine and laid back in lounge chairs. In the economy cabin, I took my seat in a row of 12 people. Row 21, seat C. I was grateful to be 116 pounds lighter. Airplane seats seemed a lot bigger! Since meditation and my ability to control my life, I had changed my diet as well as my way of thinking.

My niece, sister and brother-in-law sat one row behind me. I texted Carla one last time. *I will miss you and Tom*, I keyed out on my phone. I explored the offerings on a television screen in front of me, which offered a plenitude of movies and music channels. My thought was, *well maybe I will watch a movie, meditate, take a nap and suddenly wake up in England.* My thoughts returned to Carla. I wished she were going on this adventure with me, to places where we had shared past lives. Instead, she was home lying on the couch with three fractured bones from a fall just two weeks earlier. I worried about Tom caring for her alone for twelve days.

As I meditated, the plane taxied down the runway. Isabella was ever present. My Spirit Guide was never far from my thoughts. If I say she has some of Carla's attitudes, it might explain my comfort with her. There is a wit, strength and directness I appreciate. Isabella assured me I would see many things in England. My adventure would include visits to areas from my past. Would I feel different? Would memories surface? The plane took off. I had time for a movie, a nap and a couple of meals. It was a long flight.

We landed in England early in the morning. With the time changes and connecting flights I had lost one whole day. We were shuttled to our hotel. Tired and excited, I did not want to miss a moment in London. Check-in would not be until the afternoon. They would keep our luggage until later. The four of us marched south from our hotel to the Museum of London.

Close to the museum, I saw a red phone booth reminiscent of the Harry Potter movies. I stopped to take a picture of my niece in the phone booth. We walked past placards on the historic buildings announcing that famous people from the seventeenth and eighteenth centuries had lived behind those walls. Most of the names I did not recognize. Sir someone or another, a Member of Parliament.

At the Museum of London, I explored art from many ages and gold crowns with jewels. A large exhibit from Egypt caught my attention. I wandered in to see a massive stone carving of Ramses II, the Egyptian pharaoh. I stared in amazement. I had seen this before. Rising up before my wondering eyes was a six-feet high carving of a great pharaoh. As I took it in, I could remember every strike of the chisel that had shaped this image. I had carved it with my own hands.

Dave was Dedu, Carla was Carlisse

DAVE, writing as Dedu

My name is Dedu. I created the stone statue I am seeing in England now, but when I first created it, we were in the Valley of the Kings, just outside Thebes. The year is 1250 BC. I am a skilled tradesman, a stonecutter.

I am a son of a slave (who happens to be Dave's father in this present life), a stonecutter like my mother's family (and my mother in this life also is my mother in this present life). My mother's family has protected my father and now me, from slavery. My father was a slave but married into a nonslave family with skilled trade, therefore releasing my father from bondage. I have worked beside by father and father-in-law (who is my present grandfather, on my mother's side) working on the same structure for nearly sixty years.

Memphis, Egypt, is hot and dry and sits at the delta of the Nile. It is a great city built to be the capital. I work here, building monuments to the pharaohs and gods. I have a crew of nine slaves who work under me. Considering my family's past, I treat them well and with respect. The overseer of the project is Tomo, an aggressive, loud and brutal man. He controls the slaves with an iron-fisted discipline. I do what I can to protect my crew from him.

Tomo's daughter is Carlisse. She is but sixteen years old. Because she is a girl and his only offspring, he speaks quietly and calmly to her. Her mother is somewhat distant, and Carlisse has begun to come to the building site with her father. She noticed me from the start. I had also noticed her. She is fairer than most women, though her skin is tanned and her hair is dark brown. I immediately noticed her steel-blue eyes. Carlisse visits the work site often, volunteering and bringing water to the workers and slaves. The first time she served me, I lingered with her just a little too long. Tomo yelled, "Watch it, that one's my daughter." I thanked her for her kindness.

The next time she visited, she brought me water right away. I again noticed her beautiful eyes and told her they were enchanting. She smiled. I then heard Tomo yell, "Dedu, take her to the sun-side of the building." Tomo, was quite angry with the slaves at this moment. He did not wish for Carlisse to witness what was coming. I walked her down the steep stairs of the structure and around the corner. I heard Tomo yell as he struck one of the guards across his helmet with a large, broad stone hammer. It knocked the guard to the ground. "Do I have to show you the discipline you should be using on the slaves?" Tomo took this guard and another over to a small, dark-haired slave. "Show him discipline!" Both guards stood and looked at him but did nothing.

Tomo again raised the hammer and struck the slave. He fell to the ground, lifeless. "Now you and these slaves have learned a lesson. Make them work harder!" I had witnessed this behavior before, but Carlisse's innocent eyes had not.

I placed my arm around her to protect her. We talked, discussing the work and the heat of the day. She commented on my strength and skill as a stonecutter. What she really had noticed, though, was my chiseled frame and dedication to hard work, or so I believed. I had been kind and polite, but there was more. She was drawn to me. I could feel it. We returned to the side of the structure where her father was standing.

While I was on the other side of the stone structure, my small crew of nine slaves had become slightly idle. Tomo noticed and back-handed one of my men as I came around into the cooler, shadowed portion of the building. I raised my voice. "Tomo, while these men work under me, let me show them discipline so that they will respect me. Also, please show some respect for your daughter." Carlisse had just witnessed her father strike a man for the first time. Tomo replied, "Young man, I am responsible for these slaves and they are not men. As for my daughter she is also my mine and not yours." I responded, "Careful what you say, that may not always be the case." Carlisse was shocked that someone had stood up to her overbearing father. It somehow pleased her. She requested that I escort her home as the day was coming to an end.

The sun was still bright in the sky, and the heat of the sun made me perspire. Beads of sweat glistened on my chest and abdomen as we walked along the shore of the Nile. Carlisse said, "Would not the water cleanse you and cool you down?" I responded, "Would you join me?"

Again, she responded, "What did you mean when you said I would not always belong to my father?" I replied, "Whatever your father believes, he does not own you. No one owns another. If you would choose, I would want you as mine." Carlisse again questioned. "What if I chose you?" I responded, "Then I would choose you also."

I untied the wrap around my waist, and it fell to the ground. I stepped into the cooling water of the Nile. I offered my hand to Carlisse as she stood on the bank. She said, "What should I do?" I responded, "Leave your garment and join me." She untied her robe, and it fell at her feet, her long legs and soft skin now visible. She took my extended hand and stepped into the water. I pulled her close. After a while, I climbed out of the water and laid my still clean shirt, which I had not worn due to the heat of the sun, on the ground. I helped her from the water. She lay down upon my shirt as I joined her. We enjoyed each other's treasures, so to speak. The sun began to set as I walked her home, shining with crimson red on the horizon. Carlisse glowed with contentment from the late afternoon activities as we strolled. She turned to me and pleaded, "Can you walk me home again tomorrow?"

We approached her home and noticed Tomo and Fauna, her mother, waiting outside. Tomo said, "You certainly walked the long way home." Her mother joined in. "It was a nice day," she said, to which I replied, "It certainly was beautiful." Carlisse smiled. Her father scowled and hurried her into the house.

The next day at the work site, Tomo approached me immediately. He mentioned that Ramses, the pharaoh had approached him with a new project just outside of Thebes in the Valley of the Kings. This was to be his burial monument. I asked, "Is this not a position of great honor? Who has requested me?" Tomo, thinking himself quite clever said, "Yes, the pharaoh, himself, has recognized your work." I asked, "He has received your recommendation?" Tomo answered, "Yes, I have told him you will come now." I responded with, "I will leave immediately if you meet my three demands." Somewhat indignant, Tomo asked me to explain.

Before I answered, I again questioned whether the pharaoh expected me. Tomo replied that he was expected to deliver me, his best stonecutter. He had skirted the question.

I pressed on with my three demands. "My first demand is for my nine-man crew to come with me. My second is that I'll need a very strong horse to carry. My third demand is your daughter, who should not have to walk that far."

Tomo stood back, angered but trapped by what I had said. "This did not turn out as I planned."

"It's turning out even better than I could have expected," I said.

Two days later, Carlisse and I left Memphis, and her parents, for Thebes. Only once did we ever return to Memphis, three years later to present our son, Joseph, Tomo and Fauna's grandchild. Joseph would follow later in my footsteps as a stonecutter.

Lessons learned from this life

- Slavery and ownership are ***conceit.*** Tomo taught his daughter to own. Dedu taught Tomo's daughter to be free.

- Parents do not own their children.

- ***Love*** is not about position. Tomo thought Dedu was not good enough for his daughter.

* Parents need to be examples for their children. Tomo killed, therefore teaching it was all right. It wasn't.

* Whether a slave or a skilled tradesman, you are still a human being. You still deserve dignity.

* Loyalty is not **selfishness**. Dedu valued his workers. Tomo did not.

I stood in the Museum of London staring at the great pharaoh, and I was in awe. What else would I experience in England? What would tomorrow bring? I hurried off to find my family. We would soon meet up with our tour guide. We were having fish and chips for dinner tonight. I had been mostly gluten-free for months while losing 116 pounds. *I might order a dark ale tonight, even if it's not gluten-free*, I thought.

The next day, as I visited various sites of London, Isabella was preparing me for an additional excursion. Two days later, I met our tour guide Tony for a side trip I had arranged to Stonehenge.

To get to Stonehenge, I had to start at Trafalgar station. A round-bellied, broad-shouldered man tapped me on the shoulder and instructed me to follow him—tour guide Tony. He could get me on his tour, he promised. Sometimes things just happen for a reason. Tony had been educated at Oxford and he had a wealth of knowledge. Isabella said, *Listen to him. You would learn a lot.*

So, I embarked on a long bus ride through the Cotswolds as Tony talked of the rolling hills and beauty of the region. The Cotwolds region includes many shires in southwest England including Wiltshire, the location of Stonehenge. We passed small homes with thatched roofs, reminiscent of homes I had seen while meditating. Isabella shared that Sarah and Robert were from the Cotswolds.

Sarah, my wife, had been born in 1604. Her parents had been indentured servants to nobility in Wiltshire. When they were released from servitude, they took the last name Freeman. They were now *FREE MEN*. They were given a small portion of land just north of Wiltshire in Gloucestershire. Sarah's father, Craig, was Carla's grandfather and namesake (Carlo) in this present life. My present grandmother (Catherine) was her mother then.

I watched intently through the windows of the bus. Isabella informed me that Sarah was a direct descendant of the people who built Stonehenge in or about 3000 BC. The summer and winter solstices were marked by a large, circular structure. The people of Stonehenge believed fervently that God and nature were one. It is an engineering feat to have built Stonehenge, as some stones weigh as much as thirty tons. The building of Stonehenge was very much a lifetime labor of *love*. The building of Stonehenge would have spanned many decades. The bus turned a tight corner on the narrow highway through the Cotswold region as Tony yelled, "Look to your left." A thirty-feet tall white horse stood high on top of the hill. He informed those on this tour that this was an old Druid statue.

The Druids were Celtics who moved to this area from northern France. Druids had believed in many gods and during that time believed in human sacrifice. They also believed in reincarnation. The English, Welsh, Irish, Gaelic and Breton are the descendants of the Celts.

Certain sects of Druids became healer-priests and led the Celtic people. They passed knowledge by word of mouth. Later sects in around AD 700 became monotheist (believing in one God). They believed human sacrifice to be wrong. May 1 was an important day, the beginning of spring and new life. Nature and the oak tree were important symbols, what we now might call a Wiccan influence. Their God had masculine and feminine qualities. Robert (me) was of Druid descent.

Soon we arrived at Stonehenge. We walked a long path up, around the gift shop, then up a hill toward the stones. The sky was now covered with dark clouds as a cool wind blew. Until now, we had avoided rain in England. I wanted to see Stonehenge before rain burst from the sky. I hurried ahead of our tour group. I lined up the large arch with two tall pillars, the cross stone and the sunstone. I stood in awe of this structure almost three thousand years old. Somehow, these stones brought meaning to the past life experiences I was uncovering. Sarah's (Carla's) relatives built this. Past lives and their lessons had followed us. I took a selfie with my phone. I sent the picture to Carla. Later I would fill in the picture.

My cell battery was dying. I had a long bus ride back to London. I would have to figure out the city train system—The Tube—by myself to get back to my hotel and my family. My mind wondered back to

Sarah and Robert. Robert had left Sarah in England and had traveled to America. I had left Carla in America and had traveled to England. I missed her. A tear rolled down my face.

Off to a New Life

Once, Bristol was a busy, sea-faring port, vital to the commerce of England. The port was built on the River Avon. At high tide, the port would fill with water for nearly twelve hours, allowing large ships to dock and be loaded, which allowed it to be a major shipping and trading port. It was also a point of passage to America during the Puritan reformation in England.

My family and I visited a suspension bridge with a local tour guide and then headed down to the original dock area. I saw a large, wooden boat with three masts. Its sails hung lifeless. I suddenly felt the breeze pick up.

I had traveled in my mind to the mid-1600s, a dock bustling with activity. The shoremen shouted out urgently as they loaded the boats, only twelve hours to launch the ships. Sails billowed on the horizon as they filled with air, pulled taut to the top of the masts. My family, with its meager possessions, had found a small, wooden stall in the hold, and along with granddaughter Elizabeth we boarded. I called her precious. (She was Brenda, our coworker.)

Elizabeth/Brenda had her mother and father traveling with her. As the boat floated from the dock, I stood alone on the main deck, my eyes closed. My wife, Sarah, would not be making this trip. A tear ran down my cheek. *No reason to open my eyes*, I thought. *Sarah is in my heart. No reason to look back, she is not here. No reason to look forward, she is not there.*

Dave as Robert of Borough, Carla as Sarah Freeman

On a cool early morning in Gloucestershire, I feel the forceful shake of my bed. I try to ignore it, but my older brother Timothy insists I get up for church. Timothy is seven years my elder (Tom, Carla's husband). My parents died when I was young. Timothy has taken care of me and the land that was my parents' land. Timothy urges me to hurry, as it would be rude to be late for services. I brush my thick dark hair and pull on my brown britches and my heavy, white cotton shirt. I run out of our yellow mud-and-stone house with a thatched roof.

We travel together on top of a dark brown workhorse named Stallion, something he certainly was not. We travel to the only church I have ever seen. It is a simple, plain church with a small steeple in the front, no markings, no cross and built of the same blond stone as our house. Inside, it is small and dark with only a few candles. The furnishings are quite bare. There are stone-and-wood pews and a small stone altar. Church was usually a task but today felt different.

We arrive at church just in time and sit in our usual spot toward the back left of the sanctuary. I notice a new family sitting to the right side of the church, a man, wife and two girls who look to be around my age. I learn later that one is named Ann and is quite loud and boisterous. Her father scolded her frequently during the service. The other's name I would discover later, is Sarah. She has strawberry blond hair and seems quiet and reserved. Yet, I see a warm fire in her eyes. Immediately, I like her.

Next week, I cannot wait to go to church. I sit in a pew on the right side close to the girls. Timothy scowls, for he has sat where our parents have sat for the past seven years. Timothy does not like change. But when he sits down, he realizes why I have sat in this row. Now he doesn't seem to mind. After services, I meet Sarah and her parents. We speak but briefly.

I am already excited for next Sunday. It seems every week that it takes longer and longer to get to Sunday. A few Sundays later, Sarah's parents invite Timothy and me for dinner.

After a bath, I get dressed in my Sunday best. Timothy laughs while I try to get my unruly hair to lie down. We again ride Stallion over to Sarah's family's house a few miles away. Her parents meet us at the door of their blond-stone cottage. Timothy is allowed to walk with Ann before dinner. Sarah and I are not. We sit in the main room at the table while her mother makes us a dinner of quail, boiled potatoes and rutabaga. Sarah helps her mother set the table. Her father is a quiet man but, on this night, he did most of the talking. When Sarah exchanged conversation, I was glued to every word. I offered to help her father repair his stone fence. Dinner felt filling, and Timothy seemed to enjoy Ann's company.

Over the next few weeks, I helped Sarah's father repair his fence. He invited me over to dinner by myself, without Timothy. Craig let me know he appreciated my help on his farm. "You are a fine young man, and I enjoy having you around." A few months pass, and Sarah's father and mother allow me to sit with her outside the front door. We talk about farming and church on Sunday. She listens while I talk about raising sheep. I want my own farm someday, I tell her.

She wants a big fireplace in the kitchen and in the bedroom. There must be a porch on the front of the house. She lets me know she thinks sheep can be quite dirty. She wants no dirty sheep-shoes in her kitchen. So, we discuss the future but never discuss marriage.

I am still excited for Sunday services. I always sit next to Sarah at services. One Sunday after church I come to dinner at Sarah's house, and her father lets me know Sarah likes me. I, of course, let him know that I like her. He smiles knowingly and does not seem surprised.

Eventually, I ask her father if I can marry his daughter. He agrees as long as Sarah accepts my proposal. I get down on one knee as Timothy has taught me. My heart leaps, and I can hardly speak when she looks into my eyes and says yes. She kisses my cheek for the first time and states she would see me next week at church. She quickly heads into her house.

Her mother then appears at the door and takes me for a walk. Katherine informs me that her daughter cannot be owned. Sarah has a strong will and makes her own decisions. She tells me of their life as indentured servants and how they had worked tirelessly to buy their freedom. She never wants Sarah to feel as she did. I agree. I am but eighteen years old. I know nothing but the love I feel for this delightful strawberry blond.

I work tirelessly to build a home at the far north end of our land, moving the yellow limestone one stone at a time. I would build the house with the large kitchen and fireplace and two bedrooms with a fireplace between. I built wooden furniture to sit on. I built a thatched bed with four posters for my soon-to-be bride. I also build a wood porch, as Sarah requested. It took nearly a year. I knew Sarah was worth the wait.

On the day we married, eighty members from our small stone church arrived. I stood in my best brown britches wearing suspenders and a vest. A tie that Sarah had made was around my neck. I stood shaking from excitement in front of our small church. Timothy was at my side. Ann was Sarah's chosen witness. Constance (Paula), was married to the church tax collector, and present. I watched as Craig and Sarah appeared at the back of the church. She was dressed from head to foot in ivory and lace. The lace extended up to her chin. A veil of ivory lace draped over her face. Her hair was curly but gathered into a loose bun behind her head. She was fair but her skin was the same color as the ivory of her dress. I thought she was beautiful.

Her father walked her up the aisle and shook my hand. She took her place beside me. The ceremony took but ten minutes. Sarah smiled through the services, except for when the minister used the word obey. Afterward, she kissed me on the cheek. We celebrated by sharing fresh fruit from my farm.

That night I carried Sarah across the threshold of our new home. She wore a long, white, cotton gown. Her hair was down as her curls caressed her shoulders. We lay together for the first time. Her soft lips kissed mine. She said, "I love you. I choose you." Then she said, "Good night. I am not yours. Robert, I will not call you husband. I will respect, not obey." She rolled over, facing away from me. I stared at the ceiling.

What am I to do now? I thought.

I heard her giggle. She rolled over and climbed on top of me, straddling my thighs. She crossed and uncrossed her arms raising the gown above and over her head. This ritual would become a nightly occurrence.

Sarah's and my life were fulfilling. She had friends. She sewed for others. My flock of sheep had grown. The potato and apple crops were ample. Our garden was bountiful. Yet, it seemed as forever for Sarah to be with child. She prayed for a child. We continued to go to services every Sunday. I knew she needed a change.

She mentioned the new minister, the Rev. Henson (Don, Carla's next-door neighbor in this life) made her uncomfortable. In private she shared with me that he was more interested in church taxes and various widows than in being a reverend.

Sarah had a childhood friend named Prudence (Hope, in this life and also a childhood friend). She had moved to the coastal city of Liverpool, which was a shipping and soon-to-be slave-trading port, also famous for its salt trade. Prudence was a seamstress and dressmaker. Sarah also made all her own clothes. I suggested a trip to Liverpool. It would be well over a four-day trip by horse.

Sarah and I made a trip to the coast of England and to Liverpool. We road Stallion. It was a great adventure, as we had never traveled. When we reached the outskirts of Liverpool, we climbed to the highest hill to view the sunset. We saw but a glimpse of orange and yellow, then a sliver of ruby red. Sarah commented on the beauty of the red. We traveled into the city to meet Prudence. I purchased a bolt of ivory cotton from Prudence's shop. I then saw a bright ruby red remnant of cotton. The red matched the sunset. I knew Sarah would have to have it. Prudence offered it at no cost.

There was excitement and purpose in Sarah as we made the trip back home to the Cotswolds. She talked of the new dress she would make. The farm crops and the sheep seemed to interest her. She was quite happy when we returned to our bed.

Sarah spent all of her waking time on her new dress. It was still quite simple and somewhat of puritan design. The collar and cuffs, however, were bright red. She could not wait until it was finished. She planned to wear it to the next Sunday services.

Sunday morning arrived. Sarah pinned her slightly darkened blond hair up in a bun. The curls still framed her lovely face. She dressed in her ivory dress, the collars and cuffs a bright ruby red. Pressed and stiff, not a wrinkle could be seen. I commented and complimented on how lovely she looked. She and I walked into services. Constance and some of the other women commented on how nice she looked. She beamed. A comment came from the back. "Is red appropriate for services?" we heard. Bernadette (my wife in this life) wears a heart-shaped faced that carries a scowl. She fashions herself a pious woman. Sarah turns on her heels and says. "It pleases my husband, and I am sure it pleases the Lord."

The Rev. Henson inserts himself, shaking my hand and saying, "Yes, Sarah, you look lovely." Sarah feels uncomfortable with the reverend's attention. Bernadette turns with her Bible under her arm and stomps off.

A few days later, the Rev. Henson arrives at our home. I was not there. Sarah tells him that I am not home. He steps across the threshold. Sarah says, "It is not proper for you to be here when Robert is not present." He reaches out and touches Sarah's shoulder. She pushes him toward the door. He says, "Now, Sarah, that's not very godly."

A few days later in church the Rev. Henson approaches me and shakes my hand. I say, "I do not believe you should be in my home when I am not there. I do not believe you were touching my wife like a sister." The reverend responds, "Robert, I believe your church taxes are in arrears."

The next day, Constance and Bernadette arrive at our home, stating that the tax situation would be an issue soon. Bernadette implies that Sarah's attitude would lead her to problems. The attitudes of the church and the taxes were mounting into a catastrophe. The church was attempting to control more and more of the wealth and power. Sarah and I discussed these issues late into the night.

Shortly after this, Sarah announced she was with child. "Robert, I have stopped bleeding and my breasts are full." She was full of joy. I held her as she cried. The pregnancy was uneventful. Like many men, during the pregnancy, I tried to change a few things up. I grew a beard and started to smoke a pipe. This was much to the disproval of Sarah. She held her tongue but let me know that no pipe would be in her house. One day she approached me and stated. "I do not know if I can kiss such a hairy and stinky face. Our baby will sure not. My time is quickly approaching." Sarah and I had not been together while the baby was in her.

The following day, I shaved my face and threw away the pipe. Sarah said she was pleased. The next day she went into labor. Mary was delivered after twelve hours of labor. I paced the living room while the midwife sat with Sarah. I cried when I heard her scream. Sarah was beaming but exhausted.

They cleaned the baby and presented her in a small, ivory sleeper with a ruby red collar Sarah had made with remaining trim from her dress. I presented Sarah with a small silver locket on a chain. She would wear it under her clothes. Jewelry could no longer be worn for adornment. The church would frown on it.

Sarah breastfed Mary, and the baby grew quickly into a healthy, happy baby. Nearly fifteen months later, Sarah kissed me as we prepared for bed. "The baby has been weaned. She no longer needs me however you do," Sarah said. "I love you, I choose you. I will not call you husband. I will respect but not obey. Good night." She rolled away to her right side and giggled. I thought, *That sounds familiar.* I lay staring at the ceiling, a smile on my face.

Many years later, Mary has grown into early womanhood and has married. The Church and the taxes have become unbearable. Mary has just delivered Elizabeth, our granddaughter, whom we call "Precious." We plan to sell all we have and buy passage to America. It will be a land of religious freedom with a new start without oppression.

Passage is available from Bristol, England. We start planning, selling off sheep and property. Sarah has not been feeling well and tires quickly. She has become short of breath. I fear she has a serious problem. She insists I continue to plan for the move. Friends and nurses come to visit and care for her while I continue our plan. She insists she will get better.

One night the nurses tell me they fear that Sarah is dying of consumption. I can hardly believe the words when spoken. My heart screams in my chest. This woman is my everything. Tears roll down my face. I straightened myself up. I think she is not aware.

I pretend that nothing is wrong. I enter our room. There is pain in my heart as I cannot tell her my true feelings. I do not want her spirit to break. I cannot bear her knowing how much I hurt.

Sarah tells me to sell her locket and use it for the neighbor and her son's passage to America. I tell her that it will not be enough. "It will be when you add it with my fare," she says. I cry. She has been so strong. She knew it would not be too long. She asks me to send the nurses away till morning. I remove my clothes and climb into our bed. She was but bones only. I held her next to me all night.

"I want you, but I am too weak," she says. I touch her and she reacts but once, and then says, "Thank you." I asked her if it hurt. She giggled and said, "Only the first time and that was still beautiful." She adds, "The ten thousand times after that were perfect." She falls asleep in my arms. The nurses return in the morning. I sit at her side for the next three days. She drifts in and out of consciousness. On the third day, she reaches her hand to my face and says, "Husband, you never tried to own me." She closes her eyes and part of me dies with her.

Years later, when Robert passed away, his tombstone read, ***"He lost his life when he lost his wife in the old country."***

Lessons learned in this life

- ✦ ***Love*** is never about ownership. Sarah knew it from the start, and Robert respected it.

- ✦ Position does not give you the right to use it against people as the Rev. Henson attempted. That is ***conceit.***

- ✦ ***Jealousy*** is criticizing another because of what they have and you do not, as in the case of Sarah's new dress with the red trim.

- ✦ Using religion to control is ***conceit.***

- ✦ Giving of yourself is never wrong. Even in death, Sarah thought about her neighbors.

- ✦ ***Love*** is playful, sharing, giving, partnering and accepting. Robert and Sarah had everything.

I opened my eyes. I could barely see the coast of England through the window of my plane. I thought how badly I wanted to get home and tell Carla about what I had learned. I could still feel a tear on my cheek. *Love cannot exist with conceit, jealous, selfishness and unforgiveness.* That is what Isabella had told me.

Chapter 11

Live without Conceit

*P*er Isabella, "With each choice, with each action, ask yourself, does this benefit just me?"

If so, this is ***conceit***. ***Conceit*** means "excessive pride in oneself." ***Conceit*** manifests as ownership, entitlement, vanity, boastfulness and prejudice.

Perhaps you think ***conceit*** is vanity, someone who is vain about his or her appearance. Of course, God expects each of us to take care of ourselves and keep our bodies healthy and happy, but God does not want us to obsess about our appearance. Vanity is choosing to spend hours having a manicure, facial or electrolysis and not giving time to a charity or service organization. Vanity is when your actions evolve around your looks and happiness. It's not how important it is to stand out in a crowd for no other reason than your clothing and appearance. Vanity is choosing your personal image over being thoughtful toward others and cultivating human connection.

But that is one simple definition of ***conceit***. You probably haven't thought of ***conceit*** in another light.

We are all guilty of looking past the many forms of ***conceit***. In her next message, Isabella decided to give us a list.

- ✦ We seek praise from others. We need that pat on the back.

- We avoid our part or avoid taking the blame for some wrongdoing.

- We seek *wealth* or *power* over others—king over subjects, pope over parishioners.

- We put our self above others. Abuse and neglect are *selfish* and *conceited.* Killing is *conceit.* We take away someone's chance to complete his or her path in life.

- We try to control others—in marriage, through slavery, through human trafficking and by bullying.

- We seek *ownership* over others in many forms—religion, politics, marriage, employment.

- We believe nationalism (colonialism) is the correct and only way to live.

- *Entitlement* is *conceit.* This can include people who believe they deserve special treatment because of wrongs against their ancestors, victims who believe they deserve restitution—believing you deserve anything. Or believing you can retaliate against those who offend you.

- A sense of privilege is *conceit.*

- *Prejudice* is *conceit,* for skin color, gender preference, religious belief or political choice. This includes Christians believing to be better than Muslims, Muslims believing they're better than Christians, whites better than blacks, blacks better than whites, men better than women, women better than men, Americans better than Russians, Russians better than Americans, Republicans better than Democrats, Democrats better than Republicans, straight people better than gay, gay better than straight, wealthy better than poor and poor better than wealthy.

- *Vanity* is *conceit.* Your good looks mean nothing. The real gift lies on the inside. If you believe you are more special than another due to your looks, skills, gifts, talents, intelligence wealth or position, you are *conceited.* This includes your sex, race, creed, religion and politics. This includes actors, singers, politicians, models, husbands, wives, men, women, clergy, scientists, teachers, garbage collectors and talk-show hosts alike.

+ Looking past poverty and forgetting that you have enough, is *conceit.* Share.

+ Looking past loneliness is *conceit.*

+ Ignoring another's needs and happiness is *conceit.*

+ *Jealousy, selfishness* and *unforgiveness* are *conceit. Love* is the only answer.

After this message, we were given many examples of our past lives in which we were *conceited.* The following are three past lives where we did not complete our lessons and, therefore, reincarnated again, given yet another chance by God to complete our paths.

Carla as Katrina Rosetta Carlotta Farnese, Dave as Giovanni Caponi

CARLA, writing as Katrina

I was born in Rome in 1504. As a child, I contracted polio, after which my right leg was withered. My pride caused me to hide it under a long cloak. I lived with a chip on my shoulder, certain others saw my weakness and judged me for it. Additionally, I was the illegitimate daughter of the future Pope Paul III. I felt entitled despite the fact my parents were not married. It was common for popes to have many consorts. I judged people, assuming I knew their opinions of me. All the while I felt them to be beneath me, due to my father's position.

My mother and I frequently traveled to the apothecary, where we purchased my polio medicine. A man named Armando owned and operated the pharmacy with his son, Giovanni, who was just a few years older than me, at eighteen. Giovanni was friendly but I couldn't allow myself to fraternize with the likes of him. He was just the son of the apothecary owner, not a pope's son or royalty. Every visit, Giovanni attempted to make small talk and I avoided him. What if he saw my leg and realized I wasn't perfect?

One day, he was speaking kindly to me, showing interest in my well-being—forcing me to have conversation with him. I spun around to face him and announced myself to be Katrina Rosetta Carlotta Farnese. Mother shouted out, "Katrina, shush!" I glared at him as though to say, "How dare you look in my direction? Who do you think you are?"

Two weeks passed, and my mother and I returned to the apothecary. When Giovanni greeted us, I turned my head. But I stumbled, and my crutch fell out from beneath my coat, exposing my frailty. I was mortified. Giovanni rushed to my side before I realized I was falling. He caught me, held me and said, "There appears to be no weakness in your spirit, even though there is weakness in your body."

I was incensed. I grabbed my crutch, never bothering to thank Giovanni. He had seen me in my reality. I stomped to the best of my ability out the door and waited for my mother. But Giovanni came out, offering candy to me. With a smirk, he said, "Here is a piece of candy. Maybe it will remove some of the sourness." I grabbed the candy, turning my back to him, while seething.

As my mother exited the apothecary, she said to Giovanni, "You know, she is quite taken with you?"

His response was, "Oh, it's hard to tell."

So, our ritual began. Giovanni would eagerly watch for my return every two weeks, placing a stool by the door for me. On the stool, waiting for me would be hard piece of cherry candy. I placated Giovanni during the visits. He would extort a response from me each time, by simply saying, "Katrina." I was coerced to respond, "Giovanni." This continued for ten more visits.

The tenth time, my mother and I left the apothecary, I learned that Giovanni had asked her for an audience with me. My mother was impressed with Giovanni's impeccable manners. She told him yes. The day arrived when Giovanni was coming to visit with me. We sat in the parlor.

"I have really enjoyed getting to know you at the apothecary," he said.

"I am not that easy to know, but I have enjoyed my time there, I guess," I said.

He seemed excited by what I had said. I hoped he wasn't getting ahead of himself.

"Your home is very nice," he said. "I would enjoy knowing you even better."

I rolled my eyes. I had just thought, I hoped he wasn't moving too fast.

"I do not know if you are refined enough for me, but I find you interesting," I said.

"I'd like you to know, I speak Latin and studied medicinal chemistry at the university," Giovanni said.

He had caught me off guard. I couldn't help but giggle. I stood up, walked to my easel, and asked him his opinion of the painting sitting on the easel. Giovanni said he liked the color.

"I painted it," I said.

Then I sat down. He had to know. He wasn't the only one with knowledge.

"I particularly like the steel blue color," he said.

"Oh, why is that?" I asked.

Like he actually knew something about painting.

"Because, Katrina, it reminds me of the color of your eyes," Giovanni said.

I felt myself soften. I believed he meant what he said. Then, I told him so. My feelings were changing. Could the son of an apothecary owner actually have my attention, Katrina Carlotta Rosetta Farnese?

My mother brought us tea, in my favorite ivory cups with the gold around the rim. I was surprised when Giovanni inquired about the cups. He asked if it was normal for us to have gold painted on a cup for drinking. I explained that it was actually gold and not paint. He apparently had never owned any of the finer things in life.

I felt it the right opportunity to ask Giovanni his intentions for us. He responded with, "I was never sure there was an 'us.'"

Then, he started to explain his plan for our future. It included his inheriting the apothecary as a means to support us.

I informed Giovanni that I was never quite sure either, whether there would be an "us." Remember, I am not completely whole, I said.

"I believe you have two blue eyes," he said.

"I don't believe a man would want a woman with a withered leg."

Giovanni quickly said, "I believe it was the fire in your eyes that I first noticed."

My response was, "I first noticed the laughter in your eyes, then, I noticed the strength in you when I fell in the apothecary and you caught me. You are also very persistent."

Giovanni and I were married in 1524. The evening of our wedding, my new husband carried me over the threshold into our new apartment, which had been prepared for us. My eyes first noticed the dining room, where the table was set for four. I saw my favorite ivory teacups with gold around the rim. I was elated to see fine china and silver in my new home. I so hoped the niceties I had grown accustomed to would follow me somehow to my new life.

In the bedroom, I stopped in amazement. Giovanni appeared to be as surprised as I was. The bedroom was adorned with a wood-carved, four-poster canopy bed draped in silk. I was thrilled, speechless. Giovanni said he had not been responsible for decorating the bedroom. We would later learn that my mother and Pope Paul III were responsible for our lavishly decorated bedroom.

Over the years, Giovanni worked long hard hours to keep our home, tending to my wants and desires. He understood I was used to the finer things in life. We had our first child the year after we married, a daughter. Two more daughters followed. When Giovanni took over the apothecary, we discussed my needs for our home. I had long felt my wishes and desires were slow to materialize. Giovanni was becoming angered. He was losing patience with me.

One day when our daughter Gabriella was about four, she walked into the dining room table, knocking off one of the gold-rimmed teacups. It shattered into pieces. "Gabriella, that teacup cannot be replaced!" I shouted. She cried uncontrollably.

Giovanni came to comfort Gabriella immediately. "Katrina," he said to me, "It was just a teacup. If you want, I can work even more long hours to buy you another teacup, but you will miss me when I'm gone."

I shot him a look that could kill. I spun around in anger, losing my balance as my crutch gave way. Giovanni was there to catch me, once more, as he had always been.

"Katrina, I will always be there for you when you fall," he said. "This won't be the only time one of our girls will fall and need you to catch them. They are just little girls."

Giovanni's words touched me. I felt ashamed. I understood his words and their importance. I crawled across the floor and over to my daughter. I comforted her and knew I had somehow changed. This was my daughter, my love, more important than a teacup.

Before our next Christmas, unbeknown to me, Giovanni visited my mother. He asked where to purchase gold-rimmed teacups. That's when she told him that when I was a child, four years old, I had also broken a gold-rimmed teacup. So, she already knew where to purchase several more in case of another accident. She had purchased eight originally, given us four as a wedding present and still had three gold-rimmed teacups.

My mother lovingly advised Giovanni to take the original three teacups, should we decide to bring additional children into the world.

The early lessons Giovanni and I learned with the gold-rimmed teacups strengthened our marriage. Those lessons taught me the importance of my husband, and why I was originally drawn to him. I loved my children and husband for who they were and not for what they could bring to me. That had been **conceited.** They were not material items, wealth or possessions, but my loves. Giovanni and I had three more children after the teacup incident, another daughter and two sons. My husband had shown me unconditional *love* when at times I probably did not deserve it. I grew from the *love* he showed me and found peace and contentment I had not known before. I learned to forget my polio. It did not define me. I learned not to be so self-centered, or **conceited.**

I had allowed my position, my polio and my wealth to bring out the *conceit* in me, constantly. I assumed people judged me for my disease and kept them at bay. When, in fact, I was judging them. Giovanni never saw my disability. He **loved** me for myself, not for what I had and not for who I was. We enjoyed each other and a long, wonderful marriage. **Love** took over where **conceit** and entitlement once lived.

Lessons to be learned

+ We are not defined by our illness or circumstances; that is vanity.

+ Possessions are just things and of no importance; you believe you are entitled.

- Never allow another person to own who you are; you cannot be owned.

- Teach your children what is important in life; *love* is most important.

- Think of others first, not yourself.

- Learn to *love* completely without judgment; judgment is God's alone.

Carla as Meritneith, Queen of the First Dynasty of Egypt, Dave as Djet, Pharaoh of the First Dynasty of Egypt

CARLA, writing as Meritneith

My husband and I were groomed as children and for our entire lives to become king and queen. Our parents chose to raise us in the same household, in Egypt, ensuring we learned together to be royalty. We were not brother and sister, as the history books suspected. We were loving friends.

Djet and I were married when I was fourteen. He did not become pharaoh of Egypt until about the year 2980 BC. He ruled for only six years because deceit was lurking in our household.

Djet was a man pure of heart. He was taught, as was I, that it was normal to have slaves and have servants do our work. Our parents believed it was necessary for kings and queens to act in a superior nature to control the people. Djet believed people should be free to choose their own decisions.

We had a son, Djet and I. His name was Den. Den was of another nature. He desired control, power, wealth and everything else that came from it. He reached adolescence with a strong desire to assume the kingdom and position of pharaoh.

Djet spoke with God. He truly was a humble and righteous man. He listened to God, unlike others in history who had the gift of hearing God. He was told to free the slaves. Djet believed it was honorable to toil and that a man did not need slaves doing his work. He spoke with Den, our son, and myself one evening, during dinner, informing us of his intentions to free the slaves.

I was apprehensive about Djet's decisions. I had been raised to believe the city and our people would be in upheaval without slaves and our control. Who would build in our city? How would the released slaves eat and live? Had Djet clearly thought this decision all the way through?

Den was furious. He argued with his father, telling him he'd ruin everything for him and his later reign.

He demanded his father not release the slaves for the consequences it would create. The next morning, Djet released six hundred slaves. He gave them land to toil and income for their work for us. Den was incensed. He only thought about the money and power he was losing. Den ordered that I speak with his father and make him stop releasing slaves. He was using his inheritance money to pay the slaves, he believed. He was giving away power that would be his. He asked, "How will we control the people?"

I was conflicted. I knew Djet to be a wonderful, loving and fair man. I could understand Den's point of view but also knew that Djet spoke with God and intended on adhering to God's desires.

I spoke with my husband, the pharaoh. I reiterated Den's questions and thoughts. Djet held fast to his intentions and beliefs, the wants of God. He reminded me that it was honorable to do a day's work. He reminded me that he was acting as God had intended him to do.

I wondered to myself just how we would control the city and the people. How would this affect us as king and queen? How would our lives change? This was not how we were schooled to behave as a king and queen. I had not changed my husband's mind. He reminded me that we were not descendants of gods and were not special.

Den was more furious than before. Djet released more slaves, giving them wages for their work again and land to toil for themselves.

Den convinced me that my beloved husband had lost his mind. He couldn't possibly be acting as a pharaoh would. And, what would become of us without power and control? Pharaohs had always controlled the city, slaves and people. Would we be ostracized by our Counsel and peers? Who would take care of us? Den said our future was doomed. We would have no money with his father giving it to the slaves. He would never become king. He said it was his birthright to have money, power, slaves and control. If we did not do something extreme to stop Djet, our lives would be over.

Den was relentless. Every day, he reminded me how our lives would change. He reminded me we would have no money or power. I began to worry. Was what my son saying all true? Would we lose our kingdom, and our way of life?

A few weeks later, Den came to me. He handed me a goblet of wine laced with nightshade. He ordered me to give it to my husband before bed. He said something had to be done. This was the easiest way, he said, and no one would suspect.

I went to my husband. I asked, "How will we control the people?" I was desperate to change the situation in any other manner than by poison. I pleaded. "If we are not descendants of the gods, if we are not their owners, and we are not in power, they will no longer need us." My husband responded, "Must we control them with fear? What about respect?"

I gave Djet, my beloved husband and pharaoh, the goblet, knowing full well that it would take his life. He announced he was "dry of mouth." He complained of nausea. His heart was palpitating, he said. My Djet retired to his bed and in doing so, he turned to me, and spoke, "I love you, my queen. It seems the wine is much stronger than I am used to."

Djet knew what I had done. I had taken the life of my beloved friend from birth. I wept. I thought, "If only I could take this back." Even to his end, Djet was a loving, forgiving, pure man at heart.

The pharaoh's funeral took place seven days after his death. I followed in the tradition of past kings and buried 140 servants, live men and women, with Djet. They were promised their king would return for them to serve. I had the tomb sealed.

After Djet's death, I was made the first female pharaoh of Egypt. Our son was not of age to take the throne and certainly hadn't reached maturity. I understood my husband's actions too late. I had plenty of time and thought about what I should do. I asked myself over and over again, "If my husband said he was not a god, then why did I just bury 140 live servants with him?"

I released one thousand more slaves, following with my husband and God's desires. I paid them for work performed and offered them land to toil. I announced to the released slaves it was a celebration for Djet. My people loved me.

I was trying to rectify a wrong. I understood what we had done. Den came to me with more anger than before. He said, "You are no better than my father!"

My son became more and more restless during my reign of two years. He undermined my every move, trying to gain Counsel's approval. They took my side. I was their queen, after all.

When Den could no longer tolerate not having control and power over me, and the people, he poisoned me slowly for about a month, using the same nightshade that took my beloved Djet's life. Den himself brought a goblet to my chambers one evening. I had guessed my son was poisoning me, just as we had his father. I no longer cared. I had gained the favor of the people by setting them free, giving them respect and honoring the life of their king, Djet.

I drank the final goblet of wine. I was ready to see my husband and leave the kingdom to Den, he so needed to control.

Den ruled as pharaoh for forty-two years. His people did not love him.

I was **conceited**. I had much too much concern for material wealth and power, entitlement and ownership. I allowed my son to dictate my beliefs and own my thoughts. I allowed Den to convince me that murder was the only alternative to our situation, instead of talking with my husband more in depth. This caused a massive misunderstanding that led to murder. I valued money and power more than my lifelong *love* and friendship of Djet, my husband. After my poisoning, I stayed in Atonement for 980 years, before reincarnating again. I faced my karma for committing murder and owning slaves. I actually reincarnated four times after this life as a dark-skinned slave. I was actually poisoned in another reincarnation. It was karma.

Lessons to be learned from this life:

- Entitlement is total *conceit*.

- You cannot allow yourself to be owned by another.

- Accept people for who they are. We revel in our differences.

- Murder is always wrong, and only justifiable by God. It ends one's path to learn.

- Ownership is wrong. No one owns another.

    ✦   Things, possessions and a way of life over *love,* is always
       selfishness.

Carla was Cao Jie, Dave was Xan

CARLA, writing as Cao Jie

My father, Cao Cao, was a powerful warlord to the last Han dynasty emperor, Xian (pronounced Chien) in the year AD 200. He gave my two sisters and me to the emperor in hopes of gaining power. One of us would be chosen his empress. I was not yet of age to marry, being just fifteen, so I was kept in a room in the palace the majority of time, without companionship. Resentment grew in my heart but I consoled myself with the thought of possibly being the next empress. Still I waited impatiently. The emperor would choose his wife based on her beauty, as well as her ability to speak politically and with intelligence. He wanted his empress to carry conversation during meetings and dinners.

Unbeknown to me, the emperor was spending time with my sisters in his private chambers but had already chosen me as his empress, awaiting my maturity.

I was lonely. Locked away in my chambers, without friends, sisters or companionship made me long in my heart for someone to speak with.

My father had assigned a guard to my chambers. He was, in fact, a soldier in my father's army and had far surpassed my father's expectations in loyalty. The position given as my guard was reward for duty well-served. His name was Xan (pronounced Zan). Its meaning in Chinese is "the defending man."

There came a day when Xan, who wasn't permitted to speak with me unofficially, asked if I was unhappy. He spoke my name as Princess Jie. I corrected him, allowing him to call me by my personal name of Xu (pronounced Zu). He then said, all right, Princess Xu and I again corrected him, just Xu. I had no friends and no contact. This was possibly my first friend, although not allowed.

After getting the formalities aside, I answered Xan's question. "No, I am not all right. No one has bothered to ask me that question since my arrival."

Over the next few days, Xan and I spoke about our lives, my situation, his position and the fact I was bound to my chambers and he to his guard.

During a discussion one day, Xan referred to me as "Princess Xian Mu." I was not happy with his insinuation. Chinese reference to Mu means to be an extension of the emperor. I corrected Xan once again and reminded my new friend, he was to refer to me as Xu, only. I wanted no titles attached.

The time of my eighteenth birthday was arriving. Four older women normally attended to my needs daily, be it dressing, bathing or taking care of any wants I may have. For two days before my birthday, I was bathed, oiled, pampered and scrubbed in preparation for my wedding to the emperor.

Before the wedding, where thousands of guests awaited, Xan again asked if I was all right. I again told him, I was not, and he was the only person concerned enough to ask. I thanked my friend.

Xan adamantly said, "This will be a great honor for you, Xu."

"It is not an honor," I said. "The emperor has already been with my older and younger sisters. I am not happy."

I was dressed in my wedding attire, not appearing as myself in the least. I was adorned with a black wig, white dress with red, gold and white belt, face painted white, thick with makeup. Guards escorted me to the ceremony. The spirit once living in my eyes was not present.

This was not my choice. Xan watched me under the wooden pergola erected for the ceremony. I needed my friend at this moment. He stood helplessly.

A large feast took place after the ceremony. Four women escorted me to the emperor's chambers. I was seated on a large bed. They pulled my wedding dress up over my head and pulled my legs up onto the bed. Two women stayed as witnesses, as the emperor entered the room, already provoked, penetrated my body, admitted semen and exited the chamber. I did not cry, I did not show emotion because there was none. The four women stayed by my bed all night and when I awoke, they returned me to my chambers.

I passed Xan standing guard as I entered my room. I spoke not a word. I cleaned up and changed my clothing.

Xan knocked on my door. He called to me, "Empress Xu?"

I was infuriated. I yelled my correction this time, "Xu!"

He asked in the manner I had grown accustomed to, "Are you all right?"

I gave Xan all the sordid details of my wedding night, as you would your most treasured friend. Then I broke down in a flood of tears. He held my hand. I knew it was not proper for my guard to touch his empress but I did not care. I needed my friend.

I never saw the emperor after the ceremony but for official functions, dinner and meetings. Xan became my companion daily and during the evening. He escorted me to visit my pet tiger on the grounds and into the town for outings.

There was a day when Xan escorted me into town. A feeble, unstable peasant man bumped me, causing me nearly to fall down. I was incensed. I had been harboring a vast reservoir of anger and unhappiness since my marriage to the emperor. I had no companion, no love or children. I felt betrayed, out of control and lifeless. For some reason, this event triggered my anger, bringing all to the surface and me, out of control. I ordered Xan to strike the man down. Xan, loudly said my name, "Empress!" He attempted to appeal to my senses. I yelled back, "It is my right as empress." Although we were in public and he not permitted to use my personal name, he again attempted to jar me. He said, "Xu!" I ignored Xan and again demanded that he strike the peasant man down. Xan looked at me in horror, pulled his sword and severed the man's head.

I had allowed my bitterness and anger toward my situation, not of my choosing, to cause a feeling of entitlement. I was **conceited.** I believed I had the right to own Xan, and he would follow my wishes, causing him to take a life that was not his to take.

No one takes a life but God. I had no right to interfere with Xan's karma. Nor, did I have the right to make Xan believe he was owned.

Three years passed before I turned twenty-one. During a conversation with Xan one day, I intimated my desire and wish to become "Xan Mu." He understood my desire. He had become my friend, my love, my everything. He reminded me how the last empress had been deposed for her disloyalty and that I should be careful with my words and actions.

A few days later, my father visited. I expressed my complete unhappiness with my marriage, life and situation. I divulged my want and interest in Xan and only Xan. He informed me, he had handpicked my guard, Xan, knowing full well his nature and personality. He further said Xan was as a son to him and was regarded in the highest manner.

"Politics are about politics, and the heart is about heart," my father said, then explained that in Chinese culture, a woman coming of age at twenty-one had a choice. She could speak her mind, politically and otherwise. This prompted me to see my husband the emperor and make him aware. "You may lay with whomever you choose, but so will I," I announced.

"What do you want?" my husband said.

"I would choose my guard and no loneliness," I said.

He lectured me. "As long as you do not dishonor or disrespect the politics, your life is your own."

I spun around on my heels and almost ran out of my husband's chambers. I returned to my quarters, motioning to Xan to follow me. He did so. He closed the door behind.

"I have become of age and wish to speak my mind," I said. "I will share my want for you to become more than just my soldier and guard."

Xan laughed at me. "I will be honored to become Xu Mu."

We both laughed. I was dressed, appropriately in my wig, formal attire and painted face to have an audience with my husband. I reached my hand out to Xan, which he accepted. He held me close for our very first time. I took his hand, leading him to my private bedroom.

I called to my maids, who helped remove my wig, face paint and gown, all the while, Xan stood by watching, waiting for the real Xu to emerge.

I said to Xan, "This is your Xu, here I am, not the empress."

"I would have given my life for you and now, I give it to you," Xan said.

Xan helped me unwrap the ties of my robe. "Your skin is that of ivory and softness. Your beauty is complete." He lay next to me.

"I choose to be with you," I said. "I had no choice before."

Xan made love to me in a manner of which I was unaccustomed. It was loving, wanted and necessary.

In the morning, as we awakened, I said to my Xan, "I would choose to be with you again."

We learned in this lifetime, controlling another and ownership is **conceited**. There was entitlement and **selfishness**. Xu's attempt at reaching gratification caused **selfishness** and the taking of a life. Anger in itself is not as much inappropriate as when used for an excuse for immediate gratification.

Needless to say, our paths were not completed during this lifetime. We would again reincarnate to learn again our lessons.

Lessons to be learned from this life

- You are no better than another. You cannot own another. It is **conceit.**

- Taking a life to prove your power is both **selfish** and **conceited.**

- **Jealousy** is a wasted emotion. Be yourself, whomever you are.

- Sometimes what you want is not what you need. **Jealousy** again is a waste.

- You are not defined by your circumstances. Rise above.

- Own your voice. No one thinks for you.

*Conceit is ownership, entitlement,
vanity and prejudice.*

# Chapter 12

Do Not Harbor Jealousy

"The definition of *jealousy* is an unhappy or angry feeling of wanting to have what someone else has. It's our own perception of what we need or want that is incorrect."

These are the words Isabella gave to us.

Our opinion is that this emotion is the most wasted of all emotions. How much do we really need to be happy? Aren't we the happiest when we *love* and are *loved?* It begins with *loving* ourselves. The world is not about competing or being better than someone else. This caused us to inquire to ourselves, "Are we envious of others and what they have and do we brag about what we do have?"

Life had taught us that for every person who seems to have it all together, somewhere there's a flaw, so to speak, in their character.

Do not find *jealousy* in another's accomplishments. You should *love* that person for their success and steadfastness. *Jealousy* is about fear of loss, and possessiveness.

If you are unhappy about where you work, live or what you own, take the plunge to better yourself, and change it, if that's your wish. It's your responsibility to be your best self. But you should not degrade a person for bettering himself because it causes you to look at your own lack of accomplishment.

We are a fortunate society. *We make our own choices.* To compare yourself to others is useless. You are different, your needs are different. We are all unique.

Some people today imply that wealth is somehow a crime, yet some of those same accusers have wealth. It's not a crime to have money and fortune. You do have an obligation, however, to pay your fair share of taxes, and are not obligated to give charitably but should feel inspired by your gifts to do so.

If every wealthy individual helped another through charity or otherwise, there would be less ***jealousy,*** poverty and more ***love.***

A great little book explains this well—*The Four Agreements* by a wise Toltec ancestor, Miguel Ruiz. He writes about ***jealousy*** and the basis for its existence.

Ruiz believes, as we do, that ***jealousy*** begins within yourself—something in one's own dissatisfaction causes your ***jealousy*** toward another. If you are content with yourself, you'll find no ***jealousy*** toward another. Examine this carefully and, by all means, read the book. It's not complicated but actually outlines why another person mistreats you. It all stems from within them and within you.

If you are dissatisfied in life, it begins with changing yourself, not blaming others. ***Jealousy*** is about lack of security and self-worth. We fail to appreciate who we are and what we have.

Carla was Julia Johansen, Dave was Samuel Renner

CARLA, writing as Julia

My name was Julia Johansen, and I lived in the early 1700s. My home was in Hill Creek, in an area that would later become South Dakota. Hill Creek was one of three small Dutch colonies in that area. Once graduating from school at age sixteen, I worked in the local eatery.

The western frontier in the 1700s was not overly inhabited. The Dutch had settled this area and organized society around the rule of marshals, who were religious and political elders in the Dutch Reformed Church.

One day the marshal who was assigned to police these colonies, Aaron Myerson, happened to be my customer at the eatery. He was quite flirtatious, ten years my senior and I, very naïve. He pursued me rather rigorously until I agreed to attend the church social with him. Two dates later, and many promises of marriage later, he forced himself on me. He took me into the country after church that particular Sunday. I thought it was the normal way men behaved with women. He had promised to marry me after all. I was young, impressionable and inexperienced.

Aaron only came through our colony about once a week. He would find me at the eatery on Saturdays, and in the beginning, offer to take me to church again the next day. Then, he started saying, "No reason to go to church." I always ended up in his room above the eatery, where he had his way with me, continuing to promise we would marry. My mother had passed away when I was young. My father, a trapper/trader, traveled most of the time.

Our affair continued for a couple of months. One day, while working in the eatery, Aaron's brother, Fred Myerson, came in. During the course of my serving his food, we talked about his brother. Fred appeared to be envious of his brother's position and notoriety throughout the colony. Fred was unaware of my relationship with Aaron. He casually mentioned his brother had a woman in every colony and was making no commitment to any of them. I never let on that I was one of those women.

Fred had just confirmed my suspicions that Aaron was never going to make a commitment to me. He had duped me for long enough. The next time he came to town, I vowed I would not be available to him.

Fred continued to frequent the eatery. Sometime during one of his visits, he asked me on a date. Although he was thirteen years my senior, the choices for a good man of the marrying kind were slim in our region. I agreed to date Fred, and within a couple of weeks, he proposed.

I agreed, of course. Wasn't that my purpose, after all? Once you graduated from school, you left your father's home, married and started your own family.

We married shortly thereafter. The night of our wedding, I was not a virgin but attempted to act as one. I was expected to be, in those days. Fred would not have been happy to learn I was not pure and that the reason was his brother.

The next morning, I felt ill. I was not sure if it was due to the circumstances of the night before or something I had eaten.

I was sick for the next six mornings in a row. The sixth day, my husband drove to Rapid Creek to file our marriage certificate with the marshal.

He arrived home hours later. He was visibly angry with me, raving and ranting out of control when he picked me up from the eatery. He started quizzing me about my relationship with his brother. He said he thought he was marrying a virgin for a wife.

"Did you not just want a wife?" I said.

That did not help the situation. He accused me all the way home. In route, he was so preoccupied he didn't even notice our eight-year-old neighbor Samuel Renner walking along the road. Samuel noticed us, however. He waved as we drove by, yelling to me, in his familiar stutter, "Hi, M-m-m-mrs. M-m-m-myers-s-son." I waved back, watching Samuel leave my view, not knowing it would be my last.

Fred was driving faster than what made me comfortable. He started to scold me for not telling him on our wedding night that I was not a virgin. He said it was too easy for me and that I should have had some pain and discomfort. He pointed out that for the past six mornings I had been ill. He said I was probably pregnant and knew it all along. He suggested it to be the reason I had married him. Quite honestly, it had never occurred to me. I was young and without a mother to discuss those things. I admitted about the relationship with Aaron and my not being pure. I was still absorbed with my thoughts about the possibility of being pregnant.

Fred drove recklessly over a bridge, abruptly halting our horse and wagon. I wasn't sure what he was doing as I was still pondering in my mind a possible pregnancy. He stood up in the wagon, a strong and big man, grabbing me from my seat, and throwing me as hard as he could, with all of his anger and force, five feet in the air to around ten feet from the wagon to the ground. I felt pain as my broken body crashed onto hard earth. Above me, I heard him, yelling in anger as he approached me. I thought he was coming to help me. Instead, the left side of my head hit something hard and cold, and then, all went dark.

Fred had killed his wife and her unborn child out of sheer *jealousy.* He had seen Aaron while at the church in Rapid Creek that day. Fred had boasted to Aaron about just having married the beautiful, young Julia Johansen. Aaron's response had sent Fred out of his mind. "Oh, well, I already had her," Aaron had said. Fred punched Aaron in his face but missed, allowing Aaron to retaliate with a punch, knocking him to the ground. Fred got up, left the church fuming, never speaking with his brother again.

Here's where karma takes over. Aaron was my first husband in my present life. I left him in this life and married Tom, my present husband, Fred Myerson in that life.

Lessons to be learned in this life

+ *Jealousy* ruined a brotherhood. Fred's lack of confidence caused the rift.

+ *Jealousy* caused murder, and it's never justified, only by God.

+ Aaron bragged and could have avoided the confrontation with his brother.

+ *Conceit* caused Fred to think that he could marry just to compete with his brother.

+ Fred was also *conceited* to think he was marrying a virgin rather than a real woman. Fred exemplifies *jealousy* because his wife lacked what was expected of her by society, meaning purity, causing him to feel loss.

+ Fear is *selfish* and was why Fred killed, to stop people from learning his wife wasn't pure.

+ Fear is *selfish* and why Julia married a man she did not *love.* She saw no other solution.

Carla was Athena of Mytilini, Dave was Gregorius, her guard

CARLA, writing as Athena

In 600 BC, I lived on the island of Lesbos, sometimes referred to as Mytilini, a capital city and the third-largest island in Greece, one of the islands closest to Turkey. My name was Athena. My grandfather had named me Athena after the mythological goddess because of her strength. At his request, I became the queen once my grandfather passed away. Many powerful men were unhappy with my becoming queen.

They believed the next ruler of Lesbos should have been a man. Despite the fact that my people loved me, a plot for mutiny began among the politicians and soldiers.

Pittacus of Mytilini, a statesman, military general and poet, was known for his wisdom. I trusted Pittacus as well as my military commanders to do what was best for the Island of Lesbos, my people and myself. Pittacus was having an ongoing love affair with Ona, the queen of Smyrna, Turkey. Ona was a greedy woman, who wanted wealth and everything available for the taking. She desired power and with that power, she desired the Island of Lesbos. Pittacus promised to help Ona conquer the Island of Lesbos, believing he would then gain control himself of the island, where he was born and continued to live.

The coup d'état unfolded. Pittacus, along with one of my military commanders, brought the news to me of Ona's plot to take Lesbos. They convinced me, being just a young woman with little military experience, that my army should attack before Ona's to protect our island.

My highest-ranking commander, Demacus, advised me not to take their advice. He feared the size of our army was not sufficient to defeat Ona's army. He thought our army should stay on the island and protect us from an invasion. We had the sea between Turkey and our island. We had an advantage in that respect only.

Hathos, also an officer under ranking Demacus, was in cahoots with Pittacus. He had an agenda of his own. Pittacus and Hathos agreed to encourage me to attack Ona's territory in Turkey.

Hathos's intention was to become head commander as well as be stationed in the palace. This would ensure him never going into battle again. Pittacus promised to give that position to Hathos if he went along with his scheme.

I ordered Demacus to take my army into battle after being convinced by Pittacus and Hathos that our Island of Lesbos was in danger.

Try as he may to provide me all the reasons my army should not go, I threatened to have him killed should he not obey. Despite the danger of their plan of attack, which included crossing the Aegean Sea and approaching Turkey at the furthest point, I ordered him to follow Pittacus and Hathos's plan. My army's commander devised his own plan, which included entering Turkey at our closest point, then traveling along the coast, to ensure a surprise attack. I did not listen and did not hear him as he pleaded with me, making me aware that Pittacus's plan would surely incapacitate our army.

Four days before my army was led to battle in Turkey, I sat in my throne, in the usual manner, with Leda, my maiden, at my feet (Brenda, our coworker).

My guard Gregorius stood across from us at the large pillar as he did every day. He had been stationed there by my General Demacus due to diligence as his soldier. Demacus had ordered him to never look in my direction other than to protect me and my surroundings.

Gregorius was steadfast in his duties as my personal guard. Although, I did catch his eyes on occasion gazing in my direction, which caused me to smirk uncontrollably. I pretended not to notice.

I wore a wreath of white Zakynthos flowers around my head that morning. I wondered if Gregorius noticed me. The next morning before he reported for duty, I had Leda place my wreath at his post. A smile formed on his lips. It gave me happiness to know he was pleased.

All day, Gregorius tried to catch my eyes on his. I tried not to stare but it became almost impossible not to gaze in his direction.

His shift was coming to an end. I sent Leda to confirm that I, indeed, had noticed him. I also instructed Leda to inquire as to whether he was scheduled for battle.

I watched as Leda asked the question and Gregorius hesitated to answer. Then, I heard him respond, "It is my honor to serve my beautiful queen." Shortly afterward, his shift was completed, causing him to leave for the day.

The next morning, I instructed Leda to place a single Zakynthos flower at his post by the pillar. This time, after finding it, Gregorius immediately looked directly into my eyes. I was not able to stop from smiling at his arrival. Our eyes locked for a moment. I melted inside. I sensed and hoped he was having the same reaction.

Four hours passed. I sent Leda to again ask about his going to battle. Leda stated to Gregorius, "The queen can arrange for you to not go to battle."

There was no hesitation this time when he responded, "It is my duty and honor to serve my queen." I believed Gregorius to be a loyal and trusted soldier. He would never desert his men in their need.

Hours later, as his shift was nearing its end, I sent a confidante, Amaranda, my older, wiser advisor, to him. She informed Gregorius rather quietly and discreetly, "At the end of your day, I will come for you. You should follow me to your queen."

It was early evening, when I heard someone enter my chamber. Excitement ran through my body as I hoped and guessed it was Amaranda, (my mother in this life) bringing Gregorius as I had requested of her. I saw him standing alone in the other room. He appeared fidgety yet standing at attention.

I was giddy and nervous at the same time, not able to look directly into his eyes as I entered the room. I thought over and over what words to choose before I finally spoke. I did not approach him at first but rather went to peer through the window so as to not lose my focus.

Finally, I spoke. "Gregorius, I find your inappropriate attention, intriguing." I had not given him permission to speak with his queen. He remained silent, as he had learned.

"I fear for you going into battle," I said. "Why do you believe you must go into battle?"

He spoke then, "To do anything else would not be honorable." It was no use. I could no longer act as his queen.

"At your station, I find your response more honorable than I would have expected," I said. "I find it an attractive characteristic in a man. So, even at your station, I am hopeful for your return."

I had to see him. I turned to face him directly. He was staring into my eyes and me into his. We were melting into each other as I felt a wave of heat come over my body.

Amaranda had arranged a table with fruit where we stood. I gestured to Gregorius and asked that he join me. He started to speak but then held his tongue.

"The wiser, older woman named Amaranda tells me that sometimes a man needs something to live for and I so want you to live. And, there's not much difference between a queen and a woman," I said.

My hand reached across the table and took his without any thought.

"My queen," he said.

"My name is Athena," I told him. "Tonight, I am a woman and don't wish you to be a soldier, but rather a man."

Placing a grape into Gregorius's mouth, past his soft lips, I watched as he kissed my hand.

There was little conversation for the remainder of the evening and into the next morning.

Before daylight, Gregorius left my bed to join his army for battle. I stood at the window and watched my army leave in boats for Turkey.

Two days later, Pittacus brought me news of the battle. He advised that my bad choice in sending our soldiers to battle with Turkey had ended tragically. All soldiers had perished under Ona's as well as my command, including Demacus and Gregorius. Pittacus had stayed on Lesbos during the invasion and Hathos had stood guard with the boats.

He further said, "Hathos will now act as senior general with the death of Demacus."

My heart ached. I heard little more. My beloved Gregorius was gone. I wept, inside and out.

Pittacus assumed power in my mourning and sorrowful state. "It was best for Lesbos that I should remain a figurehead for my beloved people," he said.

He proposed marriage and confessed his interest in me for quite some time. I could think of no one but my Gregorius. I refused his proposal.

Pittacus betrayed Ona. He never relinquished control of Lesbos to her or Turkey. He kept reign over the Island of Lesbos for ten years. Hathos's *jealousy* and deceitfulness paid off. He assumed Demacus's position as senior general, stationed in the palace.

Conceit, *jealousy*, *selfishness* and deceitfulness, stole *love* from Athena and Gregorius. Ona and her troops murdered Lesbos's army for nothing. Nothing was gained or accomplished. Greed and power took lives and *loved* ones.

Lessons to be learned from this life

- You *love* who you *love*, regardless of who they are and what they are.

- *Jealousy* and *conceit* took center stage during this life. Lives were murdered to gain nothing.

+ Striving for power is ***conceited.***

+ Deception in all forms is ***conceit,*** Ona's, Pittacus's and Hathos's. It is also ***selfish.***

+ Believing you deserve to live like a queen and be with a queen is ***conceited.***

+ Hathos knowingly and willingly allowed death just for stature. That is ***conceit*** and ***selfishness.***

> ***Jealousy is being conceited enough to believe you deserve what others have.***

Chapter 13
Be without Selfishness

These *five simple rules* are so very intertwined yet distinct on their own. Now, we come to the third rule to follow with each of our daily actions.

Selfishness is being *conceited* enough to believe you deserve what you have or better, according to Isabella.

Selfishness by definition means to be concerned excessively or exclusively with oneself; seeking or concentrating on one's own advantage, pleasure, or well-being without regard for others. It is putting ourselves at the center of our existence and being concerned with self-satisfaction or self-gratification alone.

Let's think about Christmas time. You have given presents to your family or friends and the day is over. Ask yourself honestly, was there more pleasure when you received your gifts or as you watched the faces of your loved ones, as they opened theirs and grew ecstatic? Hopefully, just seeing them happy gave you great joy and peace. The giving of gifts should not be to receive in return. That would be *selfish.*

Are you a people pleaser? Do you please for praise, or do you please out of *love*? If you try to give the best, biggest, most expensive gifts and brag about it just to receive accolades, then you are giving incorrectly. The size and cost of the gift should never be the consideration but rather the time and *love* spent thinking about it.

Sometimes, it is *selfish* to not speak up or speak your mind. Are you in a relationship where you allow yourself, *selfishly,* to be cared for? You have the wherewithal to take care and give your 50 percent but you allow another to carry all the burden. That is *selfishness.* And, if that person does not speak up for himself, that is laziness, which equals *selfishness.*

Do you avoid conflict and allow yourself to be owned? That's just another form of *selfishness.* You avoid becoming your best self because you choose to let another own you. Again, that is *selfishness.* You are affecting that person's karma. You are allowing that person to own you and be *conceited.*

Being deceitful and telling lies is also considered *selfish.* You are looking out for yourself only, and not considering others.

Holding somebody back and purposefully putting yourself ahead of them, whether it be something simple like taking the bigger piece of cake, is just plain *selfishness.*

Taking credit for someone else's accomplishments is sheer *selfishness* and *jealousy.*

We were created to work together for common goals not to put ourselves or our interests before others.

If we choose to put others before ourselves, it's pure *love.*

This next part will grab your attention.

If sex is for self-gratification, it is *selfish.* Actually, making *love* should please both partners. The act of making *love* is between two people to comfort, please and show *love.* It is not meant for one person to be satisfied while the other is just along for the experience.

Because actual *love*-making is more than intercourse. *Selfish* is as *selfish* does.

Any form of withholding is ownership and *selfishness.* That means not giving your *love,* self, time, attention or sex is *selfishness.*

Selfishness and *jealousy* will kill a relationship because it will break one's spirit. A broken spirit loses its ability for choice to complete its path.

It is *selfish* to have more than you will ever need and not share it with others. If you are living in excess, it is *selfishness* knowing there are others who are hungry and in need. It's one thing to plan for your future and your family's future but take into consideration how much you really need.

To share must be taught by parents and teachers and must be an expectation of society.

It is *selfish* to use up our environment. The future needs the resources.

Remember how karma works. You reap what you sow. Therefore, if you are hoarding money, wealth and power, you are probably returning to a future life of poverty, without power.

Selfishness is a possessiveness of things and *jealousy* is a possessiveness of people and time and also about ownership.

And, as Isabella reminds us, *"Selfishness and jealousy cannot live without conceit, and conceit cannot exist without jealousy and selfishness."*

Carla's present life

CARLA, writing as Carla

My parents were happy in the beginning, my mother said. Early pictures of them in South Dakota seemed to reveal a couple in *love* while Daddy was in the U.S. Army Air Force, as it was called in those days.

It took my parents five years to conceive. For a Catholic couple not producing children immediately, they were frowned upon.

Daddy was 100 percent Italian, and Mother was English-Scottish. Their union was not favored by my Italian side, simply because Mother was not Italian. Then, for my father's new bride to not produce children right away, there was plenty of complaining.

Finally, a daughter arrived, Sharyn. She was loved and adored by both sides. She could do no wrong in any of my family's eyes. Less than two years later came Cleo. Then, in another two years came Patrice.

After Sharyn died, my parents were devastated, as were their parents and everyone who knew Sharyn. Cleo was probably most affected by the loss of her big sister.

Paula was born in 1954. My parents were still in mourning. I can only imagine their pain. Having waited five long years for a child, only to cherish the very essence of her, then having her gone in an instant. There was no preparation for their loss, not that it could have helped.

Paula resembled Sharyn with light hair and hazel eyes. It should have comforted my mother. It did not. She did not want to hold another baby. She wanted Sharyn. My mother admitted it took months before she could lovingly look at Paula and not see Sharyn. She was ashamed when she spoke of it but I understood. I always knew my mother loved every one of her daughters.

Two years after Paula came Joan, and less than eighteen months after that, I was brought into this world. By that time, my parents were numb. The loss of their daughter seriously strained the relationship. The grief and dysfunctionality were just another symptom of a bad marriage. They were not meant for each other. They had ballroom dancing in common, and that was about the extent of it.

They separated over and over again. They would reconcile, give it another try, then separate again. Somewhere in there, my parents fell in love with other people.

I have no ill will about them needing someone or something to ease their pain and give comfort. I did not live their life or circumstances. The pain was theirs and theirs alone to endure.

But, unfortunately, my parents had a fearful Catholic upbringing that forced them to try to rekindle a relationship that was impossible to rekindle, over and over again. The other persons they fell in love with also were hurt over and over again. They waited on the sidelines for my parents to make their decisions on whether to stay as a family or separate permanently.

I always felt my father never loved me. I always felt my mother did. We were not permitted to talk to him when he'd return home from work. He'd tell Mother to keep us quiet. He wanted to watch television in peace. He yelled at us for playing and laughing as kids do.

One day Cleo asked him for ten cents to ride the bus so she wouldn't be late to school. His response is etched in my mind forever. He said, "If I give you ten cents, I won't be able to buy an orange for my snack on break." Isn't it funny, what a seven-year-old child will remember? I also remember one Saturday when he kicked Joan and me up the steps to our room for making breakfast in bed for our older two sisters. Strange and upsetting, the things I recall about my father.

I do have two fond memories of Daddy. Of course, as I already said, I was a bed wetter. Cleo or Patrice would call him home from the ballroom to change my sheets, then he'd return to the ballroom. In my early years, he played the harmonica. The song that lingered in my mind was, "You are my sunshine, my only sunshine."

During the time my mother and father were still together, I have no recollection of him taking an active part in our lives. He didn't do dishes, he didn't do laundry, he never cleaned the house. Only after Mother left him would he think about cleaning. Still, I wished I could remember him holding my hand, coloring with me or taking me to a Daddy-daughter dance. There was none of that.

My mother felt the pain of leaving her children and marriage. She missed all of us. She just simply couldn't take one more day of being in an empty marriage. This was her choice.

It was mother and daughters. Never husband, father, wife and family. She ran.

A good Catholic woman in those days would never leave her husband, despite the unhappiness. Her doctors told her she was having a nervous breakdown and to get out. She couldn't afford to take the five of us. I know her intent was always to get on her feet and come back for us. She wasn't able to right away. It tugged at the deepest parts of her heart. She told me in later years, "It was the biggest mistake I ever made."

Daddy escaped to the ballroom at night. He worked during the day, then went to his part-time job as a coat- and hat-check man at the ballroom. His real reason for going there was not the money, although we needed it. It was really the love of dance. He had also found his other lover there where he continued to see her.

Again, I really don't care who went outside the marriage first, only that five little girls needed their parents' attention and instead it was given to strangers, full-grown adults, not part of our family. They spent a lot of years, frightened by the church's demands, avoiding the prospect of divorcing someone you did not *love*. Mother and Daddy tried to *love* each other many times. We romantically *love* who we *love* and can't *love* who we don't. And, Daddy was a male chauvinist, believing his word was "THE" word. My mother would keep her mouth closed for just so long, then her opinions and thoughts flew out, not welcomed by Daddy. If you've watched television from the 1950s, you have witnessed how the man made the household decisions and owned the household as well as his wife and family. Daddy did as he pleased, most of the time. He lived in his world, most of that time without his wife and us.

A person cannot be forced to feel romantic *love* if there is no common ground. Their five daughters were the only thing holding them together—and the Catholic Church. Eventually, even we couldn't achieve the impossible.

My parents were very different creatures. Neither better than the other, or more correct, just not meant for each other.

Daddy *loved* Mary. They had more in common. Mother *loved* Paul. They apparently had parallel thoughts.

My childhood was not stable, to say the least. I never blamed my parents for their failed marriage but only wished I could have had parents who realized earlier they had five young, impressionable daughters. We needed them. They needed to make up their minds and get on with life. They were so damaged. First by their own parents, then by the loss of their beautiful, beloved daughter, and not to mention, the guilt of the church and their very Catholic parents urging them to make it work at all costs.

Daddy had a bitter, unhappy mother, forced into an arranged marriage straight from Italy. She married my grandfather, and her two sisters married his two brothers. She *loved* another man back in Italy. She spewed her unhappiness at everyone in her path for as long as I knew her. Mother was sexually and emotionally abused at the hand of her alcoholic father throughout her young life.

The last time my mother left my father, she moved to Ohio to live with her aunt. She was physically ill with pneumonia and drove nearly fourteen hours by herself, in the winter.

She had moved home one last time. For whatever reason, this time, she saw five girls, a man and a woman. Not a marriage and not a family. It finally occurred to her.

Her marriage over, her family gone, she was depressed and felt forced to leave her children. The saying goes, "Once you admit and realize the problem, you have to do something about it." She did.

So, after her lover Paul turned her down, she fled to Ohio, her tail between her legs, so to speak. I can feel the pain she must have had, alone, scared, sick and confused, not knowing what to do or where to turn. She finally divorced my father when I was eight years old. But she had lost her one true *love,* Paul.

She had a funny saying about when a woman really loved a man. "She would eat beans for him," she would say. My mother would have eaten beans for Paul. Instead, she went hungry.

I told you previously my mother remarried in Michigan, about a year and a half later, to a man she had known through her parents since adolescence. She came back to Boston, right afterward, to introduce our new stepfather to all of us. She seemed happy and well. She smiled a lot, I remember thinking.

The summer after my fourth-grade year, Mother and her new husband came with a moving truck and drove us, lock, stock and barrel, to Michigan to live. I was sad I couldn't take my navy-blue stroller given to me by the fire department when I was four years old. Mother had said there wasn't room for all of our toys because four of us were moving to Michigan in the U-Haul. I was, however, able to take my brown, stuffed teddy bear, named Cherry Nose, also given to me by the fire department at four years old. I have Cherry Nose to this day.

My last memory of leaving Massachusetts that day, as I looked back at the upstairs apartment window where we had lived, was of Daddy, holding our cat, crying. My stepmother was not in the window, however. I felt bad for Daddy, but not for long. He had asked us time and time again during that past year to choose which parent we would live with. A parent should never put his children in that situation.

We, of course, gave him the answer he wanted during that year but, in the end, chose to live with our mother. She was our mother and we **loved** her.

I told you my few memories of Daddy. They were not happy ones. My memories of Mother, however, were of all five of her girls dancing the "Hully Gully" and playing cards at the kitchen table. You see, she called and came back even when they were separated. She never left us totally. She came back on the weekends. Took us to the beach and the zoo, walking for miles to get there, because we had no car or money to ride a bus. I remember my mother buying us pretty, new dresses, doing our hair and taking us to church. She **loved** us.

But, she was a mess, mentally, where her husband was concerned. She was home for holidays and birthdays and when she had reconciled with Daddy. I remember her being there on Christmas Eve, placing cookies and milk out for Santa Claus. And, being with us on Easter, all of us in pretty spring dresses with hats and coats for church. She took us out to breakfast after making our First Communion and on our birthdays. She's the one who sent us for dancing lessons to learn tap, ballet and jazz. She did so, after leaving Daddy, using her money on bettering us.

Later in life, when we were teenagers, on Wednesdays after school, she sat us down for etiquette lessons. She taught us how to set a dinner table properly, and behave during a dinner, proper things to say and do and about sending thank-you notes. Most importantly, she bestowed on us the necessity of being thoughtful and kind to all people. She tried to give us the tools to get through life. How we chose to use them was not her doing, but our own.

The first time my mother left us, she hired a woman, Nadine, to care for Joan and me as we were just four years old and eighteen months. Nadine cared for us during the day until I was four years old and able to start kindergarten. Our parents reconciled in between those years, off and on. She hired Peggy after that. Peggy stayed for two years. She disliked Daddy's girlfriend staying in the house and thought it improper. Daddy wouldn't come home from work. Instead, he would go to Mary's house after work. Peggy grew tired of his unreliability and voiced her opinion. They agreed to part ways. Next, Daddy hired Ann, the spouse of his coworker. She was young, bossy and lazy, apparently. Cleo, at thirteen, told my mother we didn't like Ann and didn't feel we needed a babysitter. She told my mother she was old enough to watch her sisters until Daddy got home. At this point, Daddy took the second job at the ballroom. He came home nights, when he was ready and not before. Cleo and Patrice, thirteen and eleven, were our parents in the evenings.

Patrice never complained, even in her later years. Cleo didn't complain until she was slightly older. She felt that the responsibility of her raising her sisters belonged with her parents, not her and Patrice. My mother's and Cleo's relationship was never the same. Cleo felt betrayed, unloved and pushed aside. She felt the burden and responsibility of having four little sisters. She never forgave my mother. To this day, my sister holds ill will toward my mother and finds it hard to utter a kind word if the subject presents itself. It's a shame, really, because she learned what it is was like to have a heartbreaking, failing marriage of her own.

My mother had quickly remarried, hoping to remedy our situation. She had a home for us, a new stepfather and a brand-new life, far away from unhappiness. She had finally gotten past the pain of losing Paul, her *love*. About a year and a half after her remarriage, Paul contacted her. He said he *loved* her and wanted to rekindle their relationship. Her decision had been made. It was too late. Their *love* was lost to poor timing.

I wish I could say my mother had a wonderful second marriage. She did not. Our life was again in upheaval. Our stepfather was a control freak—mean, vindictive and backstabbing. His goal became to turn us to him and against our mother. It was a long, unhappy marriage, turbulent and damaging to all of us involved. They fought every weekend, holiday and vacation. There was either yelling or silence. Either way, my goal became to get the hell out of Dodge as soon as I graduated high school.

My sisters and I grew up having no confidence in the male species at all. Men had let us down our entire lives. Mother and "Stepdaddy Dearest" learned to get along after we had all flown the coop. It really was simply because they were tired of fighting. They were too old to divorce and getting to the age where health and welfare took precedence over anything else. They existed. They subsisted.

Daddy lost Mary to cancer about ten years before his death. Funny, right after her death, he placed the 8-by-10 photo of my mother back on his entryway wall for all of us to see. He had placed a shrine in his living room to his five daughters and former wife. Every inch of his living room tables and walls were literally filled with pictures of his daughters. He had ten years alone to think about the family he had *selfishly* lost.

My mother died, luckily, before my stepfather. She finally had peace away from all the men whom she had allowed to disappoint her. Her fear of the church and lack of confidence had stopped her from doing the correct thing for her children and causing her to lose the *love* of her life. Fear is *conceit.*

My parents were *conceited* and *selfish,* and I *loved* them anyway. I still do. And, I forgave them.

Lessons to be learned from this life

+ It was *selfish* for my parents to think of their own needs while not considering their children's.

+ My father was *conceited,* thinking his needs and wants should be met while his children's needs weren't. He would buy records, cameras and movies for himself but let us go wanting.

* My mother allowed herself to be owned by her father and then her husbands, which meant her spirit was broken, making her unavailable to nurture and *love* her children properly.

* The death of one child should not take away the living of the others. Remorse can be a trap.

* It's *selfish* to live in your pain, forgetting another's pain.

* Divorce is neither right nor wrong but both right and wrong. *Forgive* each other. *Forgive* your parents.

***Selfishness is being conceited enough to believe you deserve what you have or better than you have.
We deserve nothing but what God graciously gives us.***

Chapter 14

Forgive Always

Are you able to turn the other cheek? If someone causes us pain, we should ignore the action and not take it personally even if the action was meant to inflict pain.

Isabella's words to us were, "Holding a grudge against someone only limits you. You are the one feeling the pain from not *forgiving* another. It stays with you, constantly, nagging away at your soul. You cannot justify another's actions. You can only be responsible for your actions, ultimately."

If in your heart you hold no anger, hurt or resentment, your soul is free to *love.* If you can *love,* you will automatically *forgive. Forgiveness* is letting go of pain, disappointment and sorrow.

If you *forgive* a person, it doesn't mean you are obligated to have that person in your life. If another person incites feelings in you that are not conducive to *love,* avoid that person. *Forgiveness* is not forgetting. Remember, there could be lessons around this action.

If you know full well this person pushes your buttons or tries hard to cause issues, keep away from that person. You can *forgive* someone yet not put yourself into situations that don't bring about your best self. But, *forgive* them and their actions.

Isabella also reminds us that above and beyond *forgiving* others, you must remember to *forgive* yourself. To not *forgive* yourself for your imperfection is *conceit.* To be unforgiving is *conceited, selfish* and

157

jealous, believing your pain, sorrow, grief or disappointment is more important than another's.

Forgiveness means, "To stop feeling anger toward someone who has done something to offend you, or to stop blaming someone or expecting restitution from them in any form." Literally, it means to let go—of resentment, hurt, anger or loss—at the hands of another, per Isabella.

Let's say you are born African American. You are well aware that your ancestors were slaves. You carry anger with you throughout life because of what others did to your people. Remember what karma is: If you hate, you will be hated. If you don't *forgive,* you will not be forgiven. Racism begets racism. Bigotry begets bigotry, and *forgiveness* begets *forgiveness.* God and God alone will take care of those slavemasters and owners. Most likely, they have already reincarnated as slaves themselves, in some form. It's not up to us to punish for their mistakes. God will prevail. The slave owners will learn the lessons of their path or be back for yet another life to learn, in an even more difficult fashion.

Remember, *forgiveness* begins with you. If you return to a life where you are now a slave because you previously enslaved someone, it is necessary to *forgive* what you have done to yourself. Enslaving can be related to working, substance abuse, alcohol, food, power, sex and people.

Retaliation is not *forgiveness.* It only perpetuates *conceit, selfishness* and *jealousy.*

Carla was Eden, Dave was Hiram

CARLA, writing as Eden

I was a slave, or rather a black-indentured servant. I lived with my husband, Hiram, and our two children on Lemon Island, now known as Bermuda, in the 1600s. My name was Eden. We loved our island and the freedom and sunshine it provided us. Lemon Island was our home. We were happy.

The English soldiers and Capt. John Smith came to capture our island in the late 1600s. They pushed us back to the middle of the island to live. The coasts were taken to erect garrisons around them for protection.

One hundred soldiers came in the beginning. Then, many more until there were a thousand. The once beautiful island was now muddy, with horses, wagons and troops galore.

Eventually, the island became not only a fort but also a trading station for slaves. The natives, including my husband and me, were taken as indentured servants. But, the constable decided the indentured servants were to be treated as the slaves, and act accordingly.

Capt. John Smith took a liking to Hiram and me. We were the first islanders he met when he arrived. He renamed us Adam and Eve and brought us into his home and plantation as caretakers of his home and family. The captain and my Hiram became more than master and slave. Each evening, the captain and Hiram would sit by the fire in the parlor, drink tea and speak about the Bible and life. Captain Smith gave Hiram a pair of his glasses and taught him to read. Mrs. Smith (Caroline), on the other hand, made sure we remembered who we were— servants. I had no choice but to do my job, be their servant and adjust. I was not content.

Our son and daughter were raised with their daughter, Jillian. I treated her children as my own. They sent their son back to England for schooling, so we never really had the chance to know him completely.

Our children naturally grew up and married. They later worked on the Smith Plantation, with us, as well.

Hiram was a righteous man. He held small church services in the barn behind the house. He was able to read the Bible to the other indentured servants and slaves. It started with maybe a dozen or so attending, then grew to about 140. We sang, learned the Bible and shared time away from our masters, with others in the same situation. It was a sort of venting of souls after the service.

There came a day when Hiram was not at home. Captain Smith came into the house in a hurry. He informed me that our daughter Moren had been sold to a plantation owner up north. I couldn't understand what he was telling me. How could this be possible? Our Moren was married and lived here on the plantation with us. I was enraged. Because Hiram was not at home, I ran from the house to head north where Mr. Thomas Silversmith (Tom, my present husband), the new slave owner, lived. He had taken my daughter away from her husband and us.

In my haste, I had forgotten to take along my papers. It was the law now that all slaves and servants had to travel with identification papers. I was stopped along the way and captured, taken to the garrison where I awaited my punishment. Captain Smith came and got me.

Hiram came home, and Captain Smith immediately relayed the events of the day. He also told Hiram I would have to be punished by lashing, which would be one hundred times for this crime. Hiram, angry and concerned all at once, blurted to Captain Smith, "No, take me instead. Eden couldn't withstand that. It would kill her."

Captain Smith was somehow able to convince the constable to punish Hiram instead of me. I was sick inside with guilt, fear and hopelessness. I had lost my daughter and now my beloved husband would face a painful punishment for my mistake.

Four English soldiers came to the door for Hiram. They took him to the square for punishment. Captain Smith took me to be with Hiram. He was lashed one hundred times, as a few slaves and soldiers watched. There wasn't a sound to be heard but the snap of the whip as it slashed the skin off my husband's back. I cried in sympathy for the pain Hiram had to endure. I was angry. Angry this was happening, angry that we had lost our freedom, happiness and our island to the English.

Captain Smith and I lifted my Hiram off the ground and took him home to be bandaged and healed. It took weeks before he was back to normal. He was a proud man. He didn't complain or show anger; he just healed slowly until he could return to his work. Captain Smith brought him tea daily and helped take over his duties. He was a kind and sympathetic man. He treated us as equals, not servants or slaves.

Our church services continued on Sundays. Unbeknown to us, our son Cellen was meeting with his fellow servants and slaves after services. It was the beginning of an uprising, if you will, because of the harsh treatment being given to his father and other servants and slaves on the island.

One night, our son and many of his friends attacked a group of English soldiers, killing almost thirty of them. Outraged, the constable hunted for the guilty parties. He believed he looked foolish not being able to control a few slaves and servants. He went from plantation to plantation seeking any information leading to the guilty murderers. He tortured one servant who gave Hiram's name in an effort to free himself from pain. The constable was almost happy to hear my husband's name. He didn't like the church services and the freedom we were given as indentured servants.

He had recently lashed a man fifty times who had defended his servant wife from being abused at the hands of a plantation owner. During the lashing this time, the square filled with many servants and slaves.

They booed during the punishment. Hiram yelled at one point, "This is a man you are beating." The constable had heard him and remembered it.

Seventy English soldiers descended on the house that day. Captain Smith tried his best to stop them from taking Hiram. He tried to defend his servant and friend, corroborating that Hiram was not responsible for the uprising or murders.

Hiram had suspicion they were coming for him. Someone had told him what they heard in the square. He dressed in the suit he wore for church, the one that Captain Smith had given him. He was escorted to the garrison square once again. This time, the streets were full of slaves, servants and soldiers. The constable tied my husband's arms over a cross, yet he stood to face me and the crowd of onlookers. His clothing was torn off his back without any regard. The lashings began. I felt the tears well up in my eyes. I had a sickening feeling in my heart and soul. Hiram stood brave; he didn't cry. He wouldn't. After a while, I couldn't hear anything, I stood there numb, wondering if this would ever stop.

My sweet, ***loving,*** pure-hearted husband slumped. His feet gave way and he hung on that cross like Jesus, limp, blood draining to the ground.

I heard myself scream but did not feel responsible for speaking the words. I yelled as loudly as I could, "Hiram, I ***love*** you." I hoped he could hear me and know that I was with him. I hoped it would somehow give him strength to hold on until we could take him down from the cross and help him.

It seemed hours while the constable administered one thousand lashings. Finally, I heard complete silence. The constable cut the ropes from Hiram's arms and wrists. He fell to the ground, lifeless.

My Hiram had been lashed to death for something he hadn't done. I hated the English soldiers. I hated living on Lemon Island. What was once beautiful was now ugly in every way.

Hiram's last words were spoken to God. He asked that God forgive the English soldiers and the constable, saying, "They do not know what they do." My husband's dying wish was ***forgiveness*** for men who had stolen his life. I never forgot what the English took from me, my daughter, my husband and my life. I never forgave the English or the life they forced upon me. I died unhappy, heartbroken and owned.

Hiram had too much pride, which is ***conceit***. Neither one of us followed the rules of the world. We were defiant, knowing full well what would happen to us.

We felt entitled to not live our lot. That was *jealousy* and *conceit.* We were not allowed to judge the English despite their actions. There should have been some way to have them evaluate themselves and their wrongdoings without pointing a finger.

Lessons to be learned from this life

+ Follow the laws of the world, or you will create unnecessary problems for yourselves.

+ Believing you are above the law is *conceit.*

+ Murder is always wrong. Only God can justify murder. Hiram's death on the proverbial cross had no meaning. Retaliation causes more *conceit, jealousy* and *selfishness.*

+ Peaceful protest is correct; all-out vigilance is not following the rules.

+ Hiram was laden with pride, which is *conceit.*

+ Hiram was *unselfish* in taking his wife's lashings. He protected her from death.

+ Nobody owns another person, regardless that they paid for them. It is *conceit.*

+ Eden never *forgave* the English for taking her Hiram. Not *forgiving* is always wrong including *forgiving* of one's self.

+ To think you are above God's will, which is nature, is *conceit.* The destruction of Lemon Island by the English was not being the best stewards of the earth.

+ The lack of *conceit,* the lack of *jealousy,* the lack of *selfishness* and the abundance of *forgiveness* and *love* equals total peace within yourself.

Unforgiveness is being conceited enough to believe another does not deserve to be forgiven due to jealousy and selfishness.

Part IV

Atonement

Isn't this what it's all about?
Mother

Chapter 15

You Own Your Karma

CARLA

On Nov. 7, 2014, Dave was awake all night. He felt as though he was given lesson after lesson. His guides explained to him that God has a difficult time getting messages and understanding to those who do not possess Dave's gift. When people do not listen, God finds other ways to get their attention.

Sometimes terrible things happen to seemingly good people because of the path they are on or were on in a previous life. They may be close to fulfilling their path. We all have or will have difficult lives. We learn and grow and complete our paths through those difficult times. We have choice before reincarnating. We know ahead of time there will be difficulties. We choose to have turbulence, in some form, in an attempt to complete our paths and fulfill our karmic debt.

When a person asks "Why did God do this to me?" the answer is easy. God didn't. You did. You are paying back your karmic debt, Isabella says.

Everyone who knows me understands that I love to sing karaoke when it's party time at our house. It was a fluke, then, when I asked Dave one day during meditation and he confirmed with Isabella, I had actually been a singer before. The flapper-me, Ruby. Yes, remember her? She was the main singer at the speakeasy in Chicago. Isn't it fascinating that my *love* of singing followed me—just as my karmic debt had?

At the beginning of November 2014, the subject of prayer came up. Isabella informed Dave that the one true prayer is The Lord's Prayer. Yes, the one that we all know from the Bible. She instructed Dave to work to use it in its most literal translation. Jesus and John the Baptist created the prayer, according to Isabella. The way I know it is as follows:

> Our Father, who art in Heaven, hallowed be thy name. Thy kingdom come, thy will be done, on Earth as it is in Heaven.
>
> Give us this day, our daily bread, and ***forgive*** us our trespasses, as we ***forgive*** those who trespass against us.
>
> And, lead us not into temptation and deliver us from evil, for Thine is the kingdom, and the power and the glory, forever. Amen.

Isabella explained that, other than the "Father" part, which should read God, not Father, it should be "The Honored One." The prayer literally says, *"Let me choose my best path. Let me forgive others. Let me choose my correct path again. Then I can return home to you, God.*

On my bookshelves, I had several books about numerology and thought I'd confirm its authenticity. Isabella and the Counsel said that it was too difficult for us to understand numerology because our calendar has changed from the original calendar started in the beginning. Numerology as we know it, is incorrect, she said. The moon affects us and our moods. The zodiac is very accurate. This has to do with our individuality. All of this she explained. Our numbers and calendars are not really true. So, when the Bible speaks of a person living to be nine hundred years old, it really is nine hundred divided by twelve which equals seventy-five. That makes more sense.

The original calendar was based on a lot of twelves—twelve tribes of Israel, twelve zodiac signs, twelve months in the year. Twelve hours in a day. Twelve apostles.

There must be something to this twelve-thing, I figured. Dave and I have discussed how we should further investigate it at a later time when we have all our other questions satisfied and are able to understand this. Maybe we will never figure that part out but at least we understand that there is merit in some of the twelves that we had questions about.

Isabella and the Counsel did say, however, that the zodiac and numerology do not affect your path or free will. It's all up to us. I have always been fascinated with the zodiac and noticed people and the way it affects them. My friends make fun of me for asking them about their own friend's sign or their birthdays. I have been asking these questions for thirty-some years. So, I had many more questions once they confirmed that there was legitimacy in it.

I wondered if, with each reincarnation a person comes back under the same zodiac sign. So, Dave asked Isabella.

She explained that, "No, indeed, we do not come back under the same sign." She said that sometimes a soul is returned under a sign that could potentially make their path a little more difficult, especially if it is getting close to the end of their path and they have almost completed their goals. We do retain some of the traits from each life and then gain new ones.

That made perfect sense. Then, we could grow.

For instance, some zodiac signs may be more stubborn or harder to get through to and others are more open-minded and more understanding.

We need all kinds of people for the world to work and as long as we all find our path, follow it and get to where we need to, that is all that matters.

I had questions about death. There is speculation about how we should be buried and whether it is acceptable to be cremated or just buried. Dave asked Isabella. Isabella simply said, "The body should be returned to the earth. The method is not of importance. Buried, burned, rotted. None of it is important as long as the body returns to the earth. We should respect the body for three days and return it to the earth. Then, celebrate the death."

Isabella said that we should respect the family also during this time and protect the spouse or partner. Although the body has no purpose again, ever, we are not to discard it before the three days.

I had more questions, as usual. What about euthanasia? It was explained by Isabella again, that we are never to end a life. Only God has the right to end one's life. We can, however, end a suffering animal's life. After all, animals are innocent and dependent on us in all ways. We should help them when they need us.

We discussed abortion before, briefly. Isabella explained that even though abortion is wrong, because only God has the authority to take a life, there is still choice.

I was very concerned about this subject because as a seventeen year old, I became pregnant and had an abortion. My older sisters learned I was pregnant and took me to the appropriate doctors, who confirmed that I was, indeed, pregnant. My sisters said I was too young to become a mother. They took me to have the abortion and paid for it. Yes, it was my choice, bottom line, but my older sisters actually made the decision. I was a teenager who was not careful about having sex, not even considering the possibilities that it would happen and, furthermore, ignoring the signs and the symptoms. Again, the decision was mine but not made by me in all actuality.

Isabella made us aware that when a woman becomes pregnant, the soul doesn't enter the fetus until shortly before the birth takes place. She confirmed that, yes, abortion is murder in God's eyes but that it is not always an actual killing because the soul may not yet be in the body. God will decide.

We have choices. I was never going to have that baby, or any other in this lifetime, because of a karmic debt that I carried with me from another life. I can only hope that God forgave me for that abortion. Ironically, I had always been against abortion unless it was a result of incest or rape. I have to reconsider my beliefs and further investigate them with Isabella and God. Because of my previous karmic debt in another life, I had to feel the loss of no children in this life. It was a hard lesson that I had to learn early in my adulthood.

During Dave's sleep last night, the end of November 2014, he was given lessons from Isabella and others in regard to justification. Justification is human-made. No one is allowed to justify an action. Only God can do that. I gave difficult examples for Dave to ask Isabella. The answers were surprising but comforting.

Because I was a teenager and became pregnant by the man I would later marry, my sisters thought they could erase that entire episode in my life. Needless to say, the event stuck with me throughout my child-bearing years and I never was able to complete a pregnancy.

I asked Dave if God would punish me for committing murder. Isabella explained that God, and only God, would make the justification. I was the age of consent by the time of the actual procedure; however, I did not make the decision on my own. It was made for me. "Who was to blame, my sisters or myself?" I asked. I will find out at Atonement.

At Atonement, when man goes into the service and is expected to obey all of the commands given by his officers and if his superior officer orders the soldier to commit murder during times of war, he is expected to obey or face court-marshal. God says that we should follow the rules of the world, which one would believe includes following your job description while in the armed services. Should the soldier worry about the act of murder that he is ordered to commit?

The answer from Isabella was simple, yet not. The soldier who enters the service for reasons of patriotism and the desire to serve his country is still expected to follow the rules when ordered to murder. Only God can justify, but God is a loving God.

The soldier, however, who enters the service with the intention of justified murdering will not be in God's favor. Imagine that you are walking down the street and someone attacks you. You respond back and defend yourself but the attacker actually dies. Isabella believes that God would find that a justifiable murder.

Here's where it becomes a bit sticky. I asked about rape and incest. No man should judge another man, we were told. We all have a just God who cares and loves each of us. God would take consideration on an abortion due to rape or incest. Murdering your rapist while in the act of protecting yourself would probably be justified by our God; however, hunting him down at a later date and not allowing the justice system to complete their job would not be justified. The killing of innocent animals for sport is never justifiable. A hunter who pursues his prey with the intention of sporting the head on his wall for boasting purposes will not have God's justification. A man who hunts an animal for the food and or hunts the animal to thin the herd for the benefit of the herd and then donates the meat or enjoys it himself, will be justifiable.

What does this all have to do with your karma? Literally, karma is not as simple as you would imagine. So, when we tell you that only

God can justify, remember that. Sometimes karma is simple, such as an eye for an eye. However, it is not up to us to decide or follow through with it. That's called retaliation, which is always an incorrect choice. We do not get to judge anyone, including ourselves.

Chapter 16

Thou Shalt Not Judge

*T*o judge is to form an opinion or conclusion about something or someone.

God says we are not to judge anyone, according to Isabella and the Bible. It is written over and over again in the Bible and some in the Quran. Common sense and history say that when we assume, no good comes from it. To believe we know someone better than they know themselves is conceit.

During Atonement we will be judged for our actions, as well as opinions we held about others.

Isabella suggested we read Matthew 12:36 in the Bible.

"I tell you, on the Day of Judgment, people will give account for every careless word they speak."

Matthew was quoting Jesus when he wrote this Scripture. Jesus told his followers and others he spoke to, as a reminder, on the day we die, and go to Atonement, God and Counsel will take us through every action and all the unkind words we have spoken. Most of us have been guilty of this.

So we should evaluate our actions. Are we keeping gossip going in the workplace with idle talk about others, assuming we know them and the lives they live? Do we purposely lie to another to get our own outcome and our own way?

Isabella tells us to remember:

+ All judgment belongs to God.

+ We shall not judge.

+ We do not know other's intentions despite what we believe.

+ They may not understand their own intentions.

+ Be gentle and encourage other persons to evaluate their own actions.

+ It is the other person's path, not yours.

+ When you point fingers, that is *judging*.

James 2:14-18 says, "What good is it, my brothers and sisters, if someone claims to have faith but has no deeds? Can such a faith save them? In the same way, faith by itself if not accompanied by action, is dead."

Some will say, "You have faith and I have deeds." Show me your faith without deeds, and I will show you my faith by my deeds. Isabella suggested to read that passage and take it to heart.

So, again, if we judge another person, we are not living our faith. We need to show by our actions that we have faith. People learn by example, not by being judged or being preached. Our words must match how we are living.

Isabella reminded us how God is like a loving parent. God gives us chance after chance to grow and learn. God is our example.

Parents, pay attention to this list. If you choose not to provide your children with the following tools for their lives, it means you are acting out of *conceit, selfishness* and not out of *love.* How can you expect them to learn if not from you? It is *conceited* and *selfish* to believe your time and thoughts are more important than your children's.

+ *Love* your children.

+ Give your time to them.

+ Live by example:

  • be kind.

- be tolerant.

- stick to your commitments; your children are watching you.

- take care of yourself.

- admit your mistakes; just because you are the parent does not mean you are perfect.

- don't be afraid to show gratitude; again, your kids are watching you.

✦ Teach them:

- to say thank you, please and all forms of gratitude and common courtesy.

- to respect; it begins at home.

- to be tolerant; not everyone is just like you are. Celebrate differences.

- to be their very best. God expects you to give what you are capable of giving of yourself.

- to be responsible for your actions. Everyone has choice and is accountable.

- to be kind; to all men, women and animals.

Isabella reminds us that our children make mistakes but we should *love* them anyway. They have to follow their path and learn. One day she asked us, "Are you telling your children to do as I say, not as I do?" That would be considered incorrect. Remember, children watch everything we say and do and learn from us. If we are bigots, our children learn to be bigots. If we are prejudiced, our children learn that also. She further said that, normally, if a man is disrespectful to his wife, he teaches his son to disrespect his spouse and all women. If a woman controls her husband and rules the roost, she teaches her daughter to act alike. And, Isabella said that, generally, if we are raised by Republicans, we generally vote Republican. Just because our child decides to vote Democrat does not mean they have not learned from us. It means we taught them to think on their own. That goes along with letting them learn their lessons and choosing their path. Teaching your children to be respectful reminds us to be respectful in life, with everyone. Remember, we are not special. Everyone is special.

The point here from Isabella is that every single path is different, yet every person's individual life is different and you cannot judge someone and their actions because you have never been them.

Carla was Cara, nobility from Spain

Dave was David, Spanish nobility

CARLA, writing as Cara

My ancestors came from what would become Porto, Portugal, arriving when the seafaring Visigoths conquered Portugal, Spain and northern Galacia during Fifth Century AD. The Visigoths ruled as kings and became nobility. My people were part of the nobles.

Two hundred years later, the Visigoth King Witiza, ruler of Hispania (which would later be known as Spain), granted land in the northern part of Spain to my family and three other noble families. That region would become Castile. Our land extended from 30 miles east of what would become Valladolid to the eastern reaches of the Douro River, approximately forty leagues by eight leagues (100 miles long by 20 miles wide) of property. This equaled 1,200,000 acres.

We were privileged. And with privilege came servants and a castle to be kept, as well as vineyards and farmland. Four stone homes were erected within our castle walls, one for each family. We shared gardens, a courtyard and protection from anyone wishing to conquer our land. Eight guards stood at our turrets at all times.

One child was born to each of the four families. Two girls and two boys. Marriages were arranged between each of the families. One boy, Fredrick, had a distant relative who had been a captain of the Visigoths. Therefore, Fredrick became a duke. David's relatives had been officers. Grier and my families had also been officers for the Visigoths. Fredrick, being a duke and thirteen years older than myself and Grier, naturally desired a duchess. My father's family had been a senior officer, higher in rank to the other families. He was also the current head of the military.

This gave him the rank and power to offer his daughter, me, to the duke, over Grier. Additionally, Grier had not yet become a woman. I married Duke Fredrick at age 14 in AD 749. Grier later married David in AD 753.

The Moors, the Muslim conquerors of the Iberian Peninsula, had already taken over all of Hispania. We maintained our positions as nobility only through paying taxes or jizya to the Moors.

Although we once had power and ownership of some four hundred families who worked for us, the Moors now essentially owned us. We had been receiving taxes from the families who worked our land, then found ourselves in the position of having to pay taxes ourselves to our rulers. We maintained our position with our tenants by forcing them to pay additional taxes to meet the Moors' demands.

The Moor conquest had not affected our standard of living. We continued to live as nobles, sacrificing our tenants, by withholding food from them and tying them to posts. Their tax money came to us regardless of whether they had ample food for their own families. Occasionally, a family would steal what we considered our food, which was anything on our land. If caught, a tenant would be tied without food or water for two days in the hot sun. We acted as judge and jury against all the families on our tenant land.

Despite the fact that I had been married to Fredrick, without any choice, my friendship remained with David. We had been inseparable as children and one would have thought the arranging of our marriages would have been to each other; however, my father saw only the marriage of his daughter to a duke. Therefore, any feelings I may have had for David were never acknowledged.

The day of my marriage, Fredrick's father performed the marriage ceremony. All four of the families, and their individual parents attended that day.

Right after the ceremony, David approached me. He kissed my cheek. He congratulated me with a tear in his eye. I wiped the tear from my own eye. We continued our lives just as they had always been.

Fredrick and I produced only one child, a son. David and Grier produced only a daughter.

Eighteen years after Frederick and I married, our son married David and Grier's daughter, living in the castle compound.

When Fredrick died at fifty-two, I was thirty-nine. Grier passed away seven years later. David's and Grier's daughter had been very shaken by the sudden loss of her mother. I spent a great deal of time trying to comfort her.

Now only four of us lived within the castle walls, David, our children and myself. It became customary for David and me to have dinner with our children each evening. After each meal, David walked me back to the door of my home. This went on for several weeks when one night, David admitted to having fond memories of our childhood. I remember my last day of childhood like it was yesterday. I said to David. "I shed my last tear that day, and it was for you."

"It was not the last tear I shed for you, Cara," David responded.

David kissed my cheek, as he had all those years before on the day of my wedding, but this time, he was not kissing me goodbye. "If you would have me, I would not stand in front of some man who's a duke. I would stand in front of our God."

David and I discussed our upcoming marriage for three months, trying to establish the most appropriate manner to have our children understand it.

David was now the acting military leader. During our dinner one evening, David asked my son, the duke, if he could lead a small group of men to Valladolid. "What is the purpose?" my son inquired.

"Our wine producers have not been satisfied with the quality of our corks," David said. "I understand the corks in the bottles of the sacramental wine in Valladolid are of the best quality."

Immediately I responded, saying, "I have never been far outside the castle. I wish to travel along to Valladolid." I suspected David's intention was to have us stand in front of God and a priest in Valladolid.

David said to my son, "I believe the closest priest is in that region." My son questioned his need for a priest when we were now subject to the Moors. "Your mother and I are subject to God."

"I can only think of one reason a man and woman would have to stand in front of God," David's daughter said. She turned to me. "Cara has always been like a mother."

Now having the understanding and permission of our children, we packed and left within three days for Valladolid. David and I stood in front of Father Juan Alejandro Pesanne and were married in God's eyes at 7:00 p.m. on a Saturday evening.

By 9:15 pm, David and I had arrived at our private quarters where a small barrel of wine awaited us, arranged by David ahead of the evening. He removed the cork from the barrel, saying, "See, I told you the cork in Valladolid was better than any other." He poured a glass of wine and toasted, saying, "The vessel has aged well, but the wine inside is as sweet as it was as a child."

I excused myself to another room in our quarters. I changed from my wedding attire to a long, white, sleeveless, wrap-around robe. I released my hair to flow around my shoulders. David was standing as I reentered our room, still sipping his wine. "Cara, there's a sweetness to this wine but it does not compare to the sweetness of this moment," he said.

I relaxed. I dropped my robe.

My husband and I returned to our home and the castle three days later. I looked through the gates of the courtyard and watched as David strutted out to his military. His step seemed a bit quicker. The next morning, I again watched him as he hoisted a bag of flour over his shoulder.

"Where are you going with the flour?" I asked.

"I know a hungry family, and this flour means nothing," he said. "I now know what it means to be rich."

Lessons to be learned from this life

* All entitlement is **conceit.**

* Judgment based on entitlement is **conceit.**

* Judgment based on what is best for you or another is **selfishness.**

* Ownership is always wrong. It also affects the karma of others.

* Punishment with judgment always belongs to God and only God.

* Our parents taught us entitlement and judgment in this life.

* **Love** is the foundation for everything.

Dave was Dotin, a shepherd boy

Carla was Raina

DAVE, writing as Dotin

The time is 3700 BC. I'm standing on the side of a green mountain, at the base which is a broad meadow. The blowing wind rustles through my hair. I'm chilled to the bone. I wrap my cloak as tight as I can.

I am but a small boy, shepherd's hook in one hand, one hundred sheep at my feet. I asked myself, *What have I done to be so cold?* I live in Thrace, which would now be known as a portion of Turkey, Greece and Bulgaria.

I am owned because my parents have died in battle and left me orphaned. I sleep in a stable among the animals. My owner's name is Draggon but I refer to him as Daniyyel, which means master, lord and judge. Daniyyel holds the title of Thracian warrior and is known for his massive wealth and power. His home and saddle are adorned with gold. Daniyyel and his wife have no children.

I have not considered why they chose to keep me and care for me. I just know I work as their shepherd, caring for their sheep and goats. My days are long and cold. Although I have a warm place to sleep and I'm not hungry, I am always alone. I often cry myself to sleep. My only conversation is with my owner, Daniyyel.

For many years, my life changed little, until age fourteen, when my life changed forever. One day, standing at the base of the mountain, I spotted another shepherd in the distance. I reported the other shepherd to my Daniyyel as an intruder on his land. Daniyyel informed me that particular side of the mountain was free range and the shepherd was not intruding. He advised me to maintain our individual herds without allowing them to commingle. To allow the herds to commingle could cause a dispute between landowners, something he wanted to prevent. The other landowner also was a wealthy Thracian warrior.

Another day shortly after that, I saw the same shepherd close to my owner's land. I called to the other boy. "This is my land and herd to keep," I said.

He scurried the herd away, saying nothing. I led my herd away as well. That night, I tell my Daniyyel about the shepherd on our land again. He advised once again to keep the herds apart and that no dispute should take place.

Several weeks passed. I was in the same area with my herd. I found stacks of branches placed as a boundary around the area where I had seen the unknown herder. The stacks are about ten feet apart and two feet high. I spent much of the day moving the branches to the other side of the meadow, out of what I considered my meadow.

Yet another day came, when my baby lamb ran past the boundaries as I chased it all the while. For nearly two hours I attempted to rescue my lamb. I headed back to my meadow only to have the other shepherd confront me.

"Is that lamb yours or mine?" he said.

He knew full well the lamb was my responsibility. Just then, the shepherd dropped the hood of the cloak, and I could see the shepherd was not a boy. Her face was smudged with dirt, hair disheveled as I stared in amazement. I first noticed her hair was much longer than mine but then was taken back by her penetrating blue eyes.

"Any lamb on this land is mine," she said.

"Any lamb on this land is mine, and I will come for it as it is my responsibility," I said.

The shepherd girl smacked the bottom of the baby lamb, which sent it running in my direction.

"See that your lamb stays on your property," she said as she again pulled her hood back to cover her head.

That evening I gave full details to my Daniyyel. He reminded me once more the importance of not commingling our herds and about getting along without dispute.

At my first opportunity I attempted to provoke the girl shepherd. I took my herd close to her owner's land on many occasions. I could see her in the distance; however, she kept far from me.

A day came when I found three stray mother sheep along with their lambs in the northern part of Daniyyel's meadow. I carefully separated them from my herd and guided them toward the female shepherd's land.

I saw her in the distance as I approached. I goaded, "My herd is suddenly larger."

Finally she spoke to me. "Did you steal my lambs?"

Immediately, I responded. "Apparently, your lambs have wandered off. I returned them because I am sure your master would have you account for them."

She spoke again, in a surly manner. "I'm sure it is your ram who stole them away from here. It is your ram who is trying to steal my sheep."

I wondered where her warmth had come from as she smiled and said, "Thanks for returning my sheep."

Again, I reported the entire incident to my Daniyyel that evening. "She is quite obstinate and difficult to deal with, this girl herder," I said. Daniyyel just smiled.

The girl herder and I had not happened onto each other for about a month until one day, I stood by her branches of markers and jumped to her side, knowing she would see me. I jumped back and forth from her side to mine, taunting her playfully. The words came from my mouth. "What should I call you?"

The girl herder flipped her hood back to expose her face. She placed both hands to her hips as she blurted out. "Raina, it means, I AM STRONG."

I wasn't responsible for what came from my mouth. It just flew out. "I think I'll call you Bayla."

She looked at me in surprise. Neither of us said it, but understood the meaning of Bayla was "beautiful."

That evening, I discussed Raina the shepherd girl with my Daniyyel. He seemed to read my complaining as "he that protests too much."

After our first real meeting and the learning of her name, whenever I saw Raina on the mountainside or meadow, I yelled to her, "Bayla." And I would continue to discuss her with my Daniyyel, complaining as to her difficult personality. My Daniyyel saw a light in me as I spoke about Raina yet never let on.

I began to notice Bayla was changing and with that, her boyish body morphing into a woman. Six months had passed since my first knowing her name. I attempted to make our interactions more frequent; however, she would just yell to me from twenty to thirty feet away.

I asked my Daniyyel one evening. "How can I know her more?"

Daniyyel, being a little awkward, said, "Why not ask Raina if she would like to know you?"

So, I approached Bayla in the meadow one day after searching and searching for her.

"Bayla, I would like to know you," I said.

Her reply was, "How exactly would you like to know me? I believe I am already owned by another."

I was very embarrassed by the forwardness of my question. I added insult to injury by then proclaiming, "If you weren't owned, could I know you?"

Bayla answered, "I believe I've already been owned once." I thought she meant, isn't one owner enough? So, I continued, "Wouldn't sheep herding be easier together?"

Bayla, apparently, did not approve of my questions as she stomped off in the other direction with her herd.

I could barely wait to discuss our conversation with my Daniyyel. "You do know what you implied?' he said. "You have made a proposal."

"What?" I did not understand the words I had spoken nor how a proposal would work.

My Daniyyel explained, "Raina has value. You must present a dowry to her owner, her Daniyyel."

I decided and spoke, "I could give one sheep and one goat to her owner."

Daniyyel laughed. "You have four sheep and three goats to call your own. You must prepare to offer three sheep and all your goats for Raina. You will retain one mother sheep with lamb for your future."

I stood up, puzzled. My Daniyyel said, "Dotin, if she has value, she is worth all of your animals. Value her not, then she is not to be proposed to."

Meanwhile, unbeknown to me, Bayla had been sharing our episodes each time with her Daniyyel, Chakkim. Chakkim asked her, "And, what do you think about Dotin's question?"

Raina's response was forced. "I think he's an awkward oaf."

"So you like him?" Chakkim said.

"Yes," she said.

Neither Bayla nor I were aware of the meetings our Daniyyels were having about us. They had already agreed between themselves on three sheep and three goats in exchange.

A short time after our individual conversations with our Daniyyels, Bayla found me in the meadow. "My master said you should talk to him about your proposal."

I agreed to meet her Daniyyel and asked Draggon to arrange our meeting.

The date came for me to discuss my proposal with Chakkim. I arrived with three sheep and three goats at his front door. He greeted me, laughed and said, "We normally don't keep the animals at our house, but it is a nice gift for Raina." I explained to her Daniyyel that the gifts were for him.

"And, what do you want in return?" Chakkim said.

I blushed, and spoke the name, "Raina."

Chakkim posed an important question. "Since you now have nothing, how will you earn your keep?"

I answered him, "We can tend the sheep and goats."

"Together?"

I thought for a moment and responded, "Yes."

Chakkim announced he would speak with my master about the arrangement of herding together.

"What do I do with these sheep and goats?" I said.

"I think you should deliver them to Raina," Chakkim said.

I did as he had suggested, searching for Bayla. When I found her, she asked, "What are you doing here?"

"Your master advised me to deliver these sheep and goats to you," I said.

"You don't have much of a herd anymore," she said. "We'll have to start our own."

The very next day, thirty laborers came to the mountain to build a three-room stone home for Bayla and me. Our masters had arranged it together.

Daniyyel came to me. "These will now be your quarters. Yours and Raina's herds can now be commingled but it will be the responsibility of each of you to keep track of the individual herds."

He presented me with a bag of root vegetables. "Plant these and you will eat."

It was the custom in our days to consummate a relationship with a rooted garden.

As the years unfolded, Bayla and I soon learned from watching the sheep and our own herd flourished.

With each child or two, I added on another room to our mountain home. Our home grew to eight rooms and our herd grew to twelve. We had four boys and eight girls. I birthed many lambs and many babies in our stone home in the mountains.

Lessons to be learned from this life

- Raina and Dotin focused on the fact they were owned and never acknowledged the parenting and *love* received from Daniyyel and Chakkim. They judged their masters as owners as opposed to caring parents.

- Chakkim had one daughter in old age, Daniyyel had none. Both masters *loved* and treated their herders as children rather than possessions. As Raina and Dotin's family grew, Chakkim's daughter married Dotin and Raina's son. They did, indeed, become family. Judging is a matter of perspective, and you can never assume what another is thinking or why he or she is behaving a certain way.

- All forms of envy are judging. We assumed our Daniyyels were complete with wealth and ownership, yet they envied our *love*, children and happiness. And, in the end, our masters found happiness in our families, not wealth.

- All judging is left to God. Because you never live another person's life, you cannot judge that person or his life.

Chapter 17

Reconciliation with God: Why Do Terrible Things Happen?

CARLA

In late November 2014, Dave was shown another of his past lives while meditating at home. This past life would take him back to the early 1700s in the western American plains frontier country that later become South Dakota. In this life, Dave was a little boy, about eight years old, named Samuel Renner. His mother died giving birth to him.

Early the same morning we learned of this very recent past life, I had received an alarming phone call from a friend named Shirley Ann. Her partner of fifteen years had hanged himself during the night, and she had been the one to find him. "Oh my God, oh my God, oh my God," was all I could say.

Tom and I had just been with them, and I also had missed any signs of unhappiness. When I called to tell Dave, I asked him to speak with his guides and find out if the man would be punished for taking his own life. My Catholic upbringing taught me that this man would be going to hell for suicide. I didn't believe it.

Dave meditated and was shown the man behind bars. He was given the feeling that the man could not communicate right then and that he felt trapped. That was the message I passed on to Shirley Ann—not that he was going to hell, also that he was all right. Later we learned it was a sign for the man waiting for Atonement. God does not send you to hell for taking your life; remember, there is no hell. Like any other lesson or mistake, when we don't get it exactly correct, only God can justify or decide whether we will reincarnate to try it again.

DAVE

That night while sleeping, I had a dream. I could smell gun smoke, and my thighs hurt from running through sand dunes toward a large fort. I ran in front of an all-black army, wearing a Union uniform. I had a feeling of pride and respect for these men following me up the hill. They were scared. I was determined that their lives would have meaning. Freedom must mean something. I felt pain in my chest as bullets pierced me. I flew backward, and simultaneously fell out of bed, hitting my head on the table. The lamp knocked to the floor. My wife was mad I had awakened her. My head hurt. What had thrown me out of bed? Why was the dream so vivid?

In the morning, I called Carla to share what I had experienced. She told me to watch an old movie, *Glory*, about the life of Col. Robert Gould Shaw, who had died in 1863 in the Civil War.

CARLA

We were so excited. While Dave was at work, Tom and I were researching on our cellphones about the main character in the movie. I was texting Dave back and forth as we found out more. Tom and I then streamed the movie and watched it again. I texted Dave, *Watch this when you can.*

The next day, Dave's wife worked, which allowed him the time to watch the movie at his leisure. He phoned in tears saying the entire movie felt like reliving a life. Indeed, Dave had been Robert Gould Shaw. He asked Isabella to confirm what he was feeling and seeing. She gave him additional details that could not be confirmed by watching the movie. I had written in my journal, early in our meditating, a day when Dave had seen Boston, identifying it by the courthouse. He remembers that my mother was with him that day but at the time he couldn't connect the dots. He was not sure why she was showing him Boston but knew that it was from an earlier time.

Apparently, I was his mother during his Civil War life. My name was Sarah Blake Sturgis Shaw. Born in Boston, Suffolk County, Massachusetts. I found that ironic because I had been born in Boston, Suffolk County, Massachusetts, in my present lifetime. This also confirmed some of the early pictures he saw of Massachusetts and a white farmhouse. My present mother was his favorite sister then. The pieces continued to fit. Dave had been a Union colonel during the Civil War and was asked to lead an all-black army. Shaw encouraged the soldiers of the Massachusetts 54th Regiment to refuse their pay until the Army gave them a wage equal to the wage of the white troops.

Shaw was from a prominent Abolitionist family in Boston. He fought in many battles during the Civil War, including the First Battle of Winchester, Cedar Mountain, Antietam, the Battle of Grimball's Landing and the Second Battle of Fort Wagner, where his troops were defeated and he died.

Remember Chapter 6, when I mentioned Silas, who had shot Dave in another life? This was the life Dave had seen earlier. And, remember, the bullet bounced off a Bible in his pocket and did not kill him. This happened during the Battle of Antietam. The pieces were coming together.

Needless to say, Dave was absolutely blown out of the water with this information. It was strangely interesting to watch a movie that was about ourselves in another lifetime. Incidentally, my present-day mother, Robert's favorite sister, was Josephine at that time.

During this meditation between Dave and Isabella, they discussed how karmic debt is repaid. Isabella actually took Dave through a partial Atonement and made him feel what everyone feels when they are judged. You are made to feel everything you inflicted or caused others during your lives. The purpose was to show him partial Atonement as Robert Gould Shaw, a white, affluent man in comparison to his incarnation as an indentured black servant. Comparing once again, he was taken from being a small, stuttering child, Samuel Renner, versus his life as a Mayan Priest who never spoke up for abused children.

Dave said he cried harder and felt worse than anything he could remember. Isabella explained to him that during the Mayan days, which we would learn about later, he never spoke up for the children who were being raped and bled. Thus, he lost a child during one lifetime, was made to stutter during another life and died a brave but very young man during yet another lifetime, even though Shaw did stand up eventually for the rights of his black soldiers.

She asked him if he now understood how our paths progress and are completed. She conveyed to Dave, he has, indeed, completed all paths now at his present life, but that he must continue to choose his path wisely. He must continue to remember and act accordingly in regard to the *five* very **simple rules.** He must not be **jealous;** he must be **forgiving;** he must not be **conceited** in any way; and he must never act **selfishly.** In other words, he must act as Jesus did during His one lifetime. He must remember to **love.**

Dave was Robert Gould Shaw

Carla was Sarah Blake Sturgis Shaw

DAVE, writing as Col. Shaw

I was born into wealth, in Boston, Massachusetts, in 1837 to abolitionist parents. I joined the Union Army in 1861, fighting in the Civil War battles of Antietam, Grimball's Landing and the Second Battle of Fort Wagner. During the Battle of Antietam, I was shot and injured by a Confederate officer. My mother had given me a Bible to carry in war. I kept it in my upper left uniform pocket over my heart for protection. I did not know at the time I placed it there, it would literally be for my protection. The Confederate bullet pierced the Bible rather than my heart that day during battle. I was stunned and injured but my life was not taken. I had simultaneously shot my pistol at my attacker, killing him. Before he died, he pulled a Bible from his own pocket and waved it at me as if to say that God was on his side. However, God was on both our sides that day.

After the Battle at Grimball's Landing, I went home for a time to Boston. Before I left for my next duty, I married my fiancé. My parents entertained many politicians. During one evening soliciting politicians for the abolitionists, I was asked to become the leader of the first all-black 54th Regiment. My father urged me to accept. Within fifteen days, I had been promoted from major to colonel. I fought for the same pay for my men, who were in the beginning, expected to get **"black wages"** only. In the end, we secured for them the same pay as any white soldier would receive.

In battle, I felt apprehensive at our start. I was unsure whether my men were capable of becoming soldiers. To my surprise, the men of the all-black 54th Regiment gained my respect and adoration. I had pride in every one of my men and his accomplishments. I was honored to fight alongside them.

We marched south through Darien, Georgia, where we were forced to participate in the burning of the town. It was nearly abandoned already, only women and children remaining since Col. Montgomery had settled his troops on St. Simons Island, just more than twenty-one miles away. Nevertheless, he ordered that my troops take part, though I adamantly refused.

After Darien, my men marched with me to Charleston, South Carolina, to take Fort Wagner. We camped on our arrival and rested, knowing full well what was to come. We were kept separate from the other white regiments that had also arrived at Fort Wagner.

On the second day after our arrival, the troops were arranged in the early hours of the morning. My men were ordered to form the central portion of the attackers, by Brig. General Quincy Gillmore. As the advance started, I became perfectly aware that my men were being sacrificed ahead of the white soldiers. One of my flagmen was shot. I picked up the flag, handed it to a soldier next to me, ordering him to carry our flag. I ran to the front, ahead of my men, as they were being shot and killed all around me. My legs and thighs burned like fire. I churned up sand as I ran, pistol in one hand, sword in the other. My only thought was that the lives of my men had to mean something. I scaled a small dune, only to be shot three times in my chest, knocking me the ground. I lay there with last thoughts of hope for my men and their survival. Then, nothing but darkness.

A small but strong hand reached toward me. The hand took my own hand. I was pulled to my feet. I felt no pain, held no knowledge of the fight still ensuing around me. Then I saw two beautiful golden wings. They lifted me. I traveled through time, space, darkness and light, at a speed that I couldn't imagine. I felt a calm, warm, peaceful feeling come over me.

I looked back. My lifeless body as Col. Robert Gould Shaw was stripped of its medals and the insignia of an officer. I had been dumped into a mass grave of black soldiers. The Confederate soldiers had treated me no better than my men. Officers were usually treated better. I heard the Confederate soldiers say, "He is no better than the n------ he led." I knew immediately that it was true. I was no better than these men. We were all just men, exactly the same, no one more special than another.

Robert had been raised with entitlement and wealth. He truly believed his worth much more in the beginning than the black men he was commissioned to lead. Although his parents raised him as an abolitionist, his true thoughts at first were of superiority. He learned in the end the value of human life and worth, regardless of the color of skin.

Lessons learned in this lifetime

+ It is **conceited** to believe your skin color makes you superior.

+ Having wealth does not entitle you to privilege. That is **conceit.**

+ Standing up for what is right is always showing **love.**

+ When life is lost in war, everyone loses. Innocent people lose their chance to correct karma.

+ Killing is wrong, and only God can justify death.

+ During Atonement you will relive all your wrongs, including murder.

+ It's **conceited** to believe your being a martyr is more important than any other soldier just because you are an officer.

DAVE

During meditation that same day, I was reminded of my Atonement for the story of Hiram and Eden, black indentured servants, or slaves, on the island of Bermuda. I was Hiram, preaching to a small, all-black slave congregation. I had spoken in a proper English dialect during that lifetime. I had experienced my death as Hiram. I heard the lashing. I heard

Eden (Carla) scream in the crowd. I was tied to wooden beams, hands stretched out much like on the cross. I could feel his anguish. I could feel the ropes tied at my wrists. Then all went black. I saw my black hand rise toward heaven. A strong yet soft hand reached for and grasped mine. I felt safety and comfort. I felt warmth, calm, peace and hope.

Two large golden wings carried me through dark and light, time and eternity. No man owns another. How could this death on a literal cross have meaning? What lessons were learned? **Love** is important; not being owned is important; **forgiveness** is important. Yet, pride is a form of **conceit.** Was my death as Hiram, in defiance, serving the greater good or was the war within himself?

I had many experiences during meditation that day. Later that same night, Carla took notes and asked questions to me while I relived my life as Samuel Renner in Dakota territory, a Dutch colony later to become part of South Dakota. I was a small boy living in a two-story farmhouse, which our guide Shelia first showed me. This meditation may be the first time I became completely lost in a character.

Two or three times, Carla stopped me while reliving this life as Samuel. I was stuttering, scared, crying, short of breath and lisping. It unnerved her to watch me literally become someone else.

Dave was Samuel Renner

Carla was Julia Johansen Myerson

DAVE, writing as Samuel

My name is Samuel Renner, from Hill Creek, a town that later would become part of South Dakota. My mother died giving birth to me eight years ago. It is the early 1700s.

I live with my father and go to a school where my teacher helps me not to stutter. My stuttering embarrasses my father. Since my mother died, he has been unhappy. It feels like he equates the loss with the birth of me, the imperfect child.

One day when I stayed late at school with Mrs. Johnson, she insisted on teaching me not to judge myself by my stuttering. You see, my tongue has been tied since I first began to speak. Try as I did to stop, my father's yelling only makes it worse. I left Mrs. Johnson feeling very happy. It was a warm, sunny day, and the wind blew as I ran home from the school about two miles.

I came to the top of the hill before I crossed the creek and paused as a wagon raced past me. I recognized Mrs. Julia Myerson as the wagon went by, and I thought she saw me because as I yelled hello to her, and she waved back. Mr. Myerson, however, did not see or notice me but rather stared straight ahead, seeming hurried. Mrs. Myerson attended school with me until recently, when she got married. I considered her my friend. She sang and read stories to me. I miss seeing her at school.

The Myersons's wagon stopped at the bottom of the hill, just over the creek. Mr. Myerson stood in the wagon, yelling at his wife. Even from a distance, I could see she was frightened. Still, she defended herself. But Mr. Myerson grabbed her by the shoulders and lifted her out of her seat. He threw her, and she landed hard on the ground. She did not move. I tried to yell down to Mr. Myerson but nothing would come out.

He jumped out of the wagon and started toward Mrs. Myerson. She lay by the tree and the edge of the creek, unmoving. Mr. Myerson bent over her body, reached for her head and picked it up, crashing it down onto a large stone. I tried to scream for help but nothing would come out.

I turned and ran toward my house. I must find someone to help Mrs. Myerson. My father would be home.

"Papa," I said, bursting into our home, "Mrs. Myerson is hurt." I stuttered it out, and my father yelled at me in anger. He ordered me to go to my room until I could speak correctly. Again, I said, "Mrs. Myerson is hurt by the creek." I went to my room and stayed there by myself. I heard my father leave the house. I hoped he had heard me and was going to help her.

I lay in my room for hours. I was hungry but my father never came home. It got dark and I fell asleep.

The next morning, my father sent me to our neighbor's house, the Myersons's, to deliver beef jerky. "Mr. Myerson may be sad and may need help because Mrs. Myerson has died," he said. I cried. I tried to stutter out that I had seen him hurt Mrs. Myerson, but my father had no patience to listen. "I know all about it!" he screamed. "Be quiet! Just take the beef jerky next door."

He instructed me specifically about what to say to the grieving Mr. Myerson, advising me to speak slowly so I would not stutter and embarrass him. I was told to say, "Sorry for your loss."

I headed to our neighbors' house just over the hill, past the bridge and around the next bend. I saw women dressed in church clothes, walking into the house carrying dishes. I walked up to the front door as my father had told me to do. Mr. Myerson answered the door himself. He glared at me. I handed him the beef jerky and said, "Sorry for your loss, Mr. Myerson." He took it without speaking. I looked at him in the eyes. I wanted him to know I had seen what he did. But I said nothing.

When I got home, I asked Papa what it all meant.

"It's none of your business," he said.

I cried. "She is my friend."

"She's dead," Papa said. "Go to your room."

I went to my room, lay on the bed and thought about what had happened. I needed to see her. My momma was dead, and now Mrs. Myerson, too. I still wanted to know what it all meant.

The next morning, I woke up to an empty house, as usual. Papa had already left the house. I dressed and headed to the Myersons's. I knew the back door would be open because nobody locked their back doors in that community. I slipped in and through the kitchen, Mrs. Myerson's kitchen. In the parlor, I saw a box. From the rim of the box, I could see the brim of a bonnet. I looked into the coffin, and Mrs. Myerson was not moving. I touched her face, and she was so cold. A blue-purple bruise spread on her forehead above her eye. It scared me. Dead meant cold. Now I understood. I ran.

At the door, strong hands grabbed my shoulders and spun me around. I fell to the floor. Something or someone lifted me up off the floor and threw me out the door and down some steps. Mr. Myerson. "What did you see?" he shouted.

I stood up. "I saw you hurt her. You threw her out of the wagon."

A hand smacked me across my face. Down I went. I felt confused and dizzy and started to cry.

A potato sack enveloped my head and body. It smelled dirty, like rotten potatoes. I could see a little light through the holes. He tied rope around my arms and body so hard I couldn't move. Mr. Myerson dragged me across the yard and tossed me into a shed. A door slammed and everything went dark.

Pain throbbed in my shoulders, and the twine cut into my biceps. I cried. I heard myself panting. It must be panic. I saw a light.

Someone was coming. A nice lady talked to me. Another voice spoke. The voices made me feel better. They said they would not leave me. I was not alone. Three days later I heard the sweet sound of Julia Myerson singing. I could still hear her singing as the world went dark. A hand reached down to me. I saw the small hand of a child, my own hand, reach toward the strong, but soft hand of a young girl. Comforting and calmly, she lifted me and held me. Two golden wings carried me as we traveled through darkness. Light, time and eternity took me along.

Lessons to be learned during this lifetime

* Because someone is different than you, that does not give you the right to mistreat him or consider him imperfect in any way. That is **conceit**. Samuel stuttered, but he couldn't help it.

* We are all connected. Always keep in mind that person you judge from afar is somehow more connected to you than you know. Mr. Myerson had no idea that Samuel was, indeed, his own biological son. Samuel's father was actually his uncle. No one is more special than another.

* All murder is **selfish** and justifiable only by God.

* The only father Samuel knew in his life never listened to him or cared about him. He felt like a burden from birth. No one should be made to feel as if he is a burden. That is **selfish** and **conceited.**

* God sees when you commit wrong. Trying to remove all evidence never works.

* We are not alone. Our spirit guides and angels are always with us, even when we can't see or feel them.

Later I asked Isabella why Samuel had to stutter, and she said, "It was because Daan had not spoken for the children during the Mayan days." So who was Daan? My next past life.

Dave was Daan

Carla was Ronna

DAVE, reliving as Daan

In the year 700 BC, I served as a low priest under Terryl, the High Priest. One morning I stood at the base of the stone temple in Chechen Itza, as the moon set and the sun came up, the sixth moon since the Summer Solstice, a time for feast and sacrifice. The golden sun rose directly behind the temple. The Chechen Itza people believe that God had sent us the Sun to care for us and provide for us. We must sacrifice to the Sun God for good crops and well-being. Only through the sacrifice of death and the blood of the innocent can we be saved from famine and despair. I am thankful. We had been at war. For the sacrifice, righteous blood was required. We captured young warriors from another tribe. They would die for us. Their blood was given in sacrifice to the Stone God of the sun.

I stood in attention in my ceremonial garb. Three lesser priests and I stand before Terryl. The head Mayan priest chanted and called for the sacrifice. He stood at a large stone altar at the pinnacle of the monument.

Deep in the temple are small, dark, stone rooms. One room held a young warrior; this man didn't know what was coming. I headed to my workroom, where carvings of a tree adorned the walls. I could not forget the tree. The bark of this tree was magic. It was light and ground easily. Fed to a person, it alleviated pain. Higher doses caused hallucination and sedation. I grabbed a wooden bowl beside the row of stuffed squirrels across the shelf edge at the top of my room. A stone was used to grind the bark. I headed to the prison cell where the young warrior was held. I mixed the bark powder with water and made the warrior drink. It was bitter but I begged him to take it all. In but a few moments he would not know where he was. I pray he would not experience what was to come.

Terryl again asked for the sacrifice. Four of us, who were dressed alike, headed down the hall and steps. The young warrior, bound at each wrist and ankle, was led up the stairs. There was still fight in his confusion. Outnumbered four-to-one, he was laid on the stone altar, then tied by his wrists and ankles across the altar. I grabbed his left ankle with all my might and held it down. The other priests also held down their corners. Terryl raised a razor-sharp, carved-bone knife over his head. I wished the warrior would stop breathing and quit struggling. The knife sliced just below his left rib cage. I heard a scream. Was it the warrior or me? A concave cup was strapped to Terryl's wrist. It, too, has razor-sharp edges. His hand and wrist disappeared into the man's chest. It severed everything. I heard one last gasp as the heart was removed from his chest. Blood splashed across my face and tunic.

I was sick to my stomach. The man twitched, then was silent. My fingers and hands ached from holding him down. I wiped the blood from my face. Terryl raised the man's heart above his head and turned to the Stone God. His mouth gaped open, he drained the blood into the beast. To my disgust, the crowd cheered.

I wrapped a soft woven cloth around the now-dead warrior. He was righteous, he fought for what he believed; his heart had been stolen for a stone idol.

Nearly a year passed. I prayed for war. Yet we were at peace. How strange it was, a Mayan priest praying for war.

The hot sun shone over the stone monument. Summer Solstice. Before the seventh day a sacrifice must be made to the God of the Sun. The sacrifice must be innocent or righteous. We were not at war. I could not sleep. I awaited Terryl's command.

Young virgin females of a family must be older than five years and younger than thirteen for the sacrifice. The family should be honored. I was horrified. Their young children will help feed the stone idol, ensuring our harvest and well-being. I led three priests into the city to the house Terryl had chosen. A father and mother stood scared in the doorway. Six young girls lived there. One was much too young. She was but three years old. The next youngest was Shanta, age five. They were all young and innocent Mayan girls. Shanta played in the small hut.

The oldest, Ronna, was soon to reach majority, the time to marry and have a family of her own. When we arrived, she was helping her mother prepare a meal. I looked at the scarred forearms of her mother. Her mother knows why I am here.

I hand the mother five white gowns to be worn by her daughters. Tomorrow I will return, I tell her. Her precious daughters will feed the Sun God tomorrow, I think to myself. They will bring honor to her family.

In the morning, I see Terryl. He is dressed in all white with a belt tied around his waist. Pieces of white cloth, stained with blood, hang from the belt. He prepares the spines. Long and sharp, they will pierce the skin easily. They will be painful. They will cause injury and scars. The wounds will fester for days. Shanta and Ronna's mother had experienced this. I knew from her scarred forearms. I head to my room and pull down my wooden bowls. I will need more bark than normal, because there are five young girls. I shudder. I have been through this with Terryl before, many times. It is what is expected of me. It is not my place to protest. I can only hope the dose will keep the young girls from remembering. Terryl is never aware of the drink I prepare. It was all I have to ease their suffering.

Early in the morning I arrived at their home. I told them they were precious and they will please the great God of the Sun. They smile, excited for the festival. They are the guests of honor. Their smiles make me cry. They have to give too much. They just don't know. Life will not be the same. I tie a Sac Nicte blossom to each one's wrist. Shanta takes my hand. It is soft, yet strong, for such a young girl.

I so wish at this moment that I could take her away from all this. She asked why I was crying. All I can say is that she looked more beautiful than the flower on her wrist. The girls walked with me toward the Great Temple.

They willingly followed me into the dark rooms at the inner portion of the temple. I prepare the bitter drink. I tell them it will purify them for the festival.

The girls, sleepy and confused, followed me and the other three priests up to the altar. Their hands tied in front of them, they lay face down across the altar, hands and forearms extended.

Terryl held the wooden cup in his left hand and the long sharp spines in his right. I shuddered as the girls cried. Sharp spines were thrust into their forearms. The wooden cup catches blood that drips from the end of the spines. I watched as young Shanta's body fell completely limp. Then Ronna struggled. Those warm familiar eyes filled with fear. I prayed that this would be the end of their torment. I knew however, it is just the beginning.

Terryl raised the wooden cup and poured the blood into the gaping mouth of the stone statue. Blood dripped from the mouth of the beast. Priests carried the girls and tied again, face down, over a much smaller stone altar. I tried to get them to drink once more, from the cup with the bitter drink.

Terryl approached the youngest and tore the back of her white gown. He spread the front of his gown. I cried and he shot me a dart of anger. "It is my right to make them bleed," he said. He finished with each young girl. He passed the cloth between their legs and tied it to his waist. The screams grew louder.

I headed to Shanta's small room. I untied her hands and held her. Her breathing was labored. Then she looked at me and smiled. I took her hands and told her she was precious. She took her last breath. I wrapped a soft woven cloth completely around her limp body.

I ran to the girls in time to see the other priests bandaging the middle sisters. I ran to Ronna. She lay over the stone, exposed and bleeding, the tale of violence marked across her body. Tools of torture are evident in a long, sharp spine still stuck in her left shoulder. She apparently refused to cry or scream. Terryl made her torture worse. I untied her and bandaged her wounds. I gave her another sip of the bitter drink. I held her while she cried. I cannot see the warm, familiar look in her eyes anymore. I think to myself, if some God wanted this, it would be better for all of us to starve.

She fell asleep, and I covered her carefully, seeking to return what dignity she has left. I held her hand and cried. I stayed with her till morning.

As the sun arose over the lower corner of the temple, I stood holding Shanta in my arms at the top of the Temple. I carried her down the steps, holding her out in front of me, my arms fully extended. My arms burned but I wanted everyone to see her. This is what we do in the name of God. As I carried Shanta home, women stood on both sides of the road, their scarred arms extended to her, showing me that they, too, were tortured by Terryl. Some asked if they could help me. "No, this is my duty," I said as I delivered her to her parents. As I watched them cry, I cried with them.

This has to end, I thought. I arranged for a young village warrior, my son Jarra, to come with me and secretly enter the Temple to kill Terryl. I was captured and took complete blame.

Now it has been three months since Shanta's death.

I had arranged for this young man to meet Ronna, prior to the killing of Terryl. He had been injured in battle as Ronna was injured in sacrifice. He had a good heart. I knew he would care for Ronna, who was ready for marriage.

My punishment for killing the high priest was death. I deserved it. I have allowed Terryl to torment and kill many young girls.

On the day of my execution, I stood before the people. Terryl's men drove two large hooks into my chest. *This pain cannot be worse than the pain suffered by all the little girls*, I thought. I felt lifted off the ground. My chest heaved for my last breath. I did not care. I was dying. I only cared that Terryl had been stopped.

All went black, again. Then I saw a soft but strong, small hand reach down for mine. It felt familiar and comforting. The hand was Shanta's. Two beautiful golden wings carried me through darkness, light, space, time and eternity. I heard a voice. *You held my hand as I died. You comforted me. I will forever reach for yours.*

Forgiveness comes in many ways. We never die alone. Shanta has decided to stay with me, through all my lives. Even though I had not spoken for the children, Shanta (I now know as Sheila), knew I had tried to ease her pain and provide comfort and I treated her with respect and dignity. Even in the end. Though I tried to do what was expected of me, I had to stop the false virtue of our religion. To stop the atrocity, I stood ready to lose everything.

What is the point of all this? I have asked over and over. Sheila can travel through space and time. She is literally an extension of God's hand. Since the Mayan life, she has crossed me and others over to the other side. We never die alone. Sheila and others like her have simply taken on a role in God's realm. She delivers me and others to Heaven. This is her gift, and the part she chooses.

It is how she shows **love**. She chose this role in Heaven. She says it is a great honor. There are many like her. They may be your sisters or brothers that have already passed. They are offered a role during Atonement to forever help others and see them through one of the most misunderstood parts of existence—our death.

Sheila also helps me travel through past lives. It is something I have learned to do, see, hear and experience. During my forty-two lives, some were short and some were long. Sheila has taken me at death, my last twenty-six times, to Heaven.

Why did they now show me all of these cruel, harmful experiences? It is what we all go through at death. It is part of Atonement. We are made to see our wrongdoings and the feelings we have inflicted on others.

Lessons we learned in these lives

- Karma does follow you. I did not speak for the children in this life. I stuttered in another.

- Fear is *conceit.* It took Daan too long to stop Terryl causing many children to suffer.

- Religion can never be used to coerce another into your way of thinking.

- Listen to your heart. The parents of these children had fear, allowing their children to suffer because of their *conceit.* Fear equals *conceit.*

- Terryl showed *conceit* in believing he had a right under his religious beliefs to take virginity from the children.

- Shanta forgave Daan despite her life being taken. We should always *forgive;* it is right.

- You face your karma in one life or another. We are all accountable.

Witnessing Others' Atonements

After all of this was revealed, and Dave had relived the parts of his past-life Atonements, he started getting visions of the Atonements for our loved ones.

CARLA'S MOTHER'S ATONEMENT

CARLA

My mother died from a brain tumor in 1996. Sheila, Dave's past life guide, escorted my mother over at death from life on Earth to the spiritual world. Once in Atonement, my mother waited for three days.

The interval acclimates us from one world to the other. During the three days, Isabella reminds us that those of us on Earth should honor the loved one's body on Earth for the family's sake.

My mother went through Atonement for seven years. While in Atonement, she was counseled, forced to see her past lives and reminded of her choices in all of her lives. During Atonement, she was then given choices to reincarnate in an attempt to learn her lessons again or take a job for God as a Gatekeeper or Animal Companion, still remaining in a different type of Atonement.

A Gatekeeper's primary occupation is to prohibit souls awaiting reincarnation from seeking out those souls on Earth. The reason is due to the possible negativity that follows the souls waiting and also to stop them from providing future information to the souls still on Earth, which could influence their choices.

The primary purpose of an Animal Companion is to oversee all the animals belonging to that soul's past lives, you are Gatekeeping. In other words, the souls you are watching over previously had pets who passed away. Those pets stay on a plane overseen by the Animal Companion. There is a lesson to be learned from Animals. If you *love* a pet, it will *love* you unconditionally. They have no expectations. They are total *love,* carrying no karma.

My mother was given the choice to reincarnate immediately or take the two jobs and hope to not to come back later. There is no guarantee when God offers you a job that you will still not have to reincarnate later. She chose the two jobs. My mother has been my Gatekeeper and Dave's since 2003. Additionally, she looked after all of our pets from every one of our lives.

One day, as I awakened, I had a vision. I saw the clouds and an opening appear, as I see just about every morning, when my Guide or Angels have a message for me. A smaller person was in front waving and jumping up and down with elation. Behind that person was something else. I had to clarify it with Dave through Isabella. It was my mother, holding my last two schnauzers who had passed. Apparently, Elizabeth, my guide, had been given permission to tell my mother of God's decision to give her permanence in Heaven. God confirmed she did not have to return to Earth. She had sufficiently completed her tasks and learned her lessons in the spiritual realm. But, as God was telling my mother she no longer had to perform her duties, and did not have to go back to Earth, Mother was concerned. She said to God, "But, how will I leave my children, Dave, Carla and my other girls when they need me so, right now?"

God so eloquently responded, "But, Cindy, isn't that what this was all about?" God knew she would choose her children and be that *selfless,* this time. She had learned her lessons. She had not been present for her children on Earth but was willing to give up her eternal happiness to be present for them now. God granted her the desire to remain our Gatekeeper, for as long as we need her.

Coincidentally, Daddy passed away in 2003. Mother was finished with Atonement as he was starting his. He finished his Atonement two years ago and was immediately reincarnated. Just previous to his reincarnation, one morning I was falling in and out of sleep and heard someone say, just as plainly as if they were sitting next to me, "We are sorry for what we did to you." Again, I had to clarify with Dave through Isabella that it was Daddy. He was telling me he was sorry for the pain he caused me through this life and all of our past lives together. We have had many.

A soul apologizes to the persons they have wronged, whether there is the ability to hear it or not, before reincarnating. Daddy was in Atonement for twelve years. I hope he learns his lessons this time and can stay in Heaven the next time he passes.

DAVE'S GRANDFATHER'S ATONEMENT

DAVE

I have so many memories of this man. He had a kind but serious smile, thinning gray hair and wire-rimmed glasses. He sat in a large brown chair next to a very organized file cabinet. The top drawer had all his important papers, and the bottom drawer was filled with silver dollars. He had been through the Depression and saw coinage as security. "Silver coins will never lose their value," he often said. One Christmas he gave me a coin collection kit so I could start saving pennies. "Now you will never be broke."

Grandpa married my grandmother when they were both young. After they graduated from high school, she became a teacher. He owned and operated a small filling station. You'll remember from an earlier chapter that one fateful night when the gas station exploded, throwing him across the street but not injuring him. The gas station burned to the ground. In an instant, their life plans were snuffed out. Ever the optimist, my grandmother told him he must be meant for something else. They moved into the big city of Lincoln, the capital of Nebraska. Looking for work, my grandfather answered a posting for a janitor's job at the University of Nebraska, walking into the admissions office. He left there that day, employed and enrolled for college. Soon he graduated and entered law school.

When we visited my grandfather, his neighbors always addressed him as "Judge." He wore a dark black fedora and a long, black wool coat when he went to work or church, where he served every Sunday as an usher. He counted the offering after Mass. To me, as a child growing up, my grandfather seemed a serious man.

Sometimes he would still be wearing dress pants but would have on suspenders and a red flannel shirt. The pants would be hiked up just a little too high. He would lean over and pull hidden ginger snaps from his well-organized drawer in a file labeled "Cookies." He always said Grandma didn't know they were there. *How funny*, I would think, *they always go grocery shopping together.* Grandma had never learned to drive. *Why wouldn't she know they were there?*

Grandpa would take me fishing, dressed in a floppy, cotton hat, black dress pants and a red flannel shirt, a fishing pole in one hand and a bucket of worms in the other. He drove me in his Mercury sedan to the lake. It was a cloudy, chilly morning. I wore a blue jacket and jeans. He spent the first thirty minutes showing me how to put a worm on the hook. "If you can't do this, you can't fish," he said. Then he explained bobbers and how to cast them. I stood in the chilly morning air for almost an hour and still no fishing. The next lecture was about catch and release. Small fish were released. We only kept what we would eat. He wanted me to understand this fishing and how much fun it was for him. I think now it was more about the quiet time alone. It was how he escaped the decisions of the Nebraska Supreme Court.

My Uncle Junior moved in with Grandma and Grandpa as they got older. Junior bought a horse and kept it on land to the south side of Lincoln. This land belonged to my mother's sister, Molly, and her husband, Sammy, a loud and boisterous man.

He drank a little too much, according to Grandma. I still remember the day Grandpa drove Junior and me to see the horse. I was excited, because I had ridden horses the summer before. I had been to Camp Okoboji and received a ribbon for being a "super duper pooper scooper." That really meant I got to brush and clean up after the horses at camp. I would be able to feed and help Junior clean up after the horse.

The day started and was overcast. Grandpa had that flannel shirt on with his dress pants. Junior wore blue jeans and cowboy boots. We drove to the small barn at the end of the road by Sammy's house. We started to pitch some hay for the horse. I heard a loud bang. Grandpa grabbed me and carried me toward the car. Junior dove behind the car and then jumped in. I heard Sammy yell, "Get off my property," sporting a rifle in his hand.

Grandpa was shaking. "That man was never fit for my daughter," he said, referring to Sammy. "Shit," he said as he floored the gas pedal. This was the only time I ever heard my grandpa swear. Gunshots rang out as we flew down the road.

By the time we arrived home, Grandpa was still shaking while making phone call after phone call. I heard later that Sammy was sent to a mental ward. Grandpa must have had some connections. My grandpa appeared to always be about the "right and wrong" of a situation and tried to teach me well.

Grandma and Grandpa were married a little over sixty years. He always held the door for her. He thanked her for every meal she cooked. He worked meticulously on his yard and the roses on the white trellis between the garage and their stone house. I always thought him a respectful, upstanding and kind man. He must have had the respect of others as well. He served on the Supreme Court of Nebraska for over twenty years.

My mother was the only one of his children to attend college. She quit college to marry my father. Grandpa was always sure to point out to my father the importance of education. He believed education to be all-important, still judging and blaming my father for my mother not finishing.

My grandfather died in 1975. He passed over and spent three days becoming accustomed to the spirit world. He then went to Atonement like all souls. He sat before his Counsel. Grandpa had to live all his past lives and transgressions as we all do. He relived every choice he had made in all his past lives. He had lived a good life this time, yet at the end of Atonement when he was given choices, as to jobs to perform for God, he requested to serve on Counsel much like the job he performed in his past life. God said no. As a judge he had used the law correctly but at times had judged based on his opinion and not purely the law. It is only God's right to judge.

My grandfather was assigned the role of "watcher" of the Counsel. He did not know whether he would return for another life or if he would fulfill his role as watcher and be able to go "over the horizon."

In July 2017 my grandmother and grandfather appeared to Carla during meditation. My grandfather had spent forty-two years watching Counsel, spending that time in observation, learning lessons. Counsel does not judge; it teaches. He learned that judgment implies superiority and putting yourself above someone else. Applying the law does not mean judging but applying the law with your personal opinion is judging and **conceited.** You cannot put yourself above others. It was a valuable last lesson for Grandpa to learn: "Thou shall not judge."

My grandfather has now passed "over the horizon."

In my grandfather's life before this one, he was Francis George Shaw, an abolitionist and social reformer who was against capitalism. He was a leader of a socialist movement in the 1870s. He was the father of Robert Gould Shaw—yes, the one who led an all-black regiment of Union soldiers in the Civil War.

In that life, my grandpa was entitled by his wealth. It is interesting to me that he was against capitalism in his past life and then lived through the Depression in this. Francis was a man of great wealth and influence in Boston. As an abolitionist, he believed in equality for all and that no man owned another. My grandfather in this life grew up a simple man who did well for himself, yet he had judged others. He had to learn after this life during Atonement that judgment belongs to God.

Earlier in chapter 12 we discussed Athena and the defeat of her Greek army. My grandfather was a general for Ona, Turkish queen and rival to Athena. He took the lives of many sons when he defeated Athena's army. As Francis George Shaw, my grandfather experienced the death of his own son at war, at age twenty-six. My uncle George, my grandpa's youngest son, also died before my grandfather in this life. Again, he lost a son. Karmic debt and lessons of Atonement go hand-in-hand.

DAVE'S FATHER'S ATONEMENT

DAVE

My father died in 2012 at age eighty-two after a struggle with Parkinson's disease. He grew up poor on a farm in Nebraska. The family lost the farm during the Depression and then moved to Lincoln, Nebraska. He played baseball and basketball, though his parents never saw him play due to lack of interest. He graduated from high school and worked full-time at a grocery store for a year before deciding he should go to college. He saved up money by working at the store and working on the railroad while in college. He also did a stint in construction and dug the basement for St. Teresa's Catholic Church in Lincoln. This was the church that my grandfather (the judge) and my grandmother attended. This was also the church in which my parents would be married Feb. 14, 1953.

My father worked his whole life trying to make up to his father-in-law, my grandfather, for marrying his daughter and taking her from completing her college. He became a teacher, then a high school principal. He always stressed the value of education, much like my grandfather.

Once during his high school principal days, my father was called about a party where senior football players had skipped school and were drinking. The team had just won second place in the state football playoffs. My father hopped in his car and drove to the party. Just as he arrived, he saw one of my friends, then a junior, walking toward the party. My father jumped up to the sidewalk and walked side-by-side with my friend John, our starting tailback. As they turned the corner to walk up to the front door together, John relayed that my father quietly said, "Maybe you should go back to school, and I will see you tomorrow." John turned back, knowing he had somehow been spared. John would go on to win the state wrestling championship that year. My father knocked on the door and discovered the entire senior boys' basketball team drinking. The rule at that time was that if you were drinking you lost the entire next season. Basketball had always been one of my father's favorite sports. The next day he met with the six seniors in his office to tell them they were suspended from basketball for the rest of the year.

Later that night I watched my father cry. He said it was one of the hardest things he had ever done. They were just kids, and they would never play competitive basketball again. Their senior year was never to be the same. It broke his heart but those were the rules. You play by the rules—that was what my father preached. The next year when I was a senior football player and the seniors were acting out at a pep rally, my father ran up the bleachers.

He stood in front of us and proclaimed, "Even if you are my son you will act like a gentleman." We had always worn football jerseys on Friday game days. From that day on we wore ties to school on game day. We needed to learn to be respectful, my father had said. These are all important lessons that I thankfully learned growing up.

Another important lesson I learned from my father was that all people should be respected. My father got to school early every day. He would make a cup of coffee and carry it down to the janitor who got there before him each day. Dad believed everyone was important, each in their own way. Emile worked some twenty years as the janitor during my father's years there. Dad always stayed after basketball games and wrestling meets to help Emile clean up. He never thought he was better than this man because of his education.

At my father's funeral, a young man walked up and introduced himself as Terry. The young man told me he had a less than perfect childhood and frequently got into trouble with drinking and running with the crowd. He said he was well on the way to dropping out of school or being expelled when my father approached him. Dad kept meeting with him, calling him to the office. He would help him with math homework and expect him to come to school daily. Sometimes Dad called his house to get him to school. Dad told him if he came to school every day, he would make sure he graduated.

My father met with him before school for almost six months. One day Terry came to my father's office to tell him that he'd gotten his girlfriend pregnant. Terry had not told his own parents yet. Dad talked to him about responsibility and stepping up to be a man. Terry said he never forgot the conversation. Shortly before graduation, Terry's girlfriend had a baby. Terry spent the entire night at the hospital and the baby was born about 6 a.m. Terry showed up at school that same morning just as he had promised my father. My father called him to the office early and said, "A father should go home and spend time with his new baby. I think there is an exception here."

Two days later, Dad told him that he had arranged for an interview at the local nursing home for a job for Terry in the housekeeping department. Terry said he only got the job because of my father's recommendation. Terry started working there the week after graduation. He worked so well, they sent him to nurse's aide training. He apparently was good with patients. Another six months had passed when my father walked into the nursing home one day. He told Terry he was on the scholarship committee at Rotary Club. They had leftover funds that year and that he had arranged a scholarship and admission papers for Terry at the local community college. Terry was to be accepted to LPN school. He would be able to earn more money and take care of his new child and soon-to-be wife. The very first invitation they sent out for their wedding was to my father, and Dad attended. Terry and his wife had now been married for many years, with three children.

Listening to Terry's story, I cried.

"Your father is the best man I have ever known and I know I am not the only one who believes that," Terry said. "He made a difference to kids over and over again. He touched many lives. We all loved him."

My father was a veteran of the Korean War. My last memory of his funeral is standing with my mother accepting the American flag. The veteran holding the flag said, "This is for a man who served his country but more importantly served this community for over twenty-three years."

One day about three years after my father passed away, he came to speak with me. My wheelchair-bound father who could no longer smile with the mask that Parkinson's disease had left on his face, stood before me, smiling. I could feel his embrace around my shoulders. He walked me to a place and pointed, saying, "Over the horizon." He turned to me. "This is where we all want to go."

I cried. My dad had made his final journey. He was done. He had gone home. He did not have to reincarnate.

Then, I received the following message, a very important lesson. Yes, there is karmic debt but it can be overcome. If you live a life that is not **conceited**, not **selfish**, not **jealous** and is **forgiving,** you do not have to come back. My father has completed his journey.

My father had passed away after the Parkinson's destroyed his body. His voice had become nonexistent, his personality all but wiped away. Upon his exact moment of death, a strong but small hand reached down and took him through light, dark, space and eternity. His grasp on her small hand was stronger than it had been in years. He held on to her during the transition although fast and confusing. He spent three days changing back from human to spirit. My grandmother, his mother-in-law was ever present, never leaving his side.

My father first noticed my grandfather, the judge (his father-in-law) sitting quietly on the sidelines when he progressed to Plane Three, which is Atonement. My grandfather raised his spiritual hand, as if to say, "Don't speak, be quiet." My grandfather did not have permission to speak or add to the Counsel proceedings. He sat quietly and observed.

Life after life passed in front of my father. The pain and sorrow he had caused others, passed before him in those other lives. He wept, then slumped. A boisterous, animated figure, who laughed and drank in a past life was passing before him. This same man had not been affected when cutting off the finger of a slave to put him in his place. This man was Horatio Volente. This had been my father in a previous life, a sailor and slave trader from the 1600s. He had been a man financed by the church to trade in human lives. He had ripped children from parents, fathers from their wives and children. He transported men and women from Africa to the small island of Bermuda, then Lemon Island. Harvey, my father, then saw himself bribing Capt. Smith to allow his slave ships to dock on the island. He watched himself herd men in chains from his boat. Horatio, as he was called then, auctioned them to the highest bidder. Strength and healthy teeth made a slave more valuable, much like the auctioning of horses.

Horatio brought laborers in the name of slaves. Soon, all of the black indentured servants, as Eden and I were, were treated just as the slaves.

My father then witnessed my death as Hiram and heard all one thousand lashings. My father in this life, as Horatio in that life, watched me as I died. He knew it was wrong. He recognized his part.

After Horatio's Atonement, he chose the life of Jonathan Wright Sr., the father of J.J. Wright, my thirty-eighth life. It was his karmic debt to feel what it was like to lose his wife and children as he had separated families as a slave trader. He experienced the death of a daughter, a wife and a son. Each time his anger at the loss was uncontrollable. He murdered his daughter's killer. His finger was lost to the mob just as he had cut off the finger of a slave. He again struck out at his child's killer, Angelo Genna, losing his own life. He could not be judge and jury. My father, as Jonathon Wright Sr. died in a dark alley outside of D'Andre's in the same place his son lost his life off of Halstead Street in Little Italy, Chicago. Just as Hiram had, he lay face down, his arms spread, bleeding until he died.

Then he felt small but strong hands lift him. He felt no fear as he traveled behind golden wings through time, space, light and darkness. He again faced Atonement as he watched his life pass in front of him.

He again chose to return as my father in this life. He became chained to his wheelchair much as he had chained slaves in the past. His boisterous personality as Horatio was silenced in this life and his face became without expression. However, he remained in good spirits and never complained. He overcame his karmic debt. He was not **conceited, selfish** or **jealous** and he followed the rules of society. He was both **loving** and **forgiving**. He lived his life as an example. His actions matched his words.

Part V

M

Metamorphosis

I am love.

God

Chapter 18
The Star-Crossed Lovers

CARLA

Around the second week of November 2014, I was anxious to know whatever happened to Ruby and J.J. While meditating around that same time, Dave saw my sister Paula in another life in which she was Jane. Jane (Paula) worked at a bank with J.J. (Dave) for Henry Spingola. Jane was married to the same man she is married to in this life. That man was a driver for Angelo Genna, Ruby's boss. When Angelo Genna married Henry's sister, Lucille Spingola, J.J. (Dave) attended. On that day at the wedding reception, Jan. 10, 1925, Ruby and J.J. met.

I must interject at this moment. Dave told me that the piano player was my present-day friend Shirley Ann and my coflapper singer was my present-day friend Ilene. Their names were Annie and Daisy.

It amazed me just how interconnected we all are and have been. The two women have been special in my heart. I have always felt a closeness with each of them in this life and, apparently, in our pasts.

The following is a conversation between Dave and me actually reliving part of the wedding.

Jonathon's (J.J.) memory of the wedding

Carla: Who do you go with to the wedding?

Dave: I go with a man from work, Phillip.

Carla: Do you know that man in this life?

Dave: Maybe. He is a teller at the bank where I work. I can see him standing with the other tellers. He looks like my friend John. John was my roommate in college.

Carla: The college you attended in this life?

Dave: Yes. One of the other tellers was his girlfriend. The other two tellers attended college with me as well. Phillip is the only male teller, though. He is in charge of all the tellers.

Carla: So, Phillip drove you to the wedding?

Dave: Yes, he is driving a small, black, boxy car. There are so many cars dropping off people. It is real busy.

Carla: Can you see a sign anywhere as to where you are?

Dave: We walk up six steps, then a landing, and six more steps. There is a sign actually above the door in the cement that reads Ashland Auditorium. We are escorted way over to the left into a very large room. They ask us if we are there for the bride or groom and we answer, "for the bride," but they escort us to the groom's side. The middle of the room is filled with church pews, and the sides are filled in with wooden chairs. We are seated in the left side in the wooden chairs. I can see an organist, and she is playing church music. I see Angelo and five other men. He is wearing a tux but the other men are not.

Carla: Can you see Ruby?

Dave: Yes, and she is singing something about a mother and child. It is a religious song. Sounds kind of familiar. She is wearing a pinkish color dress. Her hair is blond.

Carla: Is it a raspberry color? Do you have a good view of her? Does she look like me?

Dave: Yes, it's raspberry color. I can see her pretty well. Yes, she looks like you *(chuckle)*. They are starting to play the wedding march now. You know that da-da-da-dah? I can hardly see Lucille though. But, she is standing there with Angelo. I can see the top of her head. They are lighting a candle together. Ruby is starting to sing. It's Ave Maria.

At this point Dave started to cry. He stopped talking. I asked him why he was crying.

Dave: This is a moment when something special happened. The room had fallen silent. Ruby is singing in a high voice. It's very spiritual, heavenly and there's not a sound to be heard. She is beautiful. I can feel myself falling for her.

Carla: Can you fast-forward, sort of?

Dave: *(Chuckle)* … yes, I will try. We are at the reception. There are thousands of people. I can see Ruby in the crowd. I try to follow her around throughout the evening to see what she is doing. She is sitting at a table with some friends, I assume.

Carla: Do you know any of them?

Dave: They are flappers from the speakeasy. I hear Angelo come over and tell them to mingle with the single men. The girls get up and make their way around the crowd.

Carla: Do you still see Ruby?

Dave: Yes. I am going over to ask her to dance. I tell her hello and introduce myself as J.J. "You have the eyes and the voice of an angel," I say. She shoots me an ornery, yet suspicious smile. She says, "Well, maybe one dance." She has your attitude *(chuckle)*.

Carla: Tell me what happens while you are dancing? How do you feel when you take her into your arms?

Dave: I feel a sense of comfort, immediately. It's familiar. It's like going home. You know that feeling? There is an excitement throughout my body. Not sexual, though. It's electric. It feels right. I know there is something very special here. I don't feel awkward or nervous as I usually would around a beautiful woman.

Carla: How many dances are there?

Dave: Just the one. It's a waltz. I am not good at it at all. Ruby tries to lead me without anger or frustration.

Carla: What happens when the dance is over?

Dave: We walk back to the table where her friends are sitting. By the way, the girls seated there are your present friends, Annie (Shirley Ann), who is also the organist and piano player in the bar and Daisy (Ilene), who sings with you, and flappers Lila (Brenda) and Camille (Jenny). I do not recognize two of the other girls. We are standing. I ask Ruby to have breakfast with me tomorrow and she ignores me.

Carla: Then what happens?

Dave: Angelo comes by and tells the girls to go back to work. The girls scurry to get up; maybe a little nervousness or fear is there. I ask her a second time if she will meet me for breakfast. She pauses, and says, "We'll see." She pauses again and says, "I will be at Marino's tomorrow at ten."

Carla: Anything else?

Dave: Ruby starts to walk away. She gets about two hundred feet away, turns to me, smiles and continues to walk. Phillip and I leave the reception shortly afterward.

Carla: Can you fast-forward again?

Dave: Yes. Phillip drops me at my place. It must be a boarding house. I have one main room with a bathroom. No kitchen or living area. I fall on the bed with my hands clasped behind my head. I am thinking, *Wow, she agreed to meet me for breakfast.* I jump up, take a clean pair of blue trousers and a white shirt from my dresser and lay them over the chair. Funny, I still lay my clothes over a chair, today.

Carla: Anything else happen? Are you wearing pajamas? It is 1925.

Dave: I put on a white undershirt and white boxers and go to bed. There is no television *(chuckle).*

Later that same month Isabella told Dave that his friend Willie was Silas, the Civil War officer who shot Colonel Robert Gould Shaw at the Battle of Antietam. It happens that, in that life, Silas was a slave-master on a plantation. Today, although this sounds genetically impossible, Willie is a blond, blue-eyed black man. Dave felt shame at the moment Isabella told him. The thought that he once shot his best friend and killed him saddened him.

Anna emerged during the meditations—Ruby Donaldson's mother in that lifetime but also a nurse named Maria who had worked for my husband, Tom, during this present life. Remember that Anna was also married to Terryl during our Mayan days. And, Terryl, was my present husband Tom.

Anna told us that Ruby's best friend at the speakeasy was Daisy, who was black. After Ruby's parents received a letter she sent them mentioning her friend Daisy, they disowned her because she was associating with a black person. Her parents were from Bulloch, Georgia, in the early 1900s. Ruby's father had been a plantation owner in his younger years, owning slaves.

Anna had a message for me. She said that I should feel honored to be loved by a man like Tom. Apparently, Anna said, Tom and I have had many lives, starting over 3,250 years ago. She was trying to have me see the positive sides of Tom's lives versus the lives where he did not make the best choices.

A few days later, Isabella informed Dave that Jane (Paula) died of preeclampsia along with the baby. Her husband, Angelo Genna's driver, was killed shortly thereafter in a shootout. Upon receiving this news about her past life, Paula felt sad, wondering who the baby was. "Had the baby ever come back to me?" she asked.

Mother came through again and spoke with Dave. She told him that he needed to slow down a little with the meditation. He was exhausted, and all the lessons were keeping him from sleeping at night.

"Call me Cindy," she said, chuckling. "I was only your mother once."

What happened next changed everything

At the start of December 2014, Dave asked Isabella during his sleeping hours, "What became of Ruby? What's the rest of the story?"

In the wee hours of the morning on Dec. 2, 2014, Isabella took Dave through an entire weekend in the year 1925, one that changed his life with Ruby—and with me. After he relived the details of Ruby's story, he asked Isabella if he could not tell me the details of that life. Isabella said he had to tell me every detail. It was necessary for my understanding.

Hours later, when he came to the office that day, he was visibly disturbed, obviously preoccupied. We went into the break room, or as it now was, our meditation room. I sat in my usual chair, the meditation music playing. But Dave did not sit down in his usual chair. Nervously, he said, "I have details from the night before. Isabella told me the rest of Ruby's story."

As he told the story, I was finishing his sentences. I was seeing and remembering it just as he was becoming J.J. and telling me the story. I was remembering myself as Ruby Donaldson in 1925. I was remembering what Ruby felt for Jonathon. My heart raced. My face and chest flushed. Dave was no longer Dave. Dave was Jonathon Wright standing before me. We avoided looking into each other's eyes. It was uncomfortable. There was a minute when it was 100 percent real. It was like it was happening at that moment as vividly as if it was happening in 1925.

Dave stood and conveyed the story of Ruby and J.J. in its entirety. I watched before my eyes as Dave became Jonathon (J.J.) Wright telling me our love story. Then something happened. The strongest feeling came over me. I remembered all of what he was saying. We were staring at each other, both knowing what the other was feeling. It was intense. It was out of our control. It was all encompassing and overwhelming. I froze and he froze. I felt the heat rise up in me. Neither one of us spoke for several minutes. We were trying to escape what had just been realized. This was not the relationship we now knew. We were friends.

I felt as if I was cheating on my husband yet I had done nothing. Feelings and thoughts flooded my brain and heart and I wanted to run, just get out of there. Soon I heard the other employees arriving to the office.

How was this possible? How could Dave and I, both at the same time, recall a life that happened in 1925 before we had even been born in this life?

I returned to my office and resumed my usual duties. I avoided looking into Dave's eyes for a few days and kept my distance.

A couple of days later, Dave said, "Carla, I am not a stupid man. I know what you are doing."

I was running from feelings that I was not allowed to have. I loved my husband. We were soul mates. I was ticked at God and Isabella for bringing these feelings to the surface. What the hell was I supposed to do now, and why had they done this to us?

Dave would later tell me that he felt a moment when he changed from himself to Jonathon (J.J.) Wright. He could not tell if he was looking into my eyes or the eyes of Ruby. He, too, felt as though he had no control of the intense feelings.

So, what's the rest of their story?

Carla was Ruby Donaldson
Dave was Jonathon (J.J.) Wright

CARLA, writing as Ruby

Two lifetimes ago, my name was Ruby Donaldson. I was born in Bulloch, Georgia, in 1904. I was one of eleven children born to parents not well off enough to care for all of us. My parents took my two sisters and me to Chicago to live with our aunt. We would have to work to support ourselves. I was a young teenager at the time and my sisters were one younger, one older. My so-called-aunt ran a sweatshop with seamstresses and potential flappers. Her love interest was ten years her junior and none other than my former husband Jaime. Jaime's name was Angelo and he ran a speakeasy in Chicago's Little Italy. Of course, it was a cover for the mob as well as a front for bootlegging.

Aunt Mae gave me a promotion at age fifteen to become a singer and sewer of flapper costumes. Unbeknown to me, I was to be a singer/dancer at the speakeasy who also made the other flappers and my own costumes. I became Angelo's star singer. Those were not my only duties. Before too long, Angelo forced himself on me and continued to. Actually, on my sixteenth birthday, he presented me with a pearl necklace, then beat and raped me. Not long afterward, he forced me to entertain other mobsters, and by that I do not mean just sing for them.

He tried to own me; in fact, he thought he did. However, he did tell the big boss one evening, "Ruby cannot be broken." The boss said, "Give her to me, I can break her." He beat and raped me. I could not be broken. No one could own Ruby.

Angelo was gunned down in May 1925. The day he died he still had never broken Ruby. He could never own me. I never forgave him.

By the time I was nineteen, I was living in my own apartment. Since my Aunt Mae (who is my sister Cleo in this life) had also been sleeping with Angelo, it would have made for a sticky situation living in her home. Aunt Mae suspected Angelo was having sex with her niece but never confirmed it. After all, Angelo was her bread and butter.

During the week, I walked to the sweatshop, passing the bank where Angelo laundered his money. The bank was a yellow stone building with large paned windows about thirteen blocks from the sweatshop. From the sidewalk, I could see the employees inside, and they could easily see me. I made this walk Monday through Thursday. On Fridays and Saturdays, I walked to D'Andre's, a bar off the alley on Taylor Street. Six days a week, unknown to me, a man in the bank watched me pass by.

As winter came, he noticed the white hat I wore pulled down over my face, my brown gloves and scarf and the light, wool herringbone coat. More importantly, he noticed my determination and the impression. This young woman was on a mission.

Day after day, as I walked past the bank, I contemplated my life situation. I felt stuck. I clung to the hopes of someday being a singer, maybe permanently at the Drake Hotel. I dreamed about opening my own dress shop in Atlanta, Georgia, closer to home. All my thoughts were about escape. I wanted to escape Angelo Genna and my current life. I hardly even noticed the cold, bitter wind blowing through Chicago that winter.

Each time I passed the bank window, I never looked directly in. Had I, I would have possibly seen the young banker looking to catch my glimpse. I wasn't aware he looked every day, hoping for a smile. I knew not that he noticed my smooth, pale skin, the light blond curls beneath my hat. I knew not that he wondered every day where I was going at 8 a.m.

That month, Angelo would marry Lucille, the sister of the man who owned the bank where the young banker watched from the window. Yes, my lover was engaged to someone else, though he was sleeping with me and every other flapper at the speakeasy. Angelo instructed me along with three other flappers to sing at the wedding. "You will sing, and Annie will accompany you on the organ," he said. I was a last-minute substitution for the singer who fell ill. Annie and I stayed up nearly all night to prepare. "Wear this dress," Angelo said. "And this jewelry."

Angelo thought he owned me. He could never own my thoughts.

Invitation to a wedding

The young man from the bank was the wholesome Jonathon Wright, a junior banker hired by Henry as a favor to his father, a longshoreman involved in the Unione Siciliana (Sicilian Union.) The president of the Sicilian Union was also the owner of the bank where Jonathon worked, as well as the owner of the speakeasy where Ruby was employed.

Jonathon had been hired under the impression that his college education and business degree had secured the position. Jonathon's father had accidentally gotten involved with the mob but insisted to Henry that his son never be involved and hold only a legitimate position.

The wedding was held in a huge hall with more than three thousand guests attending. Inside the hall, a church was created to accommodate the attendees because no other church in Chicago had the capacity. When Jonathon arrived, he was astonished to see the number of automobiles dropping off guests. Entering the church, he noticed the vocalist—the beautiful blond who walked by the bank each day! It was her. He was mesmerized. At last he had seen her wonderful, alluring, steel blue eyes. He could not look away. He knew at that moment he loved this woman. He could think of nothing else but how to be near her. The feeling was urgent. He wanted to be close to her, now and forever. He knew this woman deep in his soul.

After the ceremony, Jonathon dragged his coworker along, searching for the singer. He desperately pushed through the hordes of guests moving toward the reception hall.

There she was. Jonathon spotted her standing at a table of friends. He walked toward her, smiling and never taking his eyes from her returning stare. "I am J.J.," he said.

"Nice to meet you," Ruby said.

CARLA, reliving and speaking as Ruby

Others were watching me. Angelo wouldn't think kindly of my engaging in too much conversation with another man. I tried to be curt and stop the conversation. J.J. was determined to make me speak with him. I saw him and thought, *This is an innocent boy. How can I possibly get involved in any way with him?*

'Voice of an angel'

Jonathon was not going to let this opportunity end. He asked the singer to dance, still not knowing her name or how to address her. He asked her to dance but, unfortunately, she denied him by saying, "Not at this time." Jonathon then blurted out, not wanting to lose her attention, "You sing beautifully. You have the voice of an angel." He was quite sincere and a bit shy and unrehearsed.

Ruby shot back a smirk, as much as to say, "Yeah, I bet you use that line a lot." However, Ruby could not help from feeling his sincerity and the pureness of his comments.

CARLA, reliving and speaking as Ruby

Oh, he was cute. I felt myself hardly able to resist him but I knew I should. Angelo had just ordered us to dance so I thought, *What harm could it do?*

May I have this dance?

Jonathon would not go away or miss his chance with Ruby. He tried not to stare but felt himself gazing into her eyes, uncontrollably, feeling her life and presence as if he'd known her forever. He tried talking with idle chitchat, to no avail. He watched her swaying and moving to the music.

He took the opportunity again to ask, "May I have this dance?"

"Maybe just this one," she said.

Jonathon reached for and took Ruby's hand, leading her about ten steps to the dance floor. He noticed the dress Ruby was wearing to be very simple and clean, bright pink with a shimmer, almost like satin. The band played a waltz made popular by Henry Burr, a famous singer of the 1920s. J.J. placed his hand on Ruby's lower back and attempted to waltz to the best of his ability. He commented on the grace in her dance steps.

"Yours also, sir," she said.

CARLA, reliving and speaking as Ruby

I could feel his gentle touch on my back. I had not experienced this gentleness before. For a split-second, I prayed to myself for the song to go on and never end. I purposely avoided looking directly into his eyes. It was so difficult as Jonathon stared into my eyes throughout the dance. I felt insecure and overwhelmed all together. I felt not pure enough to be in this man's arms.

I tried not to talk to him, saying I had to get back to work. He took this chance to ask for me to meet him for breakfast the next day. I denied him, saying that I just wouldn't be able. He pushed it, once again asking, "Breakfast tomorrow at Marino's at ten?" I just kept thinking I couldn't get involved. I didn't have permission to be with Jonathon. I was owned property of Angelo Genna. I wanted to say yes. In fact, I wanted to scream it out. YES! YES! YES! I was determined to refuse J.J. again. I would just not answer him and walk away. This time, as I walked away, my dress swirling in haste, I turned back to him from about twenty feet away and said, "Maybe, we'll see, Marino's at ten." I didn't mean to say it. The words just flew out of my mouth. Jonathon had caught my eye.

Meeting at Marino's

Jonathon believed at that moment Ruby would be at Marino's the next day. He knew something in her eyes wanted to be there, and Jonathon saw it. His heart was full. His heart was satisfied.

The next morning Jonathon Wright Jr. entered Marino's thirty minutes early, wearing a long, black, woolen trench coat, hair slicked back, sporting the hope of Ruby walking through the door. He chose a seat facing the door, placing his coat over the back of the chair. He waited, ordering a glass of water only.

He sat, looking at the door, then his watch, the door, his watch, until three minutes until ten when in stepped the beautiful woman, in a long, light-colored wool coat, white hat pulled down over her head with blond curls peeking out. He would recognize that woman anywhere.

Jonathon stood up too quickly and nearly knocked over the chair in his haste, grabbing his coat. He reached to pull Ruby's chair out in a gentlemanly manner.

CARLA, reliving and speaking as Ruby

When I arose this morning, I was sure I couldn't chance meeting Jonathon for breakfast. I so wanted to, but knew it was dangerous for myself and for him. Despite my fears, I got ready, thinking of nothing but Jonathon. It was a typical cold, windy January morning in Chicago but I did not care. I couldn't wait to see him. Twice, I stopped and turned back to walk home. The last three blocks, I almost ran, in an attempt to stop my apprehension. At the door, I took one last big breath, opened it, saw Jonathon smiling and that was it. I couldn't leave him.

I love to sing

She removed her hat as he assisted her with her coat, and then he noticed what she was wearing. He couldn't help but take into his eyes, her clear, ivory skin, gray woolen skirt just below her knees with a white blouse, and a black belt resting at her hips.

"You can call me Jonathon," he said. "Or J.J."

"You may call me Ruby."

Thoughts whirled in J.J.'s head. Ruby appeared even younger and sweeter than she had the night before. She wore no heavy make-up or lipstick, yet she was still beautiful. He knew not what to say. He was taken with Ruby.

Ruby ordered one egg, one piece of toast and coffee. She poured water into her coffee in an attempt to cool it down but never did drink it. Jonathon ordered corned-beef hash, one egg, one piece of toast and tea. He hardly ate, too engrossed in conversation, and Ruby.

They traded stories about their lives and jobs. Jonathon watched as Ruby finished her egg, and one half of the toast. He wasn't hungry, he wasn't thirsty. He was in absolute awe of this beautiful Ruby.

"Would you like to walk by the lake?" he said.

Ruby agreed. She took his left arm as they walked along Lake Michigan, sharing their dreams for the future. The wind blew hard and cold but never stopped them from dreaming of Ruby's fine dress shop in Atlanta or J.J.'s promotion at the bank.

Ruby confessed to her love of singing as J.J. confessed to his love of her singing. The couple agreed to their individual desire for four children and a home with a fireplace. The windier and colder the day became, the more Ruby snuggled close to Jonathon.

CARLA, reliving and speaking as Ruby

I struggled with my own thoughts during our walk. I asked myself why I had to push him away. I wondered why I didn't deserve this life we discussed—one he could offer me. I thought over and over, *Do I run, or do I hope he kisses me?*

She climbed the three steps

Approaching Ruby's apartment, the two paused at her doorway. Ruby climbed the three steps as Jonathon asked if he could see her yet again. He noticed the blond curls blowing beneath her hat and then, the sadness in her face as she said, "I am not of your world, and I don't want you to be part of mine." She turned, pushed the glass door open and was gone.

Jonathon stood there dumbfounded, staring at the closed door. His heart felt heavy. He turned and walked briskly back to his apartment. What had he done? What had happened? He felt so confused. He spent the remainder of the day thinking about Ruby and what went wrong. Was this it? Would he ever see her again?

*CARLA, reliving and speaking as **Ruby***

I cried all the way up the stairs and into my apartment. I sat there alone for the rest of the day and did nothing but think. I convinced myself that my decision to push Jonathon away was in his best interest. I was denying myself a relationship I so wanted but couldn't drag him into a dangerous situation. He did not deserve that or what came along with me.

Jonathon gets an invitation

Monday morning, Jonathon watched for Ruby to walk past the bank as usual but she never did. His boss, Henry, had a special assignment for J.J. that day. A small package wrapped in brown paper was to be delivered to his new brother-in-law at The Belmont Hotel.

Jonathon had never delivered a package to the Belmont. This was a first. He was delivering this particular package for the newlyweds who were about to embark on their honeymoon.

He entertained the notion during the drive to the Belmont as to how he could approach the subject of Angelo's and Lucille's wedding vocalist. How could he nonchalantly gain information about Ruby without being obvious?

Angelo greeted J.J. at the door and invited him into a small entryway, where J.J. noticed the lavish marble floors and dark woodwork. Angelo wore dark pinstriped slacks and a clean, crisp white shirt. He was a man small in stature, rather stocky with a square jaw and a stern expression.

J.J. slightly fumbled for words. He thanked Angelo for the invitation to the wedding. "I enjoyed it very much, especially the young woman vocalist," he said.

Angelo's face softened. "Young man, sometime you should come to my club. You might enjoy her singing again." He signed a business card and handed it over to Jonathon, inviting him specifically.

Jonathon accepted the card graciously as Angelo said, "This is your invitation."

With that, Jonathon left Angelo as the heavy door closed behind him. Jonathon lifted the card and said to himself, "This is my pass to Ruby."

Wednesday morning, Jonathon saw Ruby walk past the bank. He watched her but stopped himself from running out after her. He told himself, *I will go to D'Andre's this weekend.*

Two days later, J.J. arrived at D'Andre's about 10 p.m., dressed in a black suit with a matching black pencil tie and shoes. When he pounded on the door, a small window opened about six inches. A broad muscular man questioned as to why he was there. J.J. showed him the card and said Angelo invited him. The big man examined the card for authenticity and invited Jonathon in. He stepped through the door.

He first noticed pale yellow light from wall sconces shining upward. Ahead was a long bar with red lighting, a mirror running the entire length. Off to his left was an empty stage. Off to his right, Jonathon noticed tables with men in suits, women in furs. Further ahead he saw tables where cards were being played with dealers wearing red-and-black striped shirts and black bands above their elbows. Each dealer wore a black bow tie. Jonathon was amazed by the existence of such a place and such happenings. He had never seen anything like this in his life.

He allowed his eyes to adjust to the dim room. He noticed a table of young, pretty women. He stared at the women until he caught the intensity of the steel-blue eyes gazing back at him. Ruby. Ruby wore a bright red blouse, a gold band in slicked-back blond hair and a white-fringed skirt above her knees. The look on her face spoke of amazement and fear. She held a long cigarette holder in her right hand, as the smoke billowed. He first noticed the red lipstick ring on the cigarette holder, then followed its imprint to her dark ruby red lips.

CARLA, *reliving and speaking as Ruby*

Damn him. Then, thank God, him. I asked myself desperately the words, *how do I get rid of him?* I hope he wants to stay. Then, *please leave, Jonathon!*

No sweet young woman should walk home alone

Jonathon stood and watched for a moment, then crossed toward Ruby. She remained in place at her table, surrounded by the other young women. As she turned away from him, Jonathon noticed an oblong, gold-filigree, ruby ring on her middle finger of her right hand.

"J.J. you should not be here," she said.

Jonathon looked into her eyes. What he heard and what she said with those blue eyes were not the same thing. Those eyes asked him not to leave her.

Ruby introduced Jonathon to the women including her best friend, Lila. J.J. ordered drinks for the entire table, the right thing to do.

"Oh, you two danced at the wedding," Lila said.

Camille turned and glared at J.J. He felt a stab of uneasiness.

As the evening wore on, Jonathon watched the flappers sing and dance, entertaining the crowd. J.J. stayed and waited until closing. He had hopes that Ruby would agree to leave with him. J.J. asked Ruby if he might walk her home.

"Jonathon, you should probably just go home," Ruby said.

"No sweet young woman should walk home in the dark, alone," Jonathon said.

My heart would not be still. He thinks I'm a sweet young thing and treats me accordingly. Little does he know. I wanted one more chance to hold onto his arm. What will I do when we get to my door?

She removed the large ruby ring from her hand

Ruby and J.J. walked the staircase arm in arm all the way up to her apartment floor. She opened the door, inviting him in. In the kitchen, J.J. sat at a small wooden table with two chairs. Ruby took note of his actions, responding with, "You didn't come here to sit in the kitchen." And, with that, Ruby took J.J. by the hand and led him through swinging doors into her bedroom. She motioned for him to sit on the bed, walked over to her dresser, removed the ruby ring from her hand, polished it slightly and carefully placed it into a box, signifying its preciousness.

Ruby emerged from the bathroom wearing only a robe, approaching J.J. seated on her bed. She stood before him, her breasts nearly touching his chest. Her sultry words stirred him as he watched her robe fall to the floor. "J.J., do what a man wants to do to a woman," she said.

He placed his hands on the small of her back and pulled her to him to kiss her. They fell back onto the bed. Ruby unbuttoned J.J.'s shirt, removed his tie, returning his passionate kisses as his lips moved longingly around her chest, then up her neck, finally finding and devouring her lips.

"J.J., do you want me?" she said.

"Yes, I want you, Ruby, but you must invite me."

"I believe telling you that I want you J.J. was the invitation," she said.

For the second time, J.J. did not hesitate to accept Ruby's invitation. He passionately rolled Ruby onto her back and did what a man does to a woman.

Two days later on Sunday morning, when Ruby and J.J. decided it was time to join the world once again, they had made love seventeen times. Ruby had failed to report to work on Saturday evening.

They were famished, as one would imagine when they finally arose that day. The couple again went to Marino's, where Ruby ordered one egg, one piece of toast and coffee. J.J. ordered hash browns, two eggs and toast. This time, there was no lingering over their breakfast. Ruby had become fidgety and slightly distant.

The two walked back to Ruby's apartment and once again she climbed the front steps quickly, ahead of J.J. He looked up at her and said, "Ruby, when will I see you again?"

Ruby's response was a shock. "You won't."

"Tell me that this weekend meant nothing; tell me you don't love me," he said.

Ruby turned away. "This weekend must mean nothing. J.J., I don't love you." She ran inside as her door closed and locked. J.J. stood there in pain, not understanding what had happened. He stood at Ruby's door for forty minutes, hoping she would return and hoping she didn't mean what she had said.

She never did come back to the door. J.J. walked home, cold wind burning the tears into his face.

All through Monday J.J. suffered, not knowing how to change Ruby's mind and not understanding why she had thrown away their love. On Tuesday, he had hope. J.J. went to the florist and bought a dozen, beautiful, long-stemmed red roses and delivered them himself to Ruby's doorstep. Along with the roses, he included a letter.

"Dear Ruby, the rose is beautiful; it's a symbol of our love. J.J."

CARLA, reliving and speaking as Ruby

Tuesday, I arrived home to find a note on my doorstep. I picked it up only to read it had come from Jonathon. I wasn't sure what it meant at first. Then, it occurred to me, roses probably came with the note, but someone had taken them. I wanted so much to respond to him. My inner, practical Ruby said he would get over me. I had to protect him.

A single black rose

Unfortunately, Ruby never saw the roses. However, when Angelo's driver confiscated the roses from her doorstep, J.J.'s love letter had fallen out onto the steps, where she found it later.

Friday morning, when J.J. reported to work as usual at 8 a.m., he found a single black rose on his desk. He thought the rose sent one of two messages. It was either a message from Ruby, or a threat from someone.

Friday night when Ruby arrived at the speakeasy, Angelo greeted her by throwing the dozen roses from J.J. in her face. "I found these on your doorstep. Who is the boy?"

"He's more of a man than you'll ever be," she said, "but he's out of the picture now."

Angelo backhanded her across the face, leaving the speakeasy in an angry huff.

The previous Saturday when Ruby did not show for work, Angelo questioned the other flappers about Ruby's whereabouts. Camille was ever too eager to fill Angelo in on the boy dancing with Ruby at his wedding. Camille had been sleeping with Angelo prior to his bringing Ruby in as a flapper. She received gifts of furs and jewelry among other things until Angelo took a fancy for Ruby. Camille was jealous and despised Ruby for no fault of her own. She had no interest in Angelo but was forced into sex with him and to be owned by him.

J.J. stewed all day and night Friday. Should he approach Ruby?

Saturday evening, J.J. could wait no more. He had to see her. He loved Ruby and could think of nothing else. He dressed in his black suit, tie and coat. He clutched the invitation card from Angelo in his hand.

He waited until ten in the evening to go to D'Andre's. He stood outside, a bundle of nerves, perspiring thinking of all the possibilities. He needed to see Ruby. He wanted her to look into his face and admit she did not *love* him. He didn't believe she could. He knew she *loved* him.

He presented the card to the doorman saying that Angelo had invited him. The bouncer, who by the way is my nephew in this life (Paula's son) permitted his entry. He kept a watchful eye on J.J. as he scanned the bar for Ruby.

J.J. spotted her standing at a table with several other flappers. When she noticed J.J., it was with a look of horror and fear.

J.J. walked toward Ruby and she toward him. "You must leave," she said. "You should not be here. It is not safe."

"Then tell me you don't *love* me," he said.

"J.J., I can't *love* you," she said. "It's not safe."

Camille stood at her left side, pointing a finger at J.J. and talking to the doorman. Two doormen immediately raced toward them. One grabbed Ruby, one J.J. The doorman who grabbed J.J. is my nephew in this life, and the doorman grabbing Ruby is my neighbor in this life.

"Get your hands off her!" J.J. shouted.

They pushed us out into the alley. Light shone down from a streetlamp. J.J. was pushed to the ground.

J.J. got up as he heard Ruby scream. He saw a bright flash in front of him. J.J. felt as if he had been punched in the left shoulder and was forced back. He felt another punch directly in his chest, forcing him to the ground. He felt something cold and wet. The light above him grew smaller and smaller.

He tried with all his might to say, "Ruby I *love* you." In the distance, he heard her shout, "J.J., I lied. I do *love* you." Then all was black, still. Nothing.

Jonathon (J.J.) Wright saw a small, soft but strong hand reaching for him from above. He witnessed two bright golden wings, each feather illuminated, lifting him up and taking him through time, space, light and dark. No longer was he cold. He felt warmth. He felt no fear.

CARLA, *reliving and speaking as Ruby*

My blood ran cold. He was dead. They had killed him. My worst fears had happened. I felt no hope for the future. My one chance for *love* was gone. We should have left together. I should have told him I *loved* him sooner. He would have taken me away from all of this life of deceit and ownership. I wept until there was nothing left in me. No tears, no thoughts, no hopes, no *love* or cares. I was dead inside. Lila and Daisy walked me home. I was but a shell of a person.

She was a sign of their love

Ruby lost her desire to live when J.J. was murdered. Her *love* of song and dance was no more. She went through the motions at D'Andre's until one day Angelo yelled at her, accusing her of not entertaining the customers.

Ruby said to Angelo without emotion or fear, "I can no longer sing for you." Angelo's response was not surprising. He told her to gather her things and get out. Angelo couldn't control Ruby, try as he may, so he tossed her aside once she had no value to him. Ruby wasn't the only flapper who left that day. Her best friend Lila went with her. They felt the danger and wanted something more for themselves and more out of life. Neither could be controlled or used again. They had made the decision to respect themselves regardless of the outcome. It was better for Ruby and Lila to struggle together than be abused and owned. Ruby's friend Daisy left to sing in an all-black bar in Chicago then married happily. Annie left the bar, continued playing the organ at church and taught private piano lessons.

Eight months later, Ruby gave birth to Jonathon (J.J.) Wright's daughter. She was beautiful. Ruby named her Rose. She was a sign of their *love.*

CARLA, reliving and speaking as Ruby

I still had a part of J.J. Our *love* had not been in vain. Our daughter was the light of my life. She was everything good, pure and made from *love.* I was determined to prove that to our daughter.

One last gentle touch

Ruby and Lila took jobs as waitresses at Amato's Italian restaurant on Halstead Street. They had an apartment together, and Ruby was grateful for Lila's help with the baby who was J.J.'s daughter. Lila and Ruby alternated their schedules to care for her. Lila brought the baby to the restaurant during all of Ruby's shifts so she could continue breastfeeding for three months.

On Jan. 10, 1926, exactly one year after Angelo's wedding, the day Ruby met J.J. Wright, Ruby was working at Amato's where Henry Spingola, J.J.'s boss, happened to be dining. A car full of mobsters unloaded machine guns into Amato's, killing Henry. Someone had called a hit, knowing exactly where he'd be.

Ruby Donaldson, at twenty-one, never suspected this would be the last day she'd see her beloved daughter. A stray bullet meant for Henry pierced her in the back, killing her immediately.

One's only solace in the events of that day was the reuniting of Ruby with her J.J.

Although Ruby did not have the gift, as Jonathon did, to see her death, as she lay on the floor, the room went dark. She thought she heard angels singing Ave Maria. For one moment, she saw J.J.'s hand holding hers. She saw his smile. The hand changed to a soft but strong, small hand, lifting her. In that moment, Ruby spun, as if in the middle of a waltz. Sheila let her feel one last gentle touch of Jonathon Wright's hand holding hers. She saw light and dark, and traveled through space and time. She felt warmth and no more fear.

Shortly after the killing of Ruby, Lila would become the wife of a Chicago policeman named Robert. The child was raised as Lila's and her new husband's daughter, the girl never knowing the brutal details of her parents' killings. Lila chose to tell her adopted daughter about her birth parents on her thirteenth birthday. She also presented her with her mother's precious ruby ring, which had belonged to Ruby's great aunt Ruby on her mother's side. Ruby's ring and her aunt were, indeed, important as she was her aunt's namesake and felt honor to bear her name as well as wear her ring. She had few things of material value in her life. She had valued most the people in her life.

Both Ruby and Jonathon's lessons were cut short by the untimeliness of their murders. Ruby denied herself true love and allowed herself to be owned. Jonathon had foolish pride, conceit. He thought he could save Ruby but hadn't gone about it in the safest manner.

Lessons learned from this very short lifetime

* Per Isabella, "The most important lesson here is that we are all victims to other persons' **conceit, jealousy** and **selfishness.**"

- Ruby and J.J. were young and innocent. They had not yet learned life's lessons. *Love* was their goal. Unfortunately, another interfered with their karma. They lost their chance at *love* and to complete their individual paths.

- None of us are completely innocent. We still need to own our responsibility, because just as Angelo affected Ruby and J.J.'s karma, Ruby and J.J. affected Angelo's karma.

- Fear is *conceit.* If fear causes inaction, which was why Ruby did not leave Angelo and the speakeasy until it was too late, it means that fear is controlling you. No one controls another.

- No one can own another. All forms of ownership are *conceit.* Ruby allowed Angelo to own her. He was *conceited.* It ultimately caused her early demise, leaving her child in another's care. However, one has responsibility to not be owned.

- J.J. was *conceited* and *selfish* in thinking that mobsters would let him waltz in and take what he wanted. He and Angelo's thugs prevented him from finishing his path and lessons.

- Affecting another person's karma can kill *love,* indirectly.

- Murder is always wrong in God's eyes. Murder is *selfish.* It takes another from their path.

- *Jealousy* of Camille's caused the death of J.J.

- *Love* should never be denied. Ruby *loved* J.J. but fear, which equals *conceit,* destroyed it.

- Angelo had *jealousy* for his women, owning them, raping them, controlling them, keeping them from their paths and lessons.

- We cannot blame or pardon the victim. That would be judging.

- The problem in today's world is there is a little bit of Angelo and Aunt Mae in all of us. And there is a little less of Ruby and J.J. in all of us. Our *conceit, jealousy* and *selfishness* affects others and their karma and path.

- Remember, Angelo had karmic debt with Ruby (which was Julia), from Hill Creek as Aaron Myerson and again later, after this life, had another chance of altering the karmic debt when married as Jaime, to Ruby as Carla.

- Innocence and *love* are paying the price because of *selfishness, conceit* and *jealousy.* But if we rid ourselves of *selfishness, conceit* and *jealousy, love* starts to become what it was always meant to be.

Angelo and Lucille did not marry out of *love* rather for financial and power reasons. It is never *love* when marriage or relationships are for convenience or personal gain. That is *conceit, selfish, jealous* and not *loving.*

Chapter 19

The Journey of the
Red Ruby Crystal

*R*uby Donaldson's ruby ring was a piece of a much greater stone carved from a cave in Scotland many hundreds of years before. Ruby's life in the 1920s was merely part of the journey of her soul.

The following is the journey of Ruby's red ring and the path it took. The soul struggles through deceit, ***conceit, jealousy, selfishness,*** power and entitlement as did Ruby's red ring. But ***love*** always prevails. Here is that story, as revealed to us by Isabella.

In the beginning, God made the Earth, complete with rubies.

Actually, geologists aren't even certain what forms a ruby. They suspect it to be part of the motion in plate tectonics, the crust of the Earth forcing deep within itself. The limestone of the Earth literally boils and leaves behind marble and silica-free aluminum. The aluminum mixes with chromium in exactly the correct amount to reflect the color red. It must occur in the complete absence of silica and iron, the most abundant minerals on Earth. Rubies cannot exist without the absence of silica and iron. Like ***love,*** it cannot exist with ***conceit, jealousy, unforgiveness*** and ***selfishness.*** Much to God's disappointment, these are the most abundant emotions to the human soul.

God created rubies for their beauty. The following story, God created for Ruby.

The finding of the crystal, AD 904

Over 1,100 years ago in AD 904, two men building a home outside of what is now Edinburgh, Scotland, wandered upon a cave. The small cave wasn't larger than five by six feet.

Amos (Dave's present father, Harvey) and Baine, who were father and son discovered it while cutting limestone for their home. They found it on a three-feet outcropping of whitish-gray marble. Embedded in the marble was a dark red crystal. They chiseled out a piece of marble approximately one foot by two feet that included the red crystal.

The uncut red crystal measured two inches by one inch. Finding it dazzling, Baine delivered it to his soon-to-be father-in-law, Oahd (Dave) as part of his dowry for his impending bride, Oahd's daughter Agnes (Brenda, our coworker).

A crystal carved from the earth was given in exchange for a woman. A woman was traded like cattle, in ownership. She had no choice. She was given no decision as to whom she wanted to marry and with whom she would share her life.

From the beginning, the red crystal was used incorrectly.

The red crystal remained with Oahd (Dave) and his wife, Fenella (Carla). The couple had been born Danes, during the Viking age. They learned in their younger years to invade, pillage and steal as their way of life.

AD 896

Vikings invade Scotland, eight years before the crystal is discovered

During their invasion of Scotland in a previous year, AD 896, they found the land and people beautiful and welcoming, deciding to settle in Scotland. Normal invasions included routine murder, rape, theft and burning of villages. Their invasion of Scotland, close to what is now Edinburgh, was different. They found the Scots poverty-stricken, penniless, without any wealth and not willing to put up a fight.

Oahd (pronounced Owed) was a leader. He recognized the destitute state of the village, the allure of their land and the peaceful pride the residents exhibited. But what happened when they reached the outer regions of Edinburgh was very different from what he planned.

A heavily armed band of thirty-some Vikings entered the village intent on destruction. Oahd met Malcomb McKay (Carla's present grandfather on her father's side) unarmed. He stood in front of his red-haired daughter, defenseless, prepared to stand at his death. Oahd was ready to strike, though. He realized Malcomb would not fight. The troops walked past Malcomb and into a grass-thatched hut. There was nothing. It was empty. They went to another hut. Two women cowered in a corner. Again, they found no wealth, no money, no food. Another stone house with thatching was entered. Oahd heard an older woman call out for Angus. A feeble, elderly man appeared, holding but a stick (Carla's grandfather on her mother's side). He swung at Oahd with his mighty stick, which Oahd swiftly confiscated and broke.

Oahd exited the hut and back to where Malcomb stood, his soldiers standing ready. Three or four additional Scots now positioned themselves behind Malcomb with their wives also standing.

Oahd felt no honor in the prospect of raiding a poor humble village without wealth. He felt shame. He addressed his men. "There is no bounty here." Some of his men came forward. "They have women." Oahd responded, "They have mothers." Another soldier yelled out, "At least take their food."

The old woman who had been in the hut with Angus appeared with a basket of brown potatoes and handed them off to Oahd. He angrily threw the potatoes toward his men, "Here, eat," he snapped.

And with that, about half of Oahd's Vikings hesitantly left toward their ship. Malcomb pointed to a gorgeous green meadow and spoke, "This could all be yours."

Oahd pulled out a small, ivory-handled carving knife, his most prized possession, and offered it to Malcomb. The Scotsman accepted, saying, "I will never draw this knife on you," to which Oahd responded, "And, I will never use this sword on you!"

Malcomb McKay invited the wayward Vikings to stay on his land. The Vikings would become known as the McKay clan, which would someday become the McKee Clan (Carla's present-day mother's family name). From that day forward, the Vikings and the Scots were family.

Oahd and Fenella took Scottish names upon changing their homeland. Malcomb chose their names. Oahd's Viking name had been Hdejh, and Fenella's had been Hleder. If they were to live as Scots, their names would reflect their land. Malcomb gave Hdejh the name Oahd, "Because of the fire in his heart." Malcomb named Hleder Fenella for her fair white shoulders.

AD 906

The red crystal changes hands

Two years later, the Vikings invaded Scotland again. The small village where Oahd and his family and former Vikings lived again was subjected. The Vikings recognized Oahd and some of the men, yet never welcomed the thought of not invading their homes, even though it was their own people.

Despite the fact only two years had passed since their last invasion, the Vikings expected Oahd and the villagers to have obtained wealth. To their dismay, the village remained in poverty. There was no wealth to be had.

Oahd pulled his sword to prove his willingness to fight. The Vikings cared not. They would take whatever little was there, be it food or women, and would destroy what was left.

Five silver coins, remnants of his pillaging days and the red crystal was all Oahd and Fenella had of value besides their children, village family and the love of their land.

"I am ready to die for my people and my land," Oahd said.

The Viking leader, Kehldr (pronounced Kahelder, and Dave's friend Willie in our present lives), Oahd's only actual brother, was also ready to have what he believed was ripe for the taking. Oahd presented his silver coins and the red crystal to stop the Vikings from invading. The red crystal was given in ransom for love.

Oahd offered an ultimatum. "Take all the wealth I possess, or else come through me!" Oahd still possessed the skill and strength to take the Viking leader's life as well as many of his men.

Kehdlr thought the offer was too good to pass up. There would be no wealth or possessions in this village; silver and the red crystal would be better than nothing at all. Deep down, Kehldr knew his brother meant business and would take the life of his only brother to protect what was his and protect what was right.

Oahd understood the importance of family and love. The red crystal and silver coins meant nothing to him without his beloved family, villagers and the country he had grown to call his own.

AD 907

The red crystal lands in the hands of the king of the Vikings

Kehldr and his Viking troop returned to their lands with the five silver coins and the red crystal and relinquished the red crystal to their Viking king, Sweyn Forkbeard of Denmark (Don, Carla's present neighbor), soon to become the first Danish king of England.

AD 986

The red crystal goes to the king of England

King Forkbeard, named for his cleft chin and split beard, had two sons. Harald, his eldest was acting regent while the king and his younger son, Canute The Great, traveled to England to force King AEthelred the Unready (Carla's brother-in-law, Dan, married to her sister Cleo) to surrender his throne. Canute The Great was given the red crystal to placate him, because his brother was chosen the acting Regent King, staying in the kingdom while Canute and his father fought in England. The red crystal was considered very valuable. Sweyn told his son the crystal was a great gem from Scotland.

Once again, the red crystal was used for power and entitlement, brother over brother.

AEthelred had King Forkbeard's sister, Gunhilde (Don's wife, Carla's neighbors), along with every Dane in England murdered during St. Brice's Day Massacre in November 1002 in one of the Danish raids occurring every year from 997 to 1001.

That year King AEthelred the Unready had been told the Danish planned to "faithlessly take his life and then all his councilors and possess his kingdom afterward." In response, he ordered all the Danish men in England be slain. Unfortunately, during the St. Brice's Day Massacre, King AEthelred's army tortured women, children and men. Women were burned alive, children impaled on lances and men died, suspended from their private parts. King Sweyn Forkbeard vowed revenge.

He did, indeed, take King AEthelred's throne in 1003, forcing AEthelred to flee to Normandy, France, with his second wife, Emma of Normandy (Carla), who was of Danish descent. King Forkbeard ruled England for just five weeks afterward, never actually being crowned, before he died. His son Canute the Great became king upon his death.

King AEthelred the Unready died in Normandy in 1016. King Canute the Great married his widow and stepmother, Emma of Normandy, in 1017, making her queen consort of England, Denmark and Norway. This was Emma's second time as Queen of England, the first while married to King AEthelred. The red crystal was kept in a silk-lined box. Canute would say it reminded him of all the bloodshed of the Danes during the St. Brice's Day Massacre.

AD 1027

To Scotland

The red crystal remained with Canute and Emma until his invasion of Scotland in 1027 to set up trade. Canute gave the crystal to King Malcomb II (Dave's grandfather Albert, on his mother's side) to create peace between the two countries.

Using the red crystal for peace between two countries was an accomplishment. However, it was to be used again for power and entitlement.

The red crystal would become part of the Scottish royal jewels and remain with other jewels, silver and gold in safety until another battle took place.

The country was full of poor, starving people, yet jewels and coins remained hidden with those who felt entitlement and power.

The red crystal had been passed back and forth as part of the Scottish, Danish, English, Danish and Scottish possessions. It would soon return back to England once again.

AD 1297

Back to England

Edward I invaded Scotland to subdue the Scottish armies, confiscating the red crystal along with other jewels, taking them back to England. The red crystal became part of the wealth of the House of Plantagenet, which ruled from 1154 to 1485. The Plantagenet name comes from Count Geoffrey Plantagenet of Anjou, France, father of Henry II. Once the House of Plantagenet lost most of its continental possessions, it became the House of Lancaster. The House of Lancaster included King Henry V (Carla's neighbor Don).

King Henry V commissioned his jeweler to create a gold-and-glass scepter with a filigree crown surrounded by precious stones. All the stones were taken from their stolen treasures. Inside the crown, he fitted the uncut red crystal.

Henry V used his scepter as a show of power, wealth and entitlement but also as a weapon. He controlled his eleven-year-old child consort, Sussan (Carla), with his scepter, beating her into submission for sex and psychological control.

AD 1297

The new king

Upon the king's early demise, his nine-month-old son inherited the throne and his scepter. Once an adult king, Henry VI (Dave) grew unhappy with wealth and entitlement. His queen was chosen for him with political gain in mind, Margaret of Anjou of France, a marriage that made Henry king of France for a time.

Displeased with his arranged marriage, he had an entire wing added to his palace at Etham, where he had moved with his beloved Sussan (Carla) from Windsor Castle. He wanted to avoid his wife, Margaret, the queen, as much as possible. Their marriage was never consummated despite her son, Edward, Prince of Wales being named his child. Henry's (Dave's) disappointment in not having his choice of a queen caused much distress.

One day while wallowing in his disappointment, he personally dug the uncut red crystal from the top of his scepter. He commissioned the royal jeweler to cut it and add two pieces to the crown of the scepter. The remaining cut of stone would be made into a pendant for his true love, Sussan (Carla).

AD 1441

To the woman he loved

King Henry VI presented Sussan with his gift. "This should be for the queen I choose," he said.

The red crystal had been used on Sussan as a child, as fear and control by Henry V and within the same family, given to her in love and honor in the end by Henry VI.

Sussan, as a child consort to Henry's father, had born a daughter with Henry V, conceived by rape when Sussan was twelve. Sussan's daughter, Agnes (Brenda, our coworker), was Henry VI's half-sister. Sussan had raised the two together as the babies were nine months apart.

AD 1461

From mother to daughter

The red crystal pendant was passed on to Agnes (Brenda, our coworker) once she reached adulthood. The purpose was to ensure her ability to live and flourish. *Agnes received the crystal in love from her mother.*

AD 1461

To the Roman Catholic Church

Agnes married and, along with her husband, purchased land from the Roman Catholic Church. Her means with which to purchase the land for their future home was the red crystal.

The church owned and controlled much of England during that time. The red crystal again became part of a treasure hidden and kept for power

AD 1525

To a bride

The red crystal remained in the possession of the Roman Catholic Church for many years. Pope Paul III, Alessandro Farnese (Carla's present stepfather Gerard) was ordained on June 26, 1519. His longtime concubine was Mattea Orsini (Carla's present mother). Upon the marriage of their illegitimate daughter, Katrina Rosetta Carlotta Farnese (Carla) to her love Giovanni Caponi (Dave), the Pope placed the red crystal pendant around her neck to wear during the ceremony.

You see, Pope Paul III was enamored with the pendant. The Pope thought the gold setting holding the crystal resembled a pope's hat. He saw several crosses in the gold setting, in his mind. That morning as the pope was readying himself to prepare for his daughter's wedding, he came across the pendant. He blessed it and decided Katrina should wear it during the ceremony.

They were special, after all, he believed. The pendant represented wealth, power and entitlement. His offspring should reflect himself.

Pope Paul III Farnese immediately retracted the pendant from his now-married daughter after the ceremony and returned it to his jewelry box for safekeeping. It remained with the church for years.

Many years later, Pope Innocent XI, revered as the most pious of all the known popes, reigned from 1676 until he died in 1689.

The hypocrisy of being known as pious while helping himself to large amounts of wealth and jewels from the church during his term, only to be used for salt trade as well as slavery, seems abhorrent. Pope "Not

So Innocent" discovered that his beloved Roman Catholic Church was not operating in the black. He wanted to be known as a hero, restoring his church to affluence at the expense of slavery.

AD 1578

From pope to slave trader

The red crystal was given to a slave trader, Horatio Volente (Dave's present father Harvey), by Pope Innocent XI to finance the ships used to steal slaves and salt from Africa to trade with other countries and islands. The sale of slaves and salt brought money back into the church coffers. *A church, representing God and Holiness took part in the purchase and selling of human lives.*

Horatio Volente, after obtaining the red crystal from Pope Innocent XI, traveled to Lemon Island with his ship of slaves stolen from Africa.

AD 1687

To the captain of an English island

Volente bribed Captain John Smith (Carla's present brother-in-law Dan, married to Cleo) on Lemon Island with the red crystal to allow slave trade on the island.

People, human beings were being sold in exchange for a crystal.

Captain John Smith was the original English officer who came to capture and inhabit the island with one hundred soldiers, for their country, England. Time brought many more soldiers and eventually thousands. Smith became more of a figurehead than the officer in control as time went on.

But he learned the value of human lives over a red crystal.

Upon reaching Lemon Island in the 1670s, his first introduction to the natives was a young black couple, Hiram and Eden (Dave and Carla). They had two children, and a third daughter, Etta (Brenda, our coworker), who had died years earlier of fever. Love, happiness and great spirit exuded from the young family.

Hiram and Eden had lived along the shore before the English came. They had dug an Adome, a home in the side of a cave on a beach with an outer thatching, protecting them from hurricanes and allowing them the beauty of the water, to fish for food, frolic and enjoy the lifestyle of freedom. The English pushed them back toward the middle of the Bermuda colony, assuming all of the coast and waters.

Things drastically changed for Hiram and Eden and their family. The life they knew and loved was lost to the English.

Smith took a strong liking to the young couple, taking them as indentured servants. Hiram, acting in a butler capacity, spent much of his time around and with Smith. A bond grew between the two men, much different than master and servant. Each evening, the ritual was for Hiram to bring Smith his tea, while they sat in the parlor and discussed life and the world, reading the Bible. Smith gave Hiram a pair of his glasses and taught him to read the Bible as well as other books. Hiram was grateful and indebted to the captain for his kindness and friendship.

Smith was a man of substance. His servants were treated as family. He cared for them and taught them his English ways. He cultured and gave them "his" religion.

His concern for Hiram and Eden's nonmarriage grew, as they were not married in a traditional religious ceremony but rather an island ceremony. Smith feared their marriage would not be appropriate in God's eyes. He paid to have a suit sewn for Hiram and a dress made for Eden. He gave them a gold band and arranged a chapel ceremony, where the two would exchange vows and the ring in an English marriage ceremony, reading from the Bible. The couple's two children attended the wedding. Smith renamed Hiram and Eden as Adam and Eve.

Eden was a strong-willed woman with a mind of her own. Although Smith treated her well, Mrs. Caroline Smith (Carla's present sister Cleo) wanted Eden to know her place. She was a servant and treated her accordingly.

Eden raised and cared for Smith and Caroline's daughter and for a short time, their son. She kept the house, cooked and tended to every cleaning detail of the home. The son was sent back to England to attend school. Jillian (Carla's present sister Patrice), the Smiths' daughter, and Moren (who later was Rose, Ruby & J.J.'s daughter), Hiram and Eden's daughter played and became friends and family. Mrs. Smith, however, continued to remember that Eden and Hiram, along with their children, were servants.

Eden remembered and missed the days on Lemon Island when she and Hiram could enjoy the sun, land and freedom they so loved. Her heart saddened and her spirit would never be the same. The island changed, and with it the beauty and peace went from green and lush to muddy, laden with horses, manure, soldiers and slaves. Garrisons were built along the shore to house the soldiers.

The island was a fort as well as a stopover for some slaves to be sold. They were put to work farming sugar cane and tobacco while they stayed.

The attitude of the soldiers and their officers changed over time as well. Their landing on Lemon Island had been friendly in the beginning. Eventually, with all the slave trade, it was declared all indentured servants on the island would be treated as the slaves in that all would carry papers of identification. No one was free on the island but the soldiers and the officers.

The plantation owners bought slaves to do their chores and farming. It was dangerous to be a native on Lemon Island now unless escorted.

Hiram continued his life as normal. Despite the fact that he was a servant and unable to make his own decisions or have a voice, he cared about his family and chose to be his best self. He was lashed on an occasion, taking punishment for Eden for traveling without her papers. He witnessed other lashings of slaves for no good reason. He continued to lead the church service on Sunday to give the slaves hope and learn to be their best.

One evening several young slave men attacked a group of thirty soldiers, killing most of them. Although the slaves escaped without recognition, the soldiers and Constable Alex Dyer (Carla's present neighbor Don) were on the lookout for who was responsible and anyone knowing anything about the attack.

Smith already had confronted Hiram, insisting he limit the attendance at his church services, which had grown from 13 in attendance to over 184. He reminded him the constable and English soldiers were now at unrest and would be watching all slaves to control any potential uprisings.

The constable was just waiting and watching for Hiram to show any signs of misconduct, ready to pounce. The young slaves had caused the constable to look foolish and not in control. Someone would have to pay for the murdering of the white English soldiers.

A slave from a neighboring plantation was tortured and forced to give a name. He named Hiram as an instigator although Hiram wasn't aware of the attack until afterward.

Seventy soldiers came for Hiram. Smith got to Hiram before they did to make him aware.

1691

From captain to constable

Smith had offered Constable Alex Dyer his most valuable possession in exchange for his friend's release, the red crystal.

Captain John Smith offered the red crystal in the name of love.

The constable agreed and greedily took the crystal. Then he ordered his soldiers to find, seize and bring Hiram to the garrison. He did not keep his word. He was not a man of honor, rather a power-seeking tyrant who chose to preserve his reputation.

Eden and Hiram held hands in prayer until the soldiers arrived. Hiram whispered to Eden. "No one will own me. Nobody owns another person."

Later, Horatio Volente (Dave's father Harvey) stood amid the crowd, having just arrived with his wife and children to live on Lemon Island.

He stood there, oblivious to what he had caused and how his actions had ruined lives and changed people forever.

The red crystal he had exchanged to buy and sell the lives of human beings had again taken a life.

Dyer prepared himself to administer one thousand lashings in punishment to Hiram.

Hiram hummed his Eden's favorite song while awaiting his death. He spoke to God, saying, "Forgive these people. They don't know what they do." His last thoughts were of Eden and the blood-curdling scream she made. He believed it to be the worst scream he had ever heard and thought only about her, proclaiming as loudly as he was able, "I love you, Eden."

Hiram never felt the sting or pain of the lashings. He only heard them. He saw two beautiful golden wings come down toward him. He knew they had come to take him back to God. He went through space and time and once again, felt the warmth of God. Eden watched as her love, her Hiram, slumped, taking his last breath.

Dyer fled the island with his stolen red crystal on Horatio Volente's next ship to America.

1691

From constable to slave trader

The ship landed in what would become Savannah, Georgia. Dyer gave the red crystal to Horatio as payment for his trip to America. He changed his name to Butler and lived in Georgia until the end of his days.

1691

From a slave trader to a family of jewelers

Twenty-two days later, Horatio sold the red crystal in Atlanta, Georgia, to a jeweler family, which became known as John Stilson Jewelry 150 years later, where the red crystal would remain as an investment for many years. Horatio stayed in America for the rest of his days.

Butler Island Plantation in Georgia was owned and operated by Colonel Pierce Butler during the 1700s and into the 1800s. He and his family owned extensive plantations and businesses in the Sea Islands of Georgia as well as Philadelphia, Pennsylvania. The colonel personally made his fortune and power starting from no means.

The family kept hundreds and hundreds of slaves working the plantations. There was said to be about five hundred slaves in total working his properties. That figure represented more slaves owned by any other person in history.

Butler, along with his daughter's son, Pierce Mease, became the most prominent members of their family, amassing their fortunes. Butler left all of his wealth to his grandsons upon his death with the stipulation their last names be changed to Butler. Captain Pierce Mease-Butler first married actress Fanny Kemble. That marriage ended in divorce after Fanny wrote and published a book called, *Journal of a Residence on a Georgia Plantation in 1838–1839* after their extensive visit on Sea Island. The book was an antislave journal, showing the awfulness of slavery. She was weakened financially and lost custody of their two daughters during their divorce.

The younger Pierce Butler had little business sense, unbeknown to his grandfather. He was a spendthrift, and by 1859 he had made a complete wreck of the business. He decided he would sell off some of his property.

On March 2 and 3, 1859, the largest sale of human beings in the history of the United States took place on a rainy racetrack in Savannah, Georgia. By the time the sale was over, 429 slave men, women and children had been auctioned off to the highest bidder, netting more than $300,000 and once again restoring Pierce Mease-Butler to his accustomed affluence.

Pierce had been courting a longtime friend of the family, Elizabeth Roseanne Harkess, who resided in Darien, Georgia, just south of Butler Plantation. She had carried a torch for Pierce since childhood. He had not seen Elizabeth (Brenda, our coworker) in that manner, she being just twelve when he married the first time.

He traveled to Philadelphia after the sale of his many slaves, tending to their northern businesses. He stopped in Atlanta, Georgia, on his way.

1859

From jeweler to a suitor

In Atlanta, Pierce visited John Stilson Jewelry Store on Whitehall Street, purchasing a large, red ruby oblong ring, beveled and weighing 2.4 carats. The stone was set in a yellow gold solitary mount with six prongs.

Pierce had purchased the engagement ring, which normally symbolizes love, with money actually gained from the sale of human lives.

From suitor to betrothed

Eleven days later, Pierce Mease-Butler presented the ruby ring to Elizabeth Harkess (Brenda, our coworker) on Dec. 25, 1859, with a proposal of marriage.

The City of Darien, just one mile north of Butler Island, Georgia, passed a resolution in 1775 condemning and outlawing slavery in its village. It was also the location of the first and oldest African American Baptist church. This was actually ninety years prior to the Thirteenth Amendment, which abolished slavery in the United States. Just a mile away, the Butler family of Butler Island Plantation and Sea Island Plantations, held the greatest number of slaves in captivity.

The Civil War erupted in 1861.

On June 11, 1863, Union troops stationed on St. Simons Island located in the Sea Islands owned by the Butler family, were ordered by Colonel James Montgomery to loot, burn and destroy the town of Darien, Georgia, twenty-five miles away. No Southern troops were stationed in Darien. In fact, most of their residents had already fled, aware that Northern troops were located on the island.

Colonel Robert Shaw (Dave) from Boston, Massachusetts, was the commander of the 54th Massachusetts Volunteers, the first all-black troop of the Civil War. They were stationed on St. Simons Island along with many other white troops.

Shaw refused to participate in the burning and looting of Darien. He stood and observed in horror as his men were forced to participate out of fear to not follow through with Montgomery's orders.

Shaw ordered his men to take only what would be useful at camp, while Montgomery's troops broke ranks and looted freely.

1863

From betrothed to colonel

During the destruction of Darien, a soldier of Shaw's, a man called Ricker, presented him with a beautiful red ruby ring. "Look what I found."

1863

From colonel to mother

Shaw took the red ruby ring and sent it back to his mother, Sarah Blake Sturgis Shaw (Carla) in Boston, along with letters describing the injustice and disgust he felt having any participation in the burning of Darien, Georgia. He would term the actions "Satanic."

Sarah and her husband, Francis George Shaw (Dave's present grandfather, Albert, on his mother's side) were abolitionists in Boston and well-known philanthropists and intellectuals.

1864

From mother to jeweler

Sarah sold the red ruby ring to a jeweler in Boston, taking the money from the sale and adding additional money, sending it to Darien for the immediate rebuilding.

Her using of the red ruby ring was of love and kindness for the city of Darien, Georgia.

Ricker, Shaw's soldier in his 54th Volunteer Army, had removed the ruby ring from the hand of a young woman killed during the burning of Darien, Georgia. Her name was Elizabeth Roseanne Harkess (Brenda, our coworker).

1865

From jeweler to a bishop of the Roman Catholic Church

In 1865, John Bernard Fitzpatrick, Bishop of Boston, Massachusetts, (and also Carla's grandfather on her mother's side) purchased the red ruby ring from the jeweler, using church money, with the intention of making it into his own ring. He allowed the stone to be removed by the jeweler while the gold was melted to create a new mounting. Fitzpatrick carried the stone to his home for safekeeping. He unfortunately died in 1866 before the ring had been completely finished.

The stone was left to the church of Boston, where it became a symbol of power and entitlement.

The first archbishop of the Boston Diocese, John Joseph Williams, was to be consecrated in 1866.

1866

From a bishop to an archbishop

The church of Boston sent the red ruby stone, along with other precious gemstones, to Italy for the creation of a special gift to be bestowed on their new archbishop during his consecration.

After all, he was a man of God. He somehow had an ability to reach our God in a manner we weren't able to, or so they thought. Shouldn't a man with that ability be given great wealth as a symbol of power and entitlement?

Our country had just endured years of a Civil War with death, theft and destruction. The Union and Confederate uniforms must not have fit over the long red robes of priests. All able-bodied men, northerners and southerners had been included in the war, expected to fight, not take confession. Were priests entitled somehow? The men of war could pray on their own. God knew what they were doing. Did they really need to say out loud they had murdered in war? Priests were allowed to hide behind their robes, feeling somehow privileged and closer to God.

The first archbishop of the Boston Archdiocese, John Joseph Williams, was consecrated on March 11, 1866, and given a symbol of his worthiness.

Italian artisans had created a solid gold chalice, twelve-and-a-half inches high, studded with precious stones, and a Gothic design. The cup was rounded for nearly three-quarters of its height by an elaborate filigree work. Between the cup and the base is a four-cornered knob at the extreme ends of which are four rare and beautiful jewels. All are deeply set in gold. One is a sapphire; the second, an aquamarine; the third an amethyst; and the fourth a red ruby of remarkable fine color. The chalice is a work of art by A. Tanfani of Rome.

1859

From jeweler to suitor

One hundred miles due north of Bulloch, Georgia, in South Carolina plantation owner Silas Williams (Willie, Dave's present friend) was in love with a woman—Ruby Wise.

He was a man of wealth and means by way of slavery, so traveling to Atlanta, Georgia, to shop was not unheard of for Silas. He found himself in the John Stilson Jewelry Store on Whitehall Street. There, he purchased a 2.1 carat, beautiful, clear, red ruby ring, rectangular in cut and set in an 18-carat gold mount with filigree surrounding the entire stone. His intention that day was to offer the red ruby ring to his love, Ruby Wise, with a proposal of marriage.

He purchased a symbol of love, the ring, with money he made working, beating and using human lives he owned.

1861

From suitor to betrothed

The Civil War outbreak changed Silas's intentions and life in many ways. He presented the red ruby ring to Ruby Wise as a promise for marriage for when he returned from battle.

His wealth and stature in the community couldn't stop the expectation that Silas would fight as a man, for his southern country.

Unfortunately, Silas Williams (Dave's friend Willie) was fatally shot by then Shaw (Dave), never returning to fulfill his promise of marriage.

Ruby Wise would always remember Silas as the love of her life.

The jeweler, John Stiltson, had decided, in 1859 when he cut the red crystal years before, to do so in four pieces, deciding it to be more saleable in smaller increments.

1890

From a jeweler to another jeweler

A jeweler from Nashville took a trip to Atlanta to purchase precious stones for his business, the Stief Jewelry Company. He purchased the two smaller stones cut from either end of the obelisk-shaped piece. The middle had been cut into two rather large portions. Those portions were much more valuable than each end piece.

The Nashville jeweler created two different rings. One was a round beveled stone in an 18-carat gold setting surrounded with diamonds. The other was an emerald-cut beveled red ruby set in a dainty platinum setting framed by a diamond-studded band. The rings were two different styles for two different women, given to each as a gift proclaiming the love of a man. These two women had more in common than ever thought possible. Both of their red ruby rings would be purchased in Nashville from the Stief Jewelry Company and both of their daughters would be abducted in Nashville.

A well-known architect (Don, Carla's present-day neighbor) in Nashville, Tennessee, in the late 1890s, whose buildings remain today, had a dark secret in his life. Although he was an architect by day, by night he was the serial murderer of little girls, all blond, all four years old.

The architect, Douglas, had been beaten as a child by his mother (Carla's neighbor, Don's wife). When she beat him, he felt helpless and not in control of himself. When he became a man, he lacked self-control, confidence and trust in women. One day he approached a blond woman, unknowingly offending her with sexual innuendo, mistaking it for the correct approach to gain a woman's attention. She scratched Douglas across his face in retaliation. This angered Douglas, bringing up the feelings he had harbored against his mother. He wanted to hurt her, needed to hurt her and needed to feel powerful against women. Those feelings simmered inside Douglas, waiting.

Years later, Douglas worked for a prestigious architectural firm in Nashville that had been commissioned to design an elementary school.

A committee comprising teachers and others met with Douglas to discuss the needs of their new school. One teacher, Carmen, decided to bring along her blond, four-year-old daughter to use as an example for table and blackboard heights. Carmen reminded Douglas of the blond woman who had scratched his face in his earlier days.

Four-year-old Lydia was not at all happy to attend the meeting. She was tired and wanted to be home with her toys.

Douglas attempted to befriend her, only to have her kick him. He was furious. His mother's actions came flooding back in his mind. He felt pain and knew his mother would have been happy about it.

The meeting ended but Douglas's anger had not subsided. He followed Carmen and Lydia home and for a couple of weeks, watched their routines, carefully taking note as to when Lydia was alone.

A day came when Douglas watched from a distance as Lydia crossed the street. He looked on the porch to see if Carmen was overseeing her daughter. Carmen was not in sight. He sped up closer to call Lydia to which she turned and acknowledged him. She recognized him from the school meeting and came toward him. Douglas halted his car and snatched Lydia up. No one saw what he had done.

1898

From jeweler to husband to wife

That morning happened to be Carmen's birthday. Before she left for school, her husband bestowed upon her a beautiful, solitary red ruby mounted in a platinum setting, purchased from the Stief Jewelry Company.

It was a symbol of his love for her birthday.

After being kidnapped, Lydia was beaten and starved for days, sustaining injuries that took her life after four days. Douglas enjoyed each time she cried and screamed. He felt as if he was somehow vindicated by what his mother had put him through.

Lydia was never discovered. Douglas was never found out.

The ring would become a reminder to Carmen of the day her daughter was kidnapped and killed.

Four years after the first brutal killing, which was Lydia, a sixth blond-haired four-year-old girl was abducted, molested, murdered and left for dead. This particular little girl happened to be Douglas's reincarnated mother (Carla's present neighbor, Don's present wife). Unbeknown to him, he had gotten the revenge he so desired. It was extremely unfortunate that Douglas didn't know it. Maybe it would have stopped the seventh killing.

1902

From husband to wife to son

Shortly after the sixth killing, a man named Jonathon Wright Sr. (Dave's present-life father, Harvey) came from Chicago with his wife, Katherine (Brenda, our present-day coworker) and their adorable, blond-haired, four-year-old daughter, Sarah (Dave's present-life sister, Lynn), to inquire about work and have a vacation all at the same time. Jonathon needed a change. He searched for work while his wife and daughter saw the city.

Jonathon passed the jewelry store window at the Stief Jewelry Company, only to be drawn in by a beautiful, solitary, red ruby set in eighteen-carat yellow gold.

He purchased the ring for his beloved Katherine as a symbol of their new beginning and the love he had for his wife and daughter.

Jonathon had no way of knowing that at the exact moment he was celebrating his family's new beginning with the purchase of the red ruby ring, their celebration had ended before ever getting started. Katherine and Sarah stood at the street waiting to cross as cars passed. Katherine held Sarah's hand as she took in the Nashville skyline. She felt Sarah's hand leave hers, immediately looking over to understand why. A strange man had grabbed Sarah and was swiftly walking away. Sarah fought to escape. Just like that, they were out of sight.

A woman standing nearby directed Katherine where to follow. But Katherine's search was fruitless. She could not believe her daughter had been abducted right from her side on the street. Dejected, she returned to the hotel where she found Jonathon frantically waiting, worried it had taken so long for them to get back. Katherine cried through telling the story of their daughter's kidnapping. Together, they ran swiftly out of the hotel and back to the area of the abduction. They searched for hours, finally coming upon a two-story brick home surrounded by a wrought iron fence. What stopped Jonathon in his tracks was what he saw in the yard. Lying in the grass was a stuffed doll belonging to Sarah.

Jonathon broke down the door of the two-story home only to find Douglas cleaning blood from his hands. Furious, Jonathon demanded to know where his daughter was. Douglas turned to Jonathon and laughed. Katherine ran for the police. Jonathon beat Douglas beyond recognition and then to death. Sarah's body was never found.

Jonathon was arrested and taken to jail for the night. The next morning, he was given the opportunity to tell his story. The police knew Douglas as a respected member of the community. They couldn't arouse fear in the community, and besides, they reasoned, he was already dead. Jonathon was released and traveled back to Chicago with his grief-stricken wife.

Upon their return to Chicago, Jonathon gave the ruby ring to Katherine, hoping to soothe Katherine's depression with the gift. But she never wore the ring.

Nine months after the loss of their daughter, Katherine gave birth to a son, Jonathon Junior (Dave). She died in childbirth. Jonathon Senior was devastated, although he had already lost his wife in every other way after the death of their daughter. He raised his son, calling him J.J. He put the red ruby ring in safekeeping, hoping that one day, *his son would present it to the love of his life.*

1904

From betrothed to namesake

Ruby Donaldson (Carla), whom you'll remember from the previous chapter, was the seventh child of James (Tom, Carla's now husband) and Anna Donaldson, and she had been named after her mother's aunt. The year Ruby was born, her Aunt Ruby was destitute, no place to go. Anna invited her to live with them. James was very displeased with another mouth to feed. Six months after Ruby was born, her Aunt Ruby passed away. But Ruby heard the family stories through her mother, including one about the love of Aunt Ruby's life, the man to whom she was promised in marriage. Silas Williams (Willie, Dave's present-life friend) had been fatally wounded during the Battle of Antietam in the Civil War.

On her deathbed, Aunt Ruby presented Anna with her most valuable and prized possession—a red ruby ring Silas had given to her on promise of marriage. She asked Anna to pass it on to her namesake. For years, Anna kept the red ruby ring a secret from her husband, fearing he would be tempted to sell the ring.

Living on the farm in Georgia wasn't easy. Ruby's mother gardened and fed her eleven children mostly from what she grew plus the chickens and eggs they raised. The girls were taught to sew their own clothes. The older children helped cook, clean and care for the younger children.

Ruby's father was an unpleasant, unhappy man. He had been privileged as a child, living on a plantation with slaves. He never had to lift a finger to perform an ounce of work. He still believed that to be true and acted accordingly. Anna did most of the work around the farm, along with raising their eleven children.

One day Anna saw a newspaper article offering to teach young women skills in sewing, promising jobs in which they could support themselves. The owner of the sewing shop and boarding house, referring to herself as Aunt Mae, published the article. With the endless worry about feeding and caring for her children, Anna wondered if this could solve their problems and provide her daughters with hope and support. She discussed the article with her husband. He agreed with anything that brought him less work and fewer mouths to feed.

So, in 1917 the Donaldson parents prepared their three youngest daughters, Nancy, Ruby (Carla) and Bessie, to take the work in Chicago, sending them on a train. Their fake Aunt Mae (Carla's present-life sister Cleo) waited at the other end. Nancy was but fifteen, Ruby thirteen and Bessie was a mere five years old. The train ride took two days, stopping in Atlanta and Nashville along the way. Early in their journey, they ran out of food. Ruby, being the most responsible of the three girls, gave her share of the snacks to her two sisters. By the time they reached Nashville, she was starving.

A young steward on the train witnessed Ruby doling out their food rations but never eating any part of it. He quickly sized up the situation and kindly offered her a crisp, red apple. The color immediately reminded Ruby of her hidden secret, the red ruby ring sewn into the hem of her dress. Her mother had sewn it in place and sworn Ruby to secrecy, advising her to use it only in an emergency. "It is the only family heirloom we possess," her mother had said. Ruby shared the apple with her sisters. She held Bessie and rocked her with the natural sway of the train, telling the story of the ring and *what it represented, their Great Aunt Ruby and the true love of her life, Silas.*

Once reaching Chicago, Ruby and her sisters were put to work in a sweatshop that was nothing like the article had described. There were no obvious opportunities. They lived in a boarding house and worked. That was their life. Many other girls were subjected to the same lifestyle being duped by Aunt Mae's advertisements.

But Ruby thrived. She happened to be a wonderful seamstress already, a skill she had polished all her life making clothing for herself and her siblings. Ruby had another love—singing. Her dream was to become a singer with a band and then someday, open her own boutique in Atlanta, Georgia.

What Ruby could not have anticipated was that her Aunt Mae would throw her into mob life to become a flapper in a speakeasy, forcing her to sew costumes and become the entertainment at D'Andre's. She also never knew that Aunt Mae had an ongoing, personal relationship with her boss, the gangster Angelo Genna (Jaime, Carla's present-day former husband). Genna paid her for Ruby's talents, as well as some of the other seamstress/flappers Aunt Mae sent his way.

At first, Ruby saw Chicago as a great opportunity to sing and sew. She learned too quickly that Angelo owned her. He paid for an apartment and forced Ruby to move from the boarding house once she turned eighteen. She was barely paid for her sewing and singing duties, with most of her money going to Aunt Mae. Ruby never knew what the arrangements were between Genna and Aunt Mae, financially or personally.

Then came the day Genna ordered Ruby to sing at his wedding, requiring her to wear the pearl necklace he had given her on her sixteenth birthday. That had been the night he presented her with the gift, then raped and beat her, taking her virginity.

After her shift ended at the speakeasy, Ruby and Annie, the pianist/organist of D'Andre's, rehearsed until the wee hours, preparing for the wedding song. She had never expected to meet a man like J.J. But she knew enough to know Genna owned her. She was not entitled to think, want or be her own person. Preparing for the wedding that day, Ruby looked at her image in the mirror, gazing at the pearls Genna ordered her to wear. She swiftly removed them, stuffed them back in the drawer and picked up a small box, revealing the red ruby ring. She slid it onto the third finger of her right hand, saying out loud, "I'm me. I cannot be owned."

At the reception, when J.J. asked her to dance, she figured him to be one of Genna's henchmen, in which case, she'd have no say as whether to dance. But he seemed persistent … and sincere.

As J.J. pulled her toward him, he noticed the red ruby ring, which appeared more vivid next to her ivory skin. He gazed at her magenta dress, to her delicate ankles, up to her steel-blue eyes. "You have the voice of an angel," he said.

But Jonathon was somehow different than the usual Genna men— pure, sweet, sincere—so she agreed to meet him for breakfast the next morning. She wore the ring to Marino's. As they walked along the shore of Lake Michigan, Jonathon asked Ruby about her ring. She told the story of her namesake, saying, "It is part of who I am." The red ruby

ring bestowed on her a sense of peace, much as J.J. did.

The next Friday night, she was singing at D'Andre's, wearing a red silk blouse and white fringed skirt, her hair slicked back and held in place by a sparkling silver band. She had painted her lips and fingernails ruby red. She wore the ring. *It is who I am*, she thought.

Of course, we know what happened that evening! J.J. came to D'Andre's, and that night, Ruby invited him into her apartment, and they shared a whole weekend together, deeply in love. J.J. remembered watching Ruby take off her ring, carefully polishing it before placing it back in the small box and tucking it in her dresser drawer.

Only once more would J.J. glimpse the ring—that fateful night in the alley. Less than a year later, Ruby was fatally shot, leaving her baby daughter Rose behind.

1939

From mother to daughter

On her thirteenth birthday, Rose received her mother's ring, along with the story of its origin. It was given in love, and became her most precious memory of her mother, Ruby (Carla).

Years later, Rose (also Moren, Eden and Hiram's daughter) married and gave birth to a daughter and two years later, a son. Katherine Anne and Jonathon Jackson became known to their family as Katie and Johnny. They were Ruby and J.J., reincarnated. They were Carla and Dave.

For reasons that Rose didn't quite understand, Katie called her little brother J.J. They were inseparable.

Rose raised her two children alone while her husband served as a fighter pilot in World War II, stationed mostly in Germany and Europe. On Christmas Eve 1942, Katie and Johnny played happily on the winding, three-story staircase as their mother wrapped presents. They climbed onto the railing and fell, fracturing their necks. Johnny died immediately; Katie died at the hospital.

Devastated, Rose found herself alone, her husband overseas, her children gone. Lila (Brenda) was there to help her once again. When her husband returned home from the war in 1944, she conceived and gave birth to their third child, Carla, still alive today, March 9, 1945. This Carla is not the author of this book, but a different Carla.

1958

From mother to daughter

When Carla turned thirteen in 1958, her mother presented her with the red ruby ring, telling the story of its origin, given in love for her and their family. Years went by, and Carla married and gave birth to a daughter. She named her Ruby.

From mother to daughter

Now Ruby was getting married. Her mother presented the ring as her "something old," telling the story of its origin, the story of how it was given in love by a mother for a daughter. The previous year, Ruby had already given birth to a son, whom she named Jonathon. This would not be the first time a girl named Ruby conceived a child out of wedlock and out of love. A year after she married her husband, Robert, Ruby gave birth to a girl, naming her Rose.

2014

From mother to suitor to betrothed

Rosie, as she was called, worked at the University of Illinois in Chicago. When her boyfriend, David, a medical student, came to Rosie's parents to seek permission to marry their daughter, her mother, Ruby, offered the red ruby ring. Her only request was that he tell her about how the ring had passed from mother to daughter for years, and stipulated that, as he proposed, he said, "Ruby, Ruby, Rose, Carla, Ruby, Rose, will you marry me?" David agreed.

She also asked him to avoid Christmas Eve, saying, "Dec. 24 is not the date for our family," referring to the deaths of Katie and Johnny, her great aunt and uncle. "You are asking Rosie to start a new life; it is not a Christmas present."

He proposed Dec. 27, 2014.

The ring had been given in love, consistently now for five generations. If only the other three portions of the "Red Ruby Crystal" could be used in the name of love, not power, entitlement, greed or ownership.

Close ... but no red ruby ring

In October 2015, Dave, Tom, Paula, Lara and I traveled to Chicago to bequeath medical items collected for years to Tom's alma mater, a university in Rosemont, Illinois, just outside Chicago. We traveled by train. On our last day in the city, we planned to go to The Art Institute. Isabella had told us that we could possibly meet Ruby and

J.J.'s descendants (our descendants) if we made specific choices. But that was all she would say. She couldn't give us instructions. The Art Institute was a hunch.

All through the museum, up and down the floors, we had our eyes peeled for a young woman wearing a ruby ring. As Dave and I walked the museum, we were J.J. and Ruby again, hoping to see our great-great-great granddaughter Rosie. But we did not see anyone with a red ruby ring. Later, Isabella told us Rosie had been upstairs when we were down, and vice versa. She further said that the day before, when we had driven to Little Italy, hoping to find a familiar site like D'Andre's, we missed something. Right at the corner of Little Italy, which sits adjacent to the University of Illinois, a sign on the corner said, "Goodbye Rosie, we will miss you."

Rosie was employed at the university, and it had been her last day and farewell before she left to marry. Twice in two days, we had just missed her.

Isabella cheered us up, though, when she told us that the young couple we met on the train coming into the city had just returned from their honeymoon. They had given up their seat for my husband, Tom, who was eighty and had felt tired with all the travel that day. That young man was Rosie's brother—our other great-great-great-grandchild as Ruby and J.J.

2016

From estate sale to its intended place

In October 2016, Dave and I traveled to Chicago for a seminar. During our trip, we found and purchased a red ruby ring in the jewelry district from a store called Ivy Rose. The ruby was mounted in an 18-carat gold setting and surrounded by diamonds. Isabella confirmed this to be the ring that Jonathon Wright Sr. purchased for his wife, Katherine, in Nashville. Once they arrived in Chicago, and their son, J.J., was born, they had always intended it to be passed down in the family, ending up on the finger of the woman J.J. would marry—the woman who would be his great love. That woman was, of course, Ruby Donaldson. On this day in 2016, it did. It's now worn on my hand.

During this same trip, Dave and I decided to visit Little Italy in the hopes of finding Ruby Donaldson's 1925 apartment. Isabella had told us the building was still standing.

We walked around the area, up and down streets, waiting for Dave to remember something familiar. Isabella would chime in, "You're getting warmer" as we turned corners.

While walking back toward the restaurant where we had made dinner reservations, I looked across the street at an apartment building, startled. Pointing to a yellow brick three-story building, I said to Dave, "Look!" The name above the door read, "Isabelle Apartments." Of course, Isabella confirmed it to be Ruby's former place of residence. Isabella confirmed the building had always had that name. "How else would you have found it?" she said.

Emotions flooded our brains as we walked around the corner, past the bank where Jonathon Wright Jr. had been employed and to the Italian restaurant to eat. We were seated next to a picture of a young blond flapper wearing a hat pulled down over her ears.

2016

From another estate jewelry store to its intended place

Just one month later, in November 2016, Dave, Paula, Tom and I traveled to Florida to Tom's grandson's wedding, stopping in Nashville on our way home. We found Lysbeth Estate Jewelry and Antiques in an antique mall in Franklin, just outside of Nashville. (Side note: Lisbeth is the pet name I call my spirit guide Elizabeth). Sure enough, we found a red ruby ring mounted in a platinum setting, clustered in diamonds, part of an estate sale, but with only one owner. We learned the ring had originally been purchased for Carmen, a schoolteacher in Nashville. Isabella confirmed it. This was the third piece of the original red ruby crystal.

We know that one piece of the red ruby crystal remains in Massachusetts with the Archdiocese of Boston, my hometown, ironically enough, stuck in a chalice. Hopefully, if this stone is to remain in a cup given to a man because of his holiness, it can somehow, sometime become something of greatness, worthy of this world and not part of conceit, entitlement or ownership in the future.

The other two pieces remain in rings, which I now wear on my hands.

The fourth piece of the red ruby crystal is worn on the left third finger of Ruby and J.J.'s great-great-great-granddaughter, Rosie.

Both the red ruby crystal and I, Carla have had thirty-four incarnations. We would call this a true metaphor for the soul.

TIMELINE OF THE RUBY RED CRYSTAL

45 million years ago	God creates rubies.
AD 896	Vikings invade Scotland
AD 904	Amos (Dave's present father) finds the ruby red crystal. He gives it to Oahd and Fenella (Dave and Carla) for his son for their daughter, Agnes's (Brenda) hand in marriage.
AD 906	Vikings invade Scotland again. Kehldr (Willie), Oahd's brother, is given the ruby red crystal as ransom for Oahd's family and land.
AD 907	Kehlder (Willie) gives the Danish king the ruby red crystal.
AD 986	Sweyn Forkbeard (Don, Carla's neighbor) becomes the king of England and owns the ruby red crystal.
AD 1015	Sweyn gives his son Canute the Great the ruby red crystal. Canute invades England and conquers King Aethelred (Dan, Carla's brother-in-law). He and his wife, Emma of Normandy (Carla), flee England.
AD 1017	Canute marries Emma of Normandy (Carla).
AD 1027	Canute invades Scotland and then sets up trade with the ruby red crystal. It becomes part of the Scottish royal jewels.
AD 1297	Edward I invades Scotland and captures the ruby red crystal, which then belonged to the House of Plantagenet and finally to the House of Lancaster. Edward I's soldiers (Dave and Willie) invade.
AD 1413	King Henry V (Don, Carla's neighbor) becomes king of England. He places the ruby red crystal in his scepter and tortures Sussan with it.
AD 1422	King Henry VI (Dave) becomes King of England.
AD 1441	King Henry VI (Dave) gives Sussan (Carla) a ruby red crystal pendant. She passes this to her daughter Agnes (Brenda).

AD 1461	Agnes (Brenda) buys land from the Catholic Church with the ruby red crystal.
AD 1525	Katrina (Carla) wears the pendant with the ruby red crystal when marrying Giovanni (Dave). Her father, the pope, loaned it to her. It remained with the Catholic Church.
AD 1678	Pope Innocent XI funds slave trade with the ruby red crystal, giving it to Horatio Volente (Dave's present-life father, Harvey). Horatio gives it to Capt. Smith (Dan), who tries to buy off Constable Alex Dyer (Don, Carla's neighbor) so he will not punish Hiram (Dave) or Eden (Carla).
AD 1691	Alex Dyer and Horatio leave the island and land in Savannah. Dyer changes his name to Butler. Horatio sells the ruby red crystal to a family who would soon become known as the John Stilson Jewelry Company. The ruby red crystal is divided into four parts.
AD 1859	Pierce Meese-Butler purchases a ruby ring for Elizabeth Harkess (Brenda) out of one-quarter of the ruby red crystal. It passes through Colonel Robert Gould Shaw (Dave) to his mother, Sarah Blake Sturgis Shaw (Carla), then back to the Roman Catholic Church to end up in a gold chalice.
AD 1890	The Stief Jewelry Company of Nashville purchases two smaller parts of the stone. Two separate ruby rings are made. Both are intended for women who end up crossing paths with Douglas the architect (Don, Carla's neighbor) in Nashville. One is purchased by Jonathan Wright Sr. (Dave's present-life father) for his wife, Katherine (Brenda), J.J. Wright Jr.'s mother.
AD 1859	Silas Williams (Willie, Dave's Friend) purchased a ruby ring for Ruby Wise before dying in the Civil War. The ruby ring passes on to her namesake, Ruby Donaldson (Carla).
AD 1925	J.J. Wright Jr. (Dave) meets Ruby Donaldson (Carla). They conceive a daughter, Rose. J.J. and Ruby die within a year of each other, and Rose is raised by Ruby's friend, Lila (Brenda). Lila gives Rose the ruby ring.
AD 1942	Rose lost two children in an accident in which they fell to their deaths, Katie and Johnny (Carla and Dave). Her third child is born in 1945. They name her Carla.

AD 1958	Rose passes the ruby ring to her daughter, Carla.
AD 1991	Carla's (Rose's daughter) daughter, whom she named Ruby, was getting married, and she passes the ruby ring to her as her "something old."
AD 2014	Ruby's daughter is about to become engaged, and she offered David, her soon-to-be son-in-law, the ruby ring as an engagement ring. She requests that when he proposes, he says, "Ruby, Ruby, Rose, Carla, Ruby, Rosie, will you marry me?" This is the way, through the memory of five generations, in which the ruby ring has been given in love.
AD 2018	One part of the ruby red crystal remains with the Catholic Church of Boston. Dave and Carla own two parts of the ruby red crystal, now fashioned as rings. The fourth part is on the hand of Ruby and J.J.'s great-great-great granddaughter, Rosie.

Chapter 20

Lives Intertwined

DAVE

We often return to new lives with the same people for one of three reasons. One, we get along well together and support each other, referring to those people as family mates. Secondly, we have karmic debt with those same persons that needs to be resolved, referred to as karmic debt mates. And lastly, we return with a person who could potentially become our soul mate. Remember, only God can choose whether two people are worthy of becoming soul mates, when it is clear that their ability to love one another is most complete.

Those closest to us continue to travel with us to new lives but not always in the same capacity. A man and woman may be husband and wife in one life and return as father and daughter in another. Or, you could be father and son only to reincarnate as brothers in another life. We all play different roles during our many reincarnations. How else will we learn?

About Willie

Willie has been my friend for eighteen years. He's six-feet-four, balding with now gray hair and blue eyes. He is pale but not albino. When he was eighteen, he wore a thick, blond Afro. He is deaf in one ear. Both of his parents were black. His parents could only afford the company doctor in southern Ohio, who was not a specialist in hearing.

The company doctor could not save Willie's hearing. They lived in company housing, worked at the company brickyard, purchased food and clothing from the company store and paid for the company doctor with company money. Not unlike slavery of the past.

I have found Willie in many past lives, often fighting beside each other as soldiers. He was my commander on the Isle of Lesbos in 600 BC. In one of his most recent lives, he was Silas, a proud Southern slave owner who died at my hand, when I was Colonel Robert Gould Shaw. He purchased the ruby ring passed on to Ruby Donaldson. Willie was a guard for Pope Paul III, Katrina Rosetta Carlotta Farnese's father.

I have had many a conversation with Willie on these subjects. One day, I shared the story of meeting Carla when I was three years old at Revere Beach in Boston, then not seeing her again for thirty-six years. As a seven-year-old boy, he would visit his uncle, a Baptist minister in southern Ohio. Over the years, he met a woman through his uncle, who called him William. Later Willie's family moved from southern Ohio and settled up in northern Ohio. Fourteen years later he saw her again on his wedding day, at the reception. He asked if she remembered him. "Yes, you just married my granddaughter," she said. We are, indeed, all connected on purpose.

About Tom

Carla's present-life husband, James Donaldson (Ruby's father), also grew up on a plantation in Georgia with slaves. He was thirteen at the end of the Civil War, born in 1851.

The comfortable lifestyle of the Old South never returned for James Donaldson. The war ended and took with it his family's wealth. He and his brothers started to farm the land owned by his parents, Mikell and Rebecca Donaldson. His father had died when he was four years old. The farm had been run by his stepfather, John Gibson, who passed away in 1863 during the Civil War, leaving the Donaldson boys to run the plantation on their own with one remaining slave.

Bucker, one of their older black slaves, agreed to stay. He tried to show the young Donaldson boys how to pick and plant cotton and tobacco. He showed them how to raise both carrots and onions in the Georgia soil. James Donaldson had broad shoulders yet detested hard work. James hated Bucker for what he was, a reminder of what was lost. He needed Bucker, or all the work would fall to him.

Bucker tolerated the young man as he had nowhere else to go. The farm underproduced but Bucker kept it working. Bucker died in 1872. The farm was failing. The land was divided between the boys.

Eventually, James Donaldson was left with nothing. No slaves, a worthless plantation, and the inability to live in wealth and entitlement.

Tom, in this life, was born in 1935. He entered my life in 1998, when I bought his medical practice. When he was James Donaldson, Ruby's father in his previous life, he died in 1934. Born as Tom again in 1935. Tom was Terryl, the high priest in the 700s BC in the Mayan civilization, and my superior. He was Tomo, the father of the woman I married, Carlisse, in 1250 BC in Memphis, Egypt. Tom was also Mr. Myerson in South Dakota, the husband of Julia Myerson and Samuel's real father. And Tom was Robert Smith's brother (me) in the Cotswold area of England in the 1600s. Tom purchased Hiram and Eden's daughter in Bermuda as Mr. Silversmith in the late 1600s. Giovanni Caponi's father in Rome, Italy, was none other than Tom in the 1500s, my father once again.

About Harvey

J.J.'s father, Jonathon Sr., was Harvey, my present-life father and a longshoreman then, on the western coast of Lake Michigan in Chicago. He stood five-feet-ten with wide shoulders and strong forearms. The work was hard but honest in the late 1800s. He had married Katherine, J.J.'s mother, and they had a daughter, Sarah. J.J.'s father lost part of his left fifth finger to frostbite while working on the docks. Later there were stories about possible mob involvement that may have cost him that finger. In 1900, J.J.'s father, mother and sister traveled to Nashville by train. J.J.'s sister was kidnapped and murdered. (By the way, Sarah is my present-life sister also).

Jonathon and Katherine made the trip back to Chicago, devastated. They could hardly speak. J.J.'s father went back to work on the docks. His mother cried continuously. Their son was born nine months later. The delivery was difficult. J.J.'s father said that his mother would have died earlier from a broken heart if not for the pregnancy. J.J. was all his father had left. He was his father's purpose in the world. He had saved the ruby ring for J.J. that he had purchased in Nashville for his wife. His thought was that one day Jonathon Jr. would give this ring to the woman he loved as a gift from both his parents to start a new life and hopefully have a better ending.

At age four, Jonathon Sr. started to call his son J.J. He read to him every night. He was not well-educated and could barely read but he bought a book called, *The Story of the Treasure Seekers*. Every night he would try to teach his son colors and words. He would then read aloud from the book. J.J. would go to bed and hear him reading to himself, slowly, sounding out the words, learning to read ahead the next chapter of the book.

The book was about a man who had been widowed and left with five children. The adventures of the children were about trying to find treasures for their sad father. One of the characters was Oswald. The story was written from Oswald's perspective. J.J. imagined himself as Oswald, with a sad father.

Shortly after he finished reading the book to his son, Jonathon Sr. brought home a new kitten. The little, buff-colored kitten with white paws had no one to love.

J.J.'s father had been given the kitten from a fellow dockworker. He somehow knew his son needed to learn responsibility and needed someone to love. J.J. named the kitten Oswald.

His father explained that cats were different than dogs. Dogs love unconditionally. Cats must choose to love you. They are independent. He taught J.J. that he should cherish the love when given and respect their space when needed. It was a lesson he would need someday.

He continued to stress the importance of an education. J.J. studied hard. He saved money to send J.J. to school where he studied accounting and banking at a business school in Chicago. He wanted something different for his son than the hard work of the docks. He used his connections on the dock with the Unione-Sicilliano (Sicilian-Union) to get J.J. a job as a junior banker.

My father, Harvey, in this life was a quiet and serious man as you remember, always concerned with the value of a good education. Jonathon Wright Sr. and my present father, Harvey, one and the same, both valued the need for a good education.

He was also the last emperor of the Han Dynasty, married to Cao Jie and none other than Horatio Volente, who gave the ruby red crystal for slave trade. Harvey was Djet's father, the one who taught Meritneith and Djet to be entitled.

About Brenda

My employee, Brenda is a thirty-six-year-old woman whom Carla and I encouraged to go back to school. She recently graduated with her BSN degree. She, too, has been in sixteen lives with us. She has been Carla's and my daughter in many past lives, about twelve times. People often asked Carla if she was her daughter because of their similar features.

Brenda was the first bride exchanged for the ruby red crystal as Oahd and Fenella's daughter Agnes in Scotland. She was Leda, Athena's handmaiden and also Jonathon (J.J.) Wright's mother, Katherine, in Chicago in the 1900s. She was Elizabeth Harkess in Darien, Georgia, during the Civil War. Brenda was Djet and Meritneith's granddaughter in Egypt. She was Ruby's closest friend, Lila, in Chicago in 1925.

About Topher

About a year and a half ago, Topher was waiting as we came home from the grocery store one evening. He was cowering under a car in the driveway, starving and scared.

Topher's mother and sister, Isabella told us, had been killed crossing the road. J.J., too, had lost his mother and sister and needed to learn about love. This cat had come to me with purpose. You could not get close to him in the beginning, yet I coaxed him into the garage with food. Isabella told us a little girl had called him Cris-Cross. The cats had been left behind when their human family moved. They were searching for food when Topher's mother and sister were hit and killed by automobiles.

I started to rehabilitate Cris-Cross. He had never lived indoors. Dan, Carla's brother-in-law, had recently passed away. He had been given the job after Atonement of watching over our animals. He sent the cat to us. We thought maybe Cleo (his widow and Carla's sister), in her loneliness, would need this cat. Trips to the vet for shots and neutering, training with a cat box, lots of loving went into Cris-Cross. This sweet, gentle, buff-colored kitten with white paws was growing on us. I began to call him Christopher. While at the veterinarian's office one day, the doctor told us about his roommate in college named Christopher. His nickname was Topher. The name seemed right.

He was called Topher from then on. He reminded me of J.J.'s Oswald. Isabella explained how Topher was a descendant of Oswald's mother, twenty-five cats between. He was meant to find us. Topher was the last of his line, with his mother, father and siblings all gone.

It was interesting that Topher came to me a stray with no one to love or give love to. I had in a way been rescued during my divorce, a stray, nowhere to go, when Tom and Carla took me in.

Topher came when I needed him, much like Oswald, when I needed to love and be loved. Topher reminded me of the lessons of Jonathon Wright Sr. and also the lessons of my father in this life. They were great memories.

About Paula

Paula, Carla's sister, has always been close by. Now, as my office assistant and as Jonathon Wright's assistant, Jane, at the bank in Chicago in the 1920s. She was Ronna and Shanta's sister in the Mayan days, brutalized by Terryl. Robert and Sarah were reminded several times by the tax-collector's wife, Paula, in England to pay their taxes or else. She sat with Sarah and cared for her during her illness and death. Mr. and Mrs. Myerson's neighbor was Abigail, a.k.a. Paula, who paid her respects at their home during Julia Myerson's wake. She played with Hiram and Eden's daughter in Bermuda as their neighbor. Paula and her husband were Oahd and Fenella's Viking friends, who stayed in Scotland with them. Paula was Henry VI's first cousin, actually being raised in the castle with Henry.

I've seen her in many other lives from our past. Paula has been our constant witness and confidant throughout this entire process. She understands because she is and has always been around us and close.

About Carla

Carla is my best friend and office manager today. She was the mother of the Civil War officer, Colonel Robert Gould Shaw, Sarah. She was

Hiram's Eden in Bermuda, and Robert's wife Sarah in the Cotswold area of England. She was Samuel's school friend and neighbor, Mrs. Julia Myerson. She was Ronna, the oldest of the five little Mayan girls, taken to the Temple. In Memphis, Egypt, she married Dedu and was Tomo's daughter, Carlisse. Carla was the first female pharaoh of Egypt, Meritneith, after murdering her husband and king Djet. Katrina Rosetta Carlotta Farnese, daughter of Pope Paul III, was none other than Carla.

Another life that we have barely mentioned—our most recent past life, in fact—is when Carla and I were Katie and Johnny, a sister and brother from Chicago, who were tragically killed together as children. Carla was also Fenella (Hleder), a Viking woman, and Emma of Normandy of Viking and Danish descent. She was also Cao Jie, the last Empress of the Han dynasty. Once she was Athena, the queen of an obscure Greek Island called Lesbos. Carla was Ruby Donaldson from Bulloch, Georgia, the flapper murdered in 1926.

About Dave

I am Carla's best friend and present employer. During the Civil War, I was her son, Colonel Robert Gould Shaw. I was Eden's husband, Hiram, in Bermuda and Sarah's husband, Robert, in England.

As a stuttering eight-year-old boy, I was Samuel Renner in South Dakota and witnessed the death of my friend, Mrs. Julia Myerson. I ever so hesitantly remember being Daan, the priest responsible for bringing young Ronna and her four siblings to the Great Temple for Terryl. As Dedu, I helped carve the Valley of Kings, after moving from Memphis, Egypt, with my wife, Carlisse. As King Djet of Egypt, I was murdered by my wife, Meritneith (Carla), after freeing slaves from bondage.

I was Giovanni Caponi, a pharmacist in Rome, Italy, who married Pope Paul III's spoiled daughter, Katrina. I was Xan, guard to the last empress of the Han dynasty, Cao Jie.

I fell to my death from a three-story staircase trying to protect my sister, Katie, in my most recent life, at age four. I was Oahd (Hdejh), a Viking transformed to a Scotsman, who was the first man to receive the ruby red crystal. I was a confused child king as Henry the VI, accused of being weak and crazy. And, as Jonathon Wright Jr., I was shot to death in a dark alley by gangsters for spending time with a lovely young flapper, Ruby Donaldson.

Again, it's fascinating, the twists of destiny and choice. We are all connected. Is it any more surprising now, that Carla and I met twice in this life, once on the beach in Boston as preschoolers and again, as adults in Ohio, thirty-five years later? It was always meant to be.

Chapter 21

Personal Change: We Are Always Becoming

DAVE

Some would say I come from a unique background. I trained as a nurse, then a doctor. Nurses treat the human response to illness and life. Doctors theoretically treat medical conditions. Much of this is based in science. There is currently a trend to encourage a more holistic approach in medical school. Certainly, treating all aspects of the spirit and soul could aid in healing.

I bring my own unhappy self to this equation. Just over five years ago I sat down at a table to meditate for the first time. I was broken-hearted. My blood pressure was 150/100.

My blood sugar was 110. My cholesterol was 240. I was Syndrome X and weighted 325 lbs. Syndrome X is a metabolic state based on being overweight and eating unhealthy.

I ate to control my unhappiness. My stress level soared at home. I lived in an unhappy marriage. I was diagnosed with a condition known as aortic stenosis. I have a heart murmur and calcification in my aortic valve. Literally, I had a broken heart.

But now, I have learned to love myself and others again. I try to give back and be my best every day. I have lost 116 pounds. I dropped 14 inches off my waist, and I no longer shop in the Big and Tall men's section. My cholesterol is 140. My blood sugar is 85. My blood pressure is 120/68. The swish of my heart murmur has lessened. I have mended my broken heart and my broken spirit.

How can I explain this? Work is still as hard—busier in fact. The stress of the divorce should have driven up my cortisol, the stress hormone that affects your metabolism. It has been implicated in people who are overweight. Yet, my stress reduced. The weight loss was easy. I walked for exercise and ate right. Did the meditation literally change me? Yes. I got in touch with myself and my God. I gained self-respect. I became self-building not self-destructive. I craved more knowledge. Somehow, Carla always knew the next question to ask. I am sure Elizabeth her spirit guide helped her.

What have I learned? First, it is great to be a good example. I have many patients who have now gone on a diet. When I say diet, I should say a life change with fewer fats and carbs, plenty of vegetables, more chicken and turkey. I choose to have no pork because the Bible tells us so. I choose to not eat scavengers or bottom feeders, also included in the Bible. I eat less red meat as well. Fruits, vegetables and lean proteins are my choices.

I have also cut out gluten. I have a wheat allergy. But I also believe, and it is confirmed medically, that heavy gluten causes inflammation, which leads to disease and pain. Going gluten-free means less inflammation. I have given up ibuprofen, which used to be two to three times per day. I work out one hour at least per day. My knees no longer hurt. I have many patients who have also lost thirty or forty pounds through my example. My sister has lost 120 pounds. I tell my patients that I had just set a goal to lose two pounds. I believed in myself and giving my best back to God. I started with just two pounds a week then I lost two pounds fifty-eight more times. It helps when you have peace of mind.

We learned that God wants us to be our best self. I was working toward that goal. My being overweight was being selfish and a burden to others. If I had a heart attack, I would have caused my employees heartache, leaving them without paychecks. I would have caused my family great concern. It was my responsibility to make myself whole and healthy. I hadn't thought about the fact that being unhealthy was being conceited. I was putting myself before others by causing their concerns. If I couldn't take care of myself, how could I be a good example to others?

This is true for society as a whole, isn't it? Those who smoke, drink too much, eat to excess and do not exercise are all health risks. Health care is a limited resource. There are ample resources if we all do our part to take care of ourselves, do our best and care for those who are truly unable, there will be no karma to repair. In other words, if we are *selfish* and *conceited* in our ability to care for ourselves and others, we will return to another reincarnation to make up for those choices.

So, if you can mend a broken heart, what else can you do with meditation, prayer, education and self-awareness? I started to engage three very similar patients. All had somehow lost their way. All were diabetic. All had diabetic neuropathy or numbness. All did not particularly take care of their mental health and overall well-being. They had shut off part of their own feelings for whatever reasons. Interestingly, it was the emotional journey that seemed to improve their healing.

Healing a broken foot, and a hurting soul

The first man was a general surgeon and a devout Muslim. He was involved in an accident with a motorcycle driver. He presented to my office with a swollen foot. His foot was changing, discolored and collapsing. He had lost feeling in both feet. I looked at my general surgeon friend and said, "I think you are diabetic and you have a Charcot foot." He said he was not diabetic. He had been to the emergency room and had blood work and X-rays. They thought he had gout. I knew he did not have gout. His X-rays showed early bone changes. Charcot is not common but starts as a small injury in diabetics, then it becomes progressively worse. It can change rapidly. I put him in a therapeutic boot to protect his foot.

He refused to take time off work. He did not believe he could stop. How would he provide for his family and the overhead for his medical practice? No one could know he was not perfect in his mind. Who would go to a broken doctor? Yet the horrific accident with the motorcycle driver had made him numb to those around him. He was unfriendly and unaware of others. Four weeks later, his blood sugar started to rise.

Six weeks after his accident, he was diagnosed with diabetes. His foot collapsed and fractured. He felt no pain. He developed foot sores and ulcerations.

He has now been through years of wound care, surgery for bone infections and prophylactic surgery to prevent repeat ulcerations. We worked together to heal his foot. We have had hours of conversations. I ask him about his Muslim beliefs and history, and he questions me on my Judeo-Christian upbringing. We have talked about our own religious experiences. We have found many things in common, including my lessons from meditation, the lessons from Moses and the Old Testament, to lessons taught by Jesus, and also by Mohamed in the Quran.

We have decided the message is often the same, just the details have been changed. Man has somehow through **selfishness** and **conceit** changed the story to control people. If only we could get past all this. He has been inspired to explore his own religious past. He has a newfound religious excitement. We worked together to heal and protect his feet in order for him to make the holy pilgrimage to Mecca.

The pilgrimage to Mecca is one of the pillars of the Muslim faith. It reenacts the journey of Hagar and her infant son Ishmael from the desert to Mecca, the holy place of all Muslims. Ishmael is the son of Abraham and the founding father of all of Islam. Just as Isaac was the son of Abraham, the founding father of the twelve tribes of Israel. He recently returned from Mecca. It was good to see the life in his eyes and the feeling returning to his heart. The numbness is still present in his feet. However, the feeling has returned to his soul. His foot is doing well and is stable.

Restoring faith

The next patient is also a man of faith, a Baptist minister. He had early numbness in his feet. His blood sugars were out of control with a diagnosis of diabetes. His wife referred him to my practice. My weight loss inspired her, and she thought I could reach him.

The pastor and I had a long discussion on diabetes, his life, his poor congregation and having to take on a part-time job as a nursing home chaplain to pay for food and housing. We discussed the nursing home at length with so many deaths and so many lonely people.

I, too, go to this nursing home. I shared stories of some of the residents and how they make me laugh and sometimes cry. One particular resident, who was 104, met me one day in her room. She wore a black dress and high heels. She was just leaving for a funeral. She said she was burying her last friend. "I have nowhere else to wear these shoes," she said. "Everyone I know is dead."

I was immediately saddened for her. She said she was praying for God to take her soon. I shared that she must still have some work to do. She always had her Bible out and was using a magnifying glass to be able to read from it. She almost always smiled. She told me that, "At least she only had to wear these shoes one more time." She also shared that she bought the shoes fifty-two years ago and only wore them to funerals. "I always hated those shoes," she said. She laughed a full belly laugh as I left her room.

The pastor started to visit with her regularly. Somehow, the work started to excite him. He found purpose in this part of his ministry and even some dignity in the end of life of these residents. He now speaks of this job as a joy. He presided at her funeral. He said it was a privilege. He tries to give his best every day to these people.

Over the next six months his weight dropped by thirty pounds. He smiles when he comes to the office. His blood sugars are nearly normal. The tingling and burning in his feet have ended.

From numb to alive

The third man is a Lutheran minister who taught college classes on religion. He carried a recessive gene for deafness, as did his wife with the same gene. All of their children are deaf. His wife recently suffered a serious liver condition. She nearly died and was still in a mental fog with liver toxicity. They suspected she would never be the same again.

My friend is a longtime diabetic, and I have treated him for diabetes-related neuropathy, which is very painful. His feet have been numb for many years. His spirit was broken too. His outward mental appearance became flat. Suddenly, his foot swelled, not unlike my general surgeon friend. His foot collapsed and ulcerated. He presented to my office with a neuropathy-related, diabetic Charcot foot. We again treated his wound for months. We placed a supportive, therapeutic boot on his foot.

During his appointments, we started to talk about religion and history. I was, of course, on my own quest and he on his. He started to research church history for me. It sparked something in his soul. He started to come to the office happy with my interest in his knowledge, somehow giving him purpose. He quit complaining about his wife's illness. He started to plan for his next church service. He sometimes shared the lesson with me he gave in his own services. Our discourse included Catholic and Lutheran history. After about a week, the wound decreased in size by 50 percent, and eventually to the size of a pencil tip. It had started out three inches by four inches. It is now completely healed.

His numbness continues in his feet but not in his soul. He comes in excited to his appointments. Interestingly, his wife also improved at the same time.

Healing the soul

I would like to believe that seeing a change in me affected a change in all three of these men. What if the soul truly needs to be healed, and therefore heals the body?

Have you noticed the snowball effect? When you change and act differently, so do others. This could be the situation with all of our actions. One simple smile creates a chain reaction. One smile leads to another, which leads to another, causing another and before long, many people are smiling and happier. All of our actions could cause positive reactions. For example, if you are not **conceited,** others will less likely act in a **conceited** way. If you don't compete with others, they'll have no reason to compete with you. Correct?

If you give of yourself, and thus are not **selfish,** others will notice and take the same action. Be an example to others in the best way. This includes everyone, but especially for parents with their children who are learning from us constantly.

So, when we ask, "What can we do to help change the world?", the response is, "Change yourself." The rest will follow.

CARLA

Before meditation, I believed in so many things. I had some con-voluted thoughts about making a living, loving people and religion.

Those thoughts made it all much more difficult to getting through life than it needed to be. Since learning from Mother, Isabella, God and Elizabeth how the universe works and how simple God's plan was from the beginning, I have a strong desire to set things right. I need to help God enlighten the people. I really don't care about me. I know I am the best I have ever been.

Throughout my life, I have become accustomed to settling for an improper fit "for my soul" with men and in other areas of my life. It seems that if men showed me a little attention like a father would have, I was willing to sacrifice my desires and self to satisfy theirs. I wasted myself and my life, or at least that was what I had been feeling, up until we started to meditate in 2014.

Knowing now that I had a purpose all along has healed me. I no longer see my life and marriages as a waste of time or bad decisions on my behalf. I know that it wasn't time for me. I was learning along the way as I'm sure my husbands were. I felt alone, discontent, underdeveloped mentally and spent a lot of time beating myself up for my imperfections. Although, I often tell my friends, "I never got the manual." I justified that way of thinking, for everyone but myself.

I like me. I have the peace and contentment for which I've always cried to God. I have my "rock of Gibraltar" as funny as that sounds. I have asked God over and over again during my life, "Where is my rock?" I found that support in Dave. He is my best friend. He is a pure-hearted man. He balances me. God has instructed us to take care of Tom for the rest of his days. I have lost my anger toward Tom.

I don't worry anymore and analyze my every move and thought. I have let go and have given my decisions and self to whatever God has planned. I know that it must be a great plan as God was able to rid me of the chains I carried around my neck for years.

I get into bed at night and thank God for letting me be content. I thank God for my actual ability to laugh now and for being happy. Despite what occurs in this life, I have peace, contentment and purpose now. That's all I need.

DAVE AND CARLA

Living life and following our individual paths is so much easier now knowing about the Five Simple Rules. We challenge ourselves daily remembering to make decisions without *jealousy, conceit, selfish-ness* and *unforgiveness.* The decision to *love* everyone who crosses our path is not as difficult. Once you've decided to rid yourself of the four barriers, the fifth simple rule comes naturally. You're free of the heavy burdens of life and, at the same time, liberated once understanding you can overcome your karmic debt.

Chapter 22

Reflections:
We Are Always Learning

A couple of years ago, we went to a past-lives conference featuring Dr. Brian Weiss, a psychiatrist who has worked for many years in regression therapy. He has documented many past-life regressions and has treated depression and anxiety through regression therapy. We know from meditation that "soul memory" exists. We can see this in each other, in all these past lives that we have had together. Traits, attitudes, looks and even injury follow us. This is also true of Carla's husband, Tom. For example, Tom has continuously exhibited a carefree nature in most of his past lives as he continues to in this present life.

Is it any different though than the current theory of DNA memory? It somehow follows us. Life to life, lesson to lesson. Researchers can now trace our origins through our DNA. Can we one day trace the markers on our soul? We hope so.

Finding out about who we were in the past and about the characters we played is fun, exciting and beyond fascinating; however, past lives do not control who we are right this moment. We can overcome who we were, if not at our best, by our choices in this life. Even if you are unaware of who you were in the past and whether your choices were unsavory, making positive choices about your actions and how they affect others now is the most important. Your attitude and actions affect you, others and your karma.

DAVE

So, have you asked yourself why Carla and I have been brought back together twenty-nine times either as mother-son, siblings, friends or spouses? We asked ourselves the same question over and over? Why us, why now and plain old why? Is it any wonder that Carla and I met at the ages of three and four and then again thirty-five years later?

God gave us another reason for being here this time, in this particular life. We have come back many times as family mates, Carla and me. Apparently, God believes we can work well together for one cause.

God asked that we write a book for all the world, reminding them of why we are all here. We needed to be reminded of our simple lessons. We needed to know what is true and what is not. We needed to understand about karma and reincarnation, which is not looked upon as reality or favorably by society. Some cultures believe in both, however. We, as a whole, have not been taught the simplicity of karma and reincarnation.

Our experience has been mystical. Those of us who pray, pray to God. Don't we think God listens and tries to respond back to us?

Some of you may be thinking this entire account seems unbelievable. We understand. However, we have lived it and it was very hard to understand for us in the beginning as well. Paula and Brenda were with us from the start. Paula has been our constant witness for the past five years. She has heard and lived every detail. She knows this to be true. We have laughed with emotion and cried endless times with the spiritual emotion that came along with our entire experience.

The past five years have been enlightening, overwhelmingly spiritual, touching our very cores, or souls, if you will. We had to share this. Although Mother, Isabella, God and Elizabeth have instructed us to journal and share all of our experiences, we would have anyway. We had to.

———

Things do not happen by coincidence. There is no such thing as coincidence. Is it any wonder that Carla's mother wore the exact type of shoe for dancing her entire life, allowing Carla and Paula to have it etched in their memory? So, when I was able to point out that same type of shoe to identify who I was talking to that third day, was it a coincidence? No.

Because at that exact moment, the third day of meditation, we made a choice. We decided to take a different path. That path made sense for the first time in our adult lives. Everything fit and fell into places. We had peace, contentment and realization for the first time in this life. The choice was easy. We chose to meditate again and again and again and continue to do so daily.

From my very first day of meditation, the energy was powerful. I first saw an infinity sign—a twirling energy, three-dimensional, oblong in shape. If I had not studied math, I don't know what I would have called it. Maybe an oblong, twisted, light-filled doughnut. Looking deep within this, I saw what I supposed to be an electrical grid. Points of light were connected in all directions. It appeared to be more square but spread out and twisted as it extended further out; almost impossible to see the end and the edge looking much like the horizon as it curved out of sight. It curved upon itself. There was no beginning and no end. Perfectly connected in its entirety. Every point of light connected to another.

I focused at the lights and saw small pods connected in all directions to other small pods. Three souls and one spirit guide are within each pod—soul sisters or brothers, as you might call them. All of this was created in an instant as God's plan or matrix. Those created "pod-souls" are directly connected, intended to be in your lives over and over again. The connected pods farther out are not as often.

My pod is directly connected to Carla's. Isabella is also in that pod. Carla's husband, Tom, is in my own father Harvey's pod directly connected to me and Carla's brother-in-law, Dan, also in that pod. This was so confusing. How was this all related? I found my mother was from Tom's ex-wife's pod. My grandmother is from Carla's mother's pod. The interconnections were so very present. As I meditated, I found Carla, Tom, my grandmother, Carla's mother, my father Harvey, Dan, Brenda, Paula and my good friend Willie in many other lives. Friends and family appear in various lives; all of these pods, close to us, entering our lives over and over again, helping us to learn our lessons.

Yet, this grid expands in all directions and connects upon itself. We are all somehow connected from the moment of the creation of all souls.

Drawn to each other, we are all part of the whole. Each pod is connected in twelve directions as in a dodecahedron, a three-dimensional shape with twelve plain faces, interlocked together with no space between.

Tom, Harvey and Dan have been my father, my brother, my father-in-law and, a few times, my sons. They have been my friend, teacher, owner, killer and, yes, adversary. Interestingly, they have all been Carla's husband, father-in law, father and owner.

Carla has been my wife, my queen, my mother, my sister and my friend, all within twenty-nine lives.

Of course, this is part of our karma. Isabella has told me that we have three reasons to return with others: Karmic Debt Mates, Family Mates or Soul Mates.

A Karmic Debt Mate is someone who you wronged or wronged you in a past life. God gives us another chance to treat each other correctly, while learning our lessons.

Family Mates are those we choose to return with because of the comfort we feel with these souls. In past lives we were able to learn our lessons alongside these mates. We are meant to help each other.

Soul Mates are not what you know from movies and television. They are rare. God and God alone determines them, by God's invitation only, after Atonement. If God determines you have completed all lessons regarding *conceit, selfishness jealousy, love* and *forgiveness,* God may ask you and another soul to be joined as one. A Soul Mate is to emulate God in completeness.

Apparently, Carla and I have worked well together, not been the best to each other always, but always helped one another grow in the best direction. Hopefully, we will continue on our paths successfully. Who knows, maybe this could be our last life.

Karma from both sides

In past lives, I was a Viking, fighting the Scottish and English. Then, I was Scottish fighting the English. That meant I was then English fighting my own Scottish descendants.

Carla had been of Viking descent and married off to an English King, ironically, to aid in ending the struggles between the Danes and the English. Dan, her brother-in-law in this life, was that King. We are all on every side. Fighting our brothers, sons and daughters and even fighting ourselves. Are we to ask which side was right? We live every side. This grid with our pod connections is the reason. We follow each other in life after life to learn. If we do not experience all sides of all situations, how can we learn what another goes through?

In karma, we may become who we hate. We pay for our past mistakes in another life. Isn't this an eye for an eye? We own and then are owned, maybe not the next life but in some life.

Some times our past life soul interactions are quick and for only a short time. Could that man you swore at, who cut you off in traffic, have been your father in a past life? Did this cause you to slow down and miss a deadly crash later? Everything is intended. Should you have thanked him for slowing you down? Before you are quick to anger, consider the possibilities.

Why do you think you are better than someone else? **Conceit** is wrong. If you are prejudiced against black people or anyone, you may come back as a black man or that person you hate. If you abuse women you may come back a woman, who is, indeed, abused. The employees you mistreat with poor wages because you think you deserve millions of dollars may be your boss in the next life. If you kill, you will be killed. You believe you are right about politics. You may be raised in a Republican family and come back a Democrat!

What have we learned?

God still listens. God never stops trying to reach us, despite some belief that all contact ended with God after the Old Testament. Sometimes, people just don't listen. **Love** is our number one goal, or God's most important Commandment.

While researching who to give credit to for making the world believe that God stopped talking to us after the Old Testament or in the present, ironically, we found no evidence. In conclusion, God is still speaking to anyone who will listen. We have just stopped listening.

The world is busy, we are **selfish** and self-centered. We are distracted with ourselves. It was just easier for us to blame God and say God stopped talking to us.

It doesn't matter who we are. When **conceit, selfishness, jealousy** or lack of **forgiveness** are involved, **love** fails.

Aaron and Mr. Myerson lost brotherhood because of **conceit** and **jealousy** over a woman. As a result, Mrs. Julia Myerson and their young neighbor Samuel, were murdered. Both pharaohs, Meritnieth and Djet were entitled and *conceited,* and in the end caused loss of life to each other. The Mayan Priests, Terryl and Daan, felt entitlement and power. Children suffered.

Angelo Genna, Ruby's gangster boss, killed Jonathon Wright Jr., Ruby's lover, because of *jealousy* and *power.* Colonel Robert Shaw fought against slavery yet believed he was better than his black men soldiers until the day he died. Hiram was an owned slave but *conceit* made him not follow the rules and ultimately caused his death. Athena of Lesbos was duped because of power and *jealousy*, causing death and heartache to many.

In war or the struggle to win, so to speak, there are no winners.

Carla and I have lived many lives that were not perfect. We chose the wrong paths many times and thus returned again to choose the correct path back to God. It's been six thousand years.

Did we finally achieve of our goals and choose the correct path this time? We hope and pray we got it right!

Where we are is part of God's creation of who we are. We shouldn't judge ourselves as something negative or be upset with who we are now. Because we are on a stage of life's creation. Our purpose is growth and to return back to home, God, Heaven or whatever you wish to call it.

We have learned that a happy man can nearly mend his own broken heart. We learned that when *love* is given it is returned and that includes loving yourself.

What is the path of the human soul? It is much like the path of the ruby red crystal created by God to be beautiful. Yet, *conceited, jealous* and *selfish, unforgiving* men and women trade their souls for power, greed and entitlement, just as they traded and used the ruby.

The ruby was traded for ownership, control and wealth. We cannot own another yet we try. We belittle, suppress and abuse each other. Only in *love* do we make a difference. That is our lesson.

That is the struggle of the soul. Let go of *conceit, selfishness*, and *jealousy,* and *forgive* those around you. *Love* all your neighbors as yourself. Once we have learned those lessons, we can return to God. If you follow these simple rules, you CAN overcome your karma.

Is this reason enough to try meditation? Through meditation, we are able to shut off all of the world's distractions and hear GOD!

If you ask the simple question, who is God, you'll hear the answer is, "I AM."

PART I: **I**nitiation: The admitting of someone into an obscure group, typically with a ritual.

PART II: **I**ntroduction: The formal presentation of one person to another.

PART III: **I**nscribe: To fix or impress deeply or lastingly in the mind, memory, etc.

PART IV: **A**tonement: The reconciliation of God and humankind.

PART V: **M**etamorphosis: When a person develops and changes into something different.

I AM

APPENDIX 1

Mysticism

Throughout time God has spoken through his mystics: The Adams and Eves, The Abrahams and Moseses, the Enochs, Jesus and Muhammed. The Ruths, Marys, Hagars and Fatimahs just to name a few. Why do we think these are the only ones? Why would God stop trying to reach us? Why would God stop at the New Testament or the Quran? When Christians say the Holy Spirit is working through them, what do they mean? Is God truly reaching us?

God's angels have appeared to humans, the angel Gabriel to many in the Old Testament and to Muhammed in the Quran; also, to Mary or Marian, Jesus's mother in the New Testament and in the Quran. The angel Michael appeared to Joan of Arc in the 1400s. Mary, the mother of Jesus, was reported as appearing to Catherine of Labourne in 1830 and to the children of Fatima in 1917.

Female Christian mystics like Hildegard von Bingen in AD 1169 have emerged into our current consciousness. Hildegard von Bingen stated she received divine intervention in her writing and she is quoted as saying woman may have been created from man but no man can be made without a woman. It is said her writing far exceeded her education. Catherine of Genoa, AD 1497, underwent a spiritual conversion within herself that included mystical visions. Julian of Norwich in 1350 wrote that during meditation, she learned both that sin was necessary so we can learn about ourselves and that God is both Mother and Father.

Julian wrote that God sees us as perfect and waits for the day when souls mature so that evil and sin no longer hinder us.

What do these female Christian mystics have in common? They were canonized or recognized by the church and their knowledge obtained by mystical prayer, otherwise known as meditation.

We would direct you to Thomas Merton, a relatively recent Catholic Trappist monk and writer who was inspired by Zen Buddhism, and the exploration of the higher self. He was one of the most prolific Christian mystics and writers of the last century. Although he died in 1968, before his death, he wrote seventy books on spirituality, social justice and pacifism. He was a proponent of interfaith understanding. He wrote about his own vision of being a Buddhist monk as a dream, most probably in a past life. He often discussed Zen Buddhism as a way to explore his own Christian beliefs and gain enlightenment. His books address nondualism and dualism as the theory of Christian growth. Nondualism teaches that humans are responsible for their own actions and choices and can only rectify this themselves versus God's forgiveness of the failings of man through Jesus. He discussed that, as a Catholic, he could only believe that the two must be together and his knowledge was gained through his mystical experiences, a.k.a. meditation. Merton encouraged self-contemplation, reminding us that everyone is extraordinary and everybody is ordinary.

Merton wrote that every moment and every event of every man's life on earth plants something in his soul. The beginning of love is to let those we love be perfectly themselves, and not to twist them to fit our own image. Otherwise, we only love our reflection we see in them.

In the last analysis, the individual person is responsible for living his own life and for finding himself. If he persists in shifting his responsibility to someone else, he fails to find out the meaning of his own existence.

In much the same way, we could direct you to Rabbi Aryeh Kaplan who died 1983. He was well versed in Kabbalah, or Jewish mysticism. Again, how does one meditate and find greater knowledge of God and himself? Jesus used the techniques of Kabbalah taught to him by the Essenes, a Jewish religious order of the time. Kabbalah is highly spiritual and engages personal meditation to reach God and greater understanding of the self. The Sefirot, or the Tree of Life, as it is referred to during Kabbalah, tries to understand the masculine and feminine side of God. During meditation, the participants of Kabbalah examine the branches of the tree, referred to as God's wisdom, mercy, justice, beauty and glory. The final thought is that God exists both as mercy and justice. Interesting that they describe mercy as masculine and justice as feminine.

The scales of Lady Justice are pictured as female and date back to early Greek and the Egyptian goddess, Themis or Maat, also referred to as Isis. The Egyptian goddess Maat is described as regulating the stars and seasons. She sets order to the chaos at the moment of creation. Why are so many stories of creation parallel? Why are there male and female counterparts to the gods in Egypt and Greece? Why are there male and female parts to God in Jewish Kabbalah? Does God keep revealing the essence of male and female?

Mystical thinking and meditation also occur in Islam. Sufi Muslims especially talk of reaching Sohbet. Sufis are one specific sect within the Muslim faith. Sohbet is a deep meditative state in which group consciousness takes over and words and meanings are more easily understood. Peace overcomes. Communication becomes easier, with the spiritual world. The Sufi experience continues yet deeper to an acceptance and knowledge of the oneness of God. For the Muslim, they would know that God created them beautiful and that beauty is inside you. You are to let yourself feel it and believe it. You are at peace. Your heart is at peace. Allah is all. **Love** is not complete until one states, "You are me, and I am you. We are one." You see that God is present in all. Meditation serves as a way to reach the divine presence. Interestingly, Muslims also describe God as having a feminine side with attributes of gentleness, providence, *love* and compassion. Yet, they would argue that God has no sex at all and is only one.

Meditation in Buddhism may seem different than the above, yet it, too, is a belief system, but with no God. Is it yet inspired? It teaches enlightenment and that all suffering is from wanting. I would say that also translates to mean ***jealousy, conceit*** and ***selfishness*** and that contentment comes from lack of ***conceit, jealousy*** and ***selfishness***. Self-awareness of your actions is what is necessary.

The Buddhist word for finding enlightenment is *upeksha* (u-peksha), meaning the wisdom of equality. It is nondiscriminatory, as we put ourselves in another's skin and become one with them. There is no self. *Love* cannot be possessive and it cannot be to satisfy the self. That is not loving.

Can you see a similarity between the beliefs of Catholics, Muslims, Buddhists and Jews? Is it possible we all have the same beliefs and are arguing over nothing?

Quietism

Another demoralizing act by Pope Innocent XI was his outlawing of quietism, along with his financing of the beginning of slavery between the Roman Catholic Church and men like Horatio Volente.

Quietism was a term given in the Roman Catholic Church to a system of religious mysticism teaching that perfection and spiritual peace are attained by annihilation of the will and passive absorption in contemplation of God and divine things; also, a passive withdrawn attitude or policy toward the world or worldly affairs. What this was, in all actuality, was meditation.

The Church could not control persons reaching peace and passivity through meditation. So, they declared it heresy. The pope believed that meditation caused humans to become whole and have no need for prayer or fasting to find God. This practice left no place for the Church or priests. A person could reach God all by himself—or herself.

Again, the need for power and entitlement over another superseded everything else. The Church was now the owner of GOD too. The Church would dictate when and if we reached our GOD.

The practice of quietism was taught by a Spanish priest, Molinos, in the latter part of the seventeenth century, and gained popularity quickly in Spain, Italy and England.

It was also referred to as Molinism. Pope Innocent XI stopped quietism quickly in 1687 and retained his control over his people and their thoughts. Luckily, he didn't control the entire world of meditators. It continued throughout other cultures.

So, ask yourself. Would you like to try meditation?

Legend of Past Lives

Dave has had forty-two lives; Carla has had thirty-four lives. Included in this story are twenty of their past lives and the sequence of each. Together, they have shared twenty-nine lives.

4000 BC David and Ariela	Dave and Carla's 1st life
3700 BC Raina and Dotin	Dave and Carla's 2nd life
2980 BC Djet and Meritneith	Dave's 6th and Carla's 4th life
1250 BC Carlisse and Dedu	Dave's 13th and Carla's 8th life
600 BC Athena and Gregorius	Dave's 17th and Carla's 12th life
AD 200 Xan and Cao Jie	Dave's 22nd and Carla's 15th life
AD 800 Cara and David	Dave's 26th and Carla's 18th life
AD 896 Oahd and Fenella	Dave's 27th and Carla's 19th life
AD 1000 Emma of Normandy	Carla's 20th life
AD 1421 Henry VI and Sussan	Dave's 31st and Carla's 23rd life
AD 1504 Katrina and Giovanni	Dave's 32nd and Carla's 24th life
AD 1604 Robert and Sarah	Dave's 33rd and Carla's 25th life
AD 1670 Eden and Hiram	Dave's 34th and Carla's 26th life
AD 1704 Samuel and Julia	Dave's 35th and Carla's 27th life
AD 1863 Col. R. Shaw and his mother	Dave's 37th and Carla's 29th life
AD 1925 Ruby and J.J.	Dave's 38th and Carla's 30th life

AD 1940 Miscarriage to Carla's mother — Dave's 39th and 40th life

AD 1944 Johnny and Katie — Dave's 41st and Carla's 31st life

AD 1950 Miscarriage to Dave's mother — Carla's 32nd and 33rd life

AD 1962 Dave and Carla — Dave's 42nd and Carla's 34th life

APPENDIX 3

Legend of Characters

BRAD

- Paula's son in her present life.

- Egypt, 2980 BC; slave at the palace of Djet and Meritneith. Freed by Djet.

- Half-brother of Cao Jie. Son to Cao Cao, China AD 200.

- Son of Paula and Argos, Isle of Lesbos, 600 BC.

- Tavern worker, Bermuda, late 1600s, with Joan. English tavern worker.

- Viking son of Paula, Scotland, AD 900s

- Bouncer, D'Andre's, Chicago, 1920s. He escorted Jonathon Wright Jr. into the alley, where he assisted in shooting him to death. He also assisted in the murder of Jonathon Wright Sr.

BRENDA

- Youngest worker in the medical office with Carla and Dave for many years.

- Daughter of Katrina and Giovanni in Italy, 1500s.

- Grandchild to Djet and Meritneith, Den's child born after their demises.

- Neighbor to Julia Johansen, bringing food to her wake.

- Handmaiden to Queen Athena, named Leda. She delivered messages for her.

- A daughter to Hiram and Eden, she died early in childhood before the English came.

- As Elizabeth, her grandparents Sarah and Robert in England, called her "precious."

- Terryl, the High Mayan Priest, never bled out his own daughter. His wife sent Brenda away before it could happen.

- Oahd and Fenella were given the Red Ruby Crystal in exchange for Brenda's hand in marriage, in Scotland during the Viking raids.

- She is Sussan's daughter, Agnes, half-sister to King Henry VI.

- In Darien, Georgia, burned to the ground by the Union soldiers during the Civil War, Brenda was Elizabeth Roseanne Harkess, engaged to Pierce Mease-Butler, who was murdered during the raid.

- Jonathon (J.J.) Wright never met his mother, Katherine (Brenda). She died giving birth to him, broken-hearted after the kidnapping and murder of her innocent four-year-old daughter, Sara Wright, in Nashville, late 1800s.

- Ruby Donaldson's best friend and coflapper was Lila. Ruby left her daughter Rose to be raised by Lila and her husband in 1920s Chicago.

CARLA

- Office manager for Dave at his medical office since 1998.

+ Tom's present wife for the past twenty-five years.

+ Sister to Paula, Cleo, Patrice, Sharyn and Joan in this life.

+ Katrina Rosetta Carlotta Farnese, Rome, Italy, 1500s, married to Giovanni Caponi.

+ Meritneith, first female pharaoh, Egypt 2980 BC, murderer of husband Djet, mother of Den.

+ Cao Jie, last Han Dynasty empress, married to Emperor Xian and in love with Xan. They had six children together, Tom, Paula, Brenda and another son and two more daughters.

+ Julia Johansen, married to and murdered by Mr. Fred Myerson; Tom in this life.

+ Schoolmate and friend of Samuel Renner, the stutterer.

+ Got pregnant by Aaron Myerson, Fred's brother, Carla's former husband in this life.

+ Athena, Queen of the Isle of Lesbos. Betrayed by Hathos and Pitticus, lover of Gregorius, her soldier.

+ Eden, an indentured servant in Bermuda in the 1600s. Married to Hiram.

+ Carlisse, daughter of Tomo and Fauna. Lover of Dedu, mother of Joseph, Egypt 1250 BC. Moved to the Valley of the Kings for her husband to carve for Rameses II.

+ Sarah, wife of beloved Robert, England, 1600s. She died of consumption, giving her locket and ticket to America to her neighbor, for passage to America.

+ Parishioner of the Rev. Henson in England, who was Don, Carla's neighbor at present.

+ Sarah Sturgis Shaw, mother of Colonel Robert Gould Shaw, Boston, Massachusetts, 1860. Sarah's husband, Francis, Robert's father, was Dave's grandfather, Albert.

- Ronna, sisters to the four Mayan little girls, tortured and bled by Terryl the High Priest in Chechen Itza 700 BC. Paula, Patrice, Sharyn and Sheila were the four other sisters.

- Fenella, Viking-turned-Scot, lover of Oahd.

- Emma of Normandy, wife and queen of King Aethelred, The Unready, and Canute, The Great Viking descedent given in marriage to England for peace.

- Sussan of England, King Henry the V's eleven-year-old consort and mother to his illegitimate daughter Agnes. Lover and stepmother to King Henry VI.

- Daughter of James and Anna Donaldson, who sent their three young daughters to Chicago to work in a sweatshop.

- Ruby Donaldson, flapper in 1920s Chicago. Murdered by gangsters. Lover to J.J. Friend to fellow flappers Lila, Daisy and pianist Annie. Mother to Rose.

- Ruby was sister to Nancy and Bessie.

CLEO

- Sister to Carla, Paula, Patrice, Sharyn and Joan, presently.

- Aunt Mae, sweatshop owner, Chicago 1920s. Lover to Angelo Genna.

- Caroline, wife of Captain John Smith and owner of Eden and Hiram, Bermuda 1700s.

- Maid to Emma of Normandy and King Aethelred, sleeping with the king.

- Nobility responsible for releasing Sarah of England's parents from servitude.

- Cousin of Ronna, the Mayan virgin; their mothers were sisters.

+ Cleo was Angus's daughter, the Scotsman attacking Oahd, the Viking with a little stick.

+ First Empress Xian before Cao Jie; ousted by Cao Pi, through a coup d'etat.

+ Aaron Myerson found comfort in her in Rapid City in between seeing Julia Johansen.

+ As a slave of Djet's and Meritneith's, she had the honor of being buried alive with her king in his tomb, in Egypt.

+ Pope Paul III's consort, Ms. Orsini, had other friends, consorts of other cardinals. She was a friend of Ms. Orsini, whose daughter played with Katrina. She was the mother of Tullia d'Aragona, the famous Italian Renaissance poet and our former editor, Maureen. Ironically, Cleo's keeper was Carla's present-life father.

DAN

+ Married to Cleo, Carla's older sister, brother-in-law to Carla, Paula, Joan and Patrice. He passed away during the writing of this book.

+ As Cao Cao, he was Cao Jie's father in China and the Warlord to her emperor husband, Xian, in the year AD 200. Xan, Cao Jie's guard, was one of his chosen warriors and guards.

+ Peasant boy who was a friend of Athena and Gregorius's son, Doros.

+ Captain John Smith, married to Caroline, and father to Jillian and her brother on the island of Bermuda in the late 1600s. He cherished his indentured servants Hiram and Eden and their children Moren and Cellen. He attempted to buy off the constable, Alex Dyer, with ruby red crystal in exchange for freeing Hiram from lashing.

- Dan was Tomo's brother, in Egypt, 1250 BC and uncle to Carlisse. He was married to Patrice in that life, his sister-in-law in this present life.

- Ronna and Shanta's uncle during the Mayan life, 700 BC, married to their mother's sister.

- As King Aethelred the Unready, of England, his arranged marriage to Emma of Normandy, of Danish descent, was an attempt to make peace between the Vikings and English.

- He was Henry VI's carriage footman, who drove Henry and Sussan to their country estate regularly, where they hid their illegitimate daughter, Elizabeth.

- Dan and Patrice were again husband and wife, in Chicago in the 1920s and were the neighbors to Aunt Mae's boarding house. Aunt Mae tried to seduce Dan many times without success. Eventually, they were responsible for alerting the police to the illegal activity at Aunt Mae's home.

DAVE

- Medical doctor at a small office in Ohio, where Carla, Paula and Brenda work.

- Giovanni Caponi, son of Armando (Tom) who owned the apothecary in Rome, Italy, in AD 1500. He married Katrina Rosetta Carlotta Farnese.

- Pharaoh of Egypt 2980 BC, Djet. Freed many slaves, only to upset his queen and son, causing his murder. Den, his son, was Carla's first love in this life, John.

- Xan, Cao Jie's guard and love; a guard who was handpicked by her father for his loyalty and personality mirroring his daughter's needs.

- The stuttering, eight-year-old Samuel Renner, who was bound, roped and left for dead in Fred Myerson's shed after witnessing Mr. Myerson's brutal murdering of his wife, Julia Johansen.

* Friend to Julia Johansen from school.

* As Gregorius, a soldier on the Isle of Lesbos, he won the heart of his Queen Athena, spending his final night before a fatal battle with her. Gregorius never met their son, Doros, who was born nine months after his death and was actually himself reincarnated.

* Hiram was a righteous, pure-hearted, indentured servant who loved his wife, Eden, in Bermuda in the late 1600s. His close relationship with his master, Captain John Smith, was not enough to stop the brutal lashing that ultimately killed him.

* Dedu, a stone cutter in Egypt late 1200s BC. He worked with his own crew under Tomo, Carlisse's tyrant father. He eventually took her away to the Valley of the Kings to carve the famous burial grounds for the Rameses kings. Their son, Joseph, followed in his father's footsteps as a stone carver. Joseph is the son of Diane in this life.

* Robert of Cotswold, England, early 1600s, loved his Sarah more than life itself. She died before they made it to America to free themselves from taxes. His tombstone read, "He lost his life when he lost his wife, in the old country." He took with him, to America, and named his granddaughter, "Precious."

* Daan. As an underling priest, to Terryl, in Mayan times 700 BC, it was his responsibility to bring virgins for bleeding to the temple. He secretly administered a tree bark, mixed with water, to lessen the pain and fear associated with the experience. He and his son, Jarra, later killed Terryl to stop the bleeding and torture. Jarra is Diane's son in this life. Daan arranged for Jarra and Ronna to marry before his own murder, knowing they both had been injured and would be suited to each other.

- Oahd was Fenella's Viking husband and leader, invading Scotland and choosing to stay in the late 800s BC. He was the original owner of the red, ruby crystal, given to him in exchange for his daughter's hand in marriage. He gave it in exchange for safety of his family and people, back to the Vikings upon their invasion in later years.

- Hugon was a child when he met and fell for Emma of Normandy, at her home in France, where his parents were servants. He gave up on Emma when her family moved away, never seeing her again.

- Henry VI was said to be crazy, so history has told. He was speaking with Isabella, not talking with demons in his head. He was son to Henry V (Don, Carla's neighbor) and to Catherine of Valois (Dave's second wife.) His half-sister was Agnes (Brenda) and a daughter with his love, Sussan (Carla) was Elizabeth. His first cousin was Paula, and her mother was her Aunt Mary in this life. His grandmother was Carla's present mother. (Henry V's mother.)

- As Colonel Robert Gould Shaw, he led the 54th Regiment, all-black Northern army in the Civil War, to their deaths in the second battle at Fort Wagner, Charleston, South Carolina. He was shot in his Bible, in a previous battle, by Silas (Willie) but actually killed by his present-day barber's father in that lifetime.

- Robert's favorite sister, Josephine, was Carla's present-day mother. Carla was his mother, Sarah.

- Robert's soldier Ricker, at the burning of Darien, Georgia, presented him with a ruby ring taken from the hand of Elizabeth R. Harkess (Brenda).

- Jonathon Wright Jr. (J.J). lost his life when killed at gunpoint by the Chicago mob for flirting with a flapper named Ruby Donaldson. His mother was Brenda, father was Harvey and killer was Carla's neighbor Don. Camille, the flapper in the bar who confirmed J.J.'s identity, which got him murdered, was Ona, Athena's rival, Meritneith's slave, a friend of Robert Gould Shaw's mother Sarah and Carla's friend in the present, Jenny.

DIANE

- Carla's friend since childhood in this life.

- Schoolmate of Julia Johansen's.

- Wife of Thomas Silversmith in Bermuda, late 1600s. Her husband bought Moren, the married daughter of Hiram and Eden, and later had six children with her.

- Carlisse's mother, Fauna. She was selfish and unavailable to Carlisse as a mother.

- Wife of Timothy, Robert's brother in Cotswold, England, in the early 1600s; also Ann, Sarah's older sister.

- During Mayan times, she is a mother of other little girls, bled by Terryl, in the village.

- Ruby Donaldson's grandmother, mother of Anna, Ruby's mother.

DON

- Was Carla/Tom's neighbor in present life.

- A soldier in Cao Cao's army, Cao Jie's father, China, AD 200.

- A soldier in Ona's army, he died at the hand of Gregorius, Athena's lover during his last battle, Isle of Lesbos, 600 BC.

- Constable Alex Dyer, tyrant responsible for lashing Hiram on two occasions, the second being fatal. He swindled the ruby red crystal from Captain John Smith under the pretense of not lashing Hiram, only to renege and flee with Horatio Volente to America. He swapped the crystal for his voyage to America.

+ He commissioned Dedu through Tomo to carve his burial tomb in The Valley of The Kings, as Rameses II, in Egypt 1250 BC.

+ As the Rev. Henson in Cotswold, England, early 1600s, he attempted to molest Sarah in her home while Robert was working. He enforced their taxes after she did not accept his advances.

+ A Mayan guard who murdered Daan in the Temple after the killing of Terryl the High Priest. Daan took the blame although it was his son's doing. 700 BC.

+ King Sweyn Forkbeard of Denmark in the late 900s. His son, Canute the Great, married Emma of Normandy after her husband King Aethelred died. Sweyn was given the ruby red crystal by Kehldr, after taking it from his brother Oahd. Canute kept the crystal until he traded it back to Scotland in later years.

+ King Henry V of England of the House of Lancaster, mid-1400s, father to Henry VI and illegitimate daughter Agnes (Brenda) by eleven-year-old consort Sussan (Carla). He placed the ruby red crystal in the top of his sceptor, using it as a weapon against Sussan.

+ Well-known architect in Nashville, late 1800s, whose secret life as a serial killer finally catches up with him when an unsuspecting father, Jonathon Wright Sr., finds clues to his daughter's whereabouts at Douglas's home and murders him.

+ Bouncer at D'Andre's in Chicago 1920s, he murdered J.J. and discarded his body in Lake Michigan. He later murdered Jonathon Wright Sr. to stop his snooping and questioning as to his son's whereabouts.

GERARD

- Stepdaddy Dearest in this life to Carla, Paula, Joan, Patrice and Cleo.

- Pope Paul III and father of Katrina Rosetta Carlotta Farnese. Born Alessandro Farnese, he went from cardinal to pope in 1534. His long-standing consort Ms. Orsini, mother of Katrina, was Carla's present-day mother.

- Servant in the palace of Emperor Xian and Empress Cao Jie, he cleaned the chamber pots and emptied the garbage, China in AD 200.

- Neighbor to Captain John Smith family and Hiram and Eden's family, Bermuda, late 1600s. His daughter, Priscilla (Paula in this life), played with Jillian, Moren and Cellen.

- Nobility in Cotswold, England, in the early 1600s, he was married to a woman (now Cleo.) They released their indentured servants, Craig and Katherine, parents to Sarah. Setting them free to begin their lives with their children and live as "Freemen," the name they adopted.

GRANDMA

- Dave's infamous, miracle-laden grandmother in the present life.

- Giovanni Caponi's mother's mother, making her his grandmother, Italy, 1500s.

- Djet's mother's mother was her again, making her Dave's grandmother in that life also.

- Mrs. Johnson, Julia Johansen's teacher, and Samuel Renner's teacher and confidant.

- Athena's mother, married to Carla's Nonu in this life, Isle of Lesbos, 600 BC. She dies before Athena reaches adulthood.

- ✦ Dedu's grandmother, on his mother's side, Egypt 1250 BC.

- ✦ Sarah Freeman's mother, Katherine, in Cotswold, England, early 1600s.

- ✦ Sister to Hdejh (later Oahd), Copenhagen, Denmark, late AD 800s.

- ✦ Maid in the estate where young Emma of Normandy lived. Hugo's parents also worked there as servants.

- ✦ Cao Jie's older maid, who attended to her always and at consummation.

HARVEY

- ✦ Father of Dave in this present life.

- ✦ Father of Djet of Egypt, 2980 BC and preceded him as King Djer. His present-day wife was his queen during his reign as pharaoh.

- ✦ As Emperor Xian, he married Cao Jie in name only but later gave her permission to live as she desired.

- ✦ Horatio Volente was the cause of slave trading on Bermuda in the late 1600s. He made a deal with Captain John Smith, offering a ruby red crystal to bribe him into allowing slave trading on the Island. He is responsible for then taking the ruby red crystal back to America along with Constable Alex Dyer during his flight from persecution.

- ✦ His father and a stone-cutter slave under Dedu, in Egypt 1250s, leaving with him to later help carve the burial sites in the Valley of the Kings.

- ✦ Amos in Scotland, who first discovered, with his son, Baine, the ruby red crystal, given in exchange for a woman's hand, Oahd's daughter.

- ✦ Edward the Peaceful, father of King Aethelred the Unready, married to Emma of Normandy. That made him Emma's father-in-law.

- Jonathon Wright Sr., a wonderful, caring father, who inadvertently placed his son in the hands of the mob. He asked for a favor from Henry Spingola, giving J.J. a job as a junior bank officer. Not knowing it was a cover for the mob, it ultimately led to his son's death. Jonathon Sr. made too many waves after his son's death, and the mob murdered him.

- His wife, JJ's mother and Sarah Wright's mother, was Brenda. Sarah, J.J.'s older sister that he never met, is his present sister today. Jonathon Sr. purchased a ruby red ring for his wife in Nashville, while his four-year-old daughter Sarah was being murdered. Katherine never wore the ring, even though it was bought through love.

ILENE

- Carla's very dear friend in the present life. They met many years ago at the YMCA.

- One of Cao Jie's personal ladies, who tended to her daily needs, China, AD 200.

- Eden's sister, Asene, Bermuda, late 1600s. She was a maid at Priscilla's house right across the street from the Smith Plantation.

- Fern, who lived in the Scottish village where the Vikings attempted to ravish her, in AD 896. She was working in the same potato patch as her friend, Fenella.

- Daisy, the other singer with Ruby at D'Andre's in Chicago, 1920s. They became good friends, causing Ruby's parents to disown her for fraternizing with colored people.

JAIME

- Carla's first husband from 1977 through 1993.

- Counsel to Den, Meritneith and Djet's son, in Egypt 2980 BC.

* Aaron, Mr. Fred Myerson's brother, he impregnated young Julia Johansen, promising to marry her. He slept with Cleo, Carla's present older sister in Rapid City, South Dakota, while performing his marshal duties.

* Husband of Bernadette (Dave's former wife this life) and a church-goer with Sarah and Robert in England, 1600s. He was a tax collector. He mentioned to Bernadette about liking Sarah's red-trimmed dress, which sent Bernadette into a tizzy, causing her to tell Sarah it was inappropriate for church.

* One of Oahd's Viking soldiers, who invaded Scotland. Although, he decided not to stay, his brother (Paula's present-day husband) chose to stay with Paula. He was the soldier who piped in with, "They have women" when Oahd decided it was not honorable to ravish them.

* Angelo Genna was a short, stocky, stern-faced, angry man. He had no respect for women, and especially Ruby Donaldson. He couldn't break or own her. But he took his revenge out on the love of her life, J.J., ordering his killing and booting her out of the bar afterward. He had ongoing affairs with Aunt Mae, Camille and attempted to with every other flapper available.

* Husband of Lucille Spingola, who is his granddaughter in the present life.

JENNY AND PAUL

* Present-day husband and wife, acquaintances of Tom, Carla and Dave.

* Jenny, a slave in the palace, Egypt 2980 BC. She is jealous of Meritneith's wealth and position. Meritneith frees her after Djet's death.

* Ona (Jenny), Athena's rival from Smyrna, Turkey, the closest land to the Isle of Lesbos, 600 BC, encourages

Pittacus (Paul) to urge Athena to attack her country, knowing she is much more powerful and Athena's army cannot win.

❖ Paul is a priest who performed the marriage of Emma of Normandy to Canute the Great, England AD 1017.

❖ Phillip (Paul) and Alexandria (Jenny) attend as friends of Sarah and Francis Shaw, in 1860s Boston, Massachusetts, to the home of Colonel Robert Gould Shaw's parents, who hosted a party for Robert's wedding.

❖ Camille (Jenny), a flapper in 1920s Chicago at D'Andre's speakeasy, who entertained as a singer and dancer. She also entertained Angelo Genna after hours until Ruby came along, that is. She had it out for Ruby. She alerted the bouncers and identified J.J. the night they murdered him. Because she no longer had Angelo's attention, she became very fond of one of the card dealers, Reggie (Paul). The two eventually left the bar, finding employment at a restaurant, and then married.

JOAN

❖ Older sister of Carla and younger sister to Paula, Patrice, Cleo and Sharyn.

❖ Male adviser to Den, son of Meritneith and Djet in Egypt, 2980 BC.

❖ Cao Pi, half-brother to Cao Jie in China, AD 200. They shared the same father Cao Cao.

❖ Joan is Cao Pi's brother, and Cao Jie's half-brother.

❖ A trapper in South Dakota, late 1700's with Julia Johansen's father, who happened to be Joan's second husband in this present life.

❖ A tavern worker in Bermuda, late 1600s. She watched from the crowd as Hiram was lashed to death.

+ Midwife, who tended to Sarah on her deathbed, Cotswold, England, early 1600s.

+ First cousin in the Mayan days to Ronna, Shanta and their four other sisters. She was bled and tortured by Terryl previous to their ordeal.

+ Customer to the D'Andre's speakeasy in Chicago, 1920s with her present husband in this life.

JOE

+ Son of Diane, Carla's childhood friend, in his present life.

+ Son, Joseph, of Carlisse and Dedu, Egypt, 1250 BC.

+ Son of Timothy and Ann in the Cotswold area of England, early 1600s. Timothy and Ann are Tom and Diane in the present life.

+ Jarra, son of Daan, who kills Terryl and marries Ronna (Carla), Mayan life, 700 BC.

JOHN

+ Present life, he was Carla's first love in high school.

+ Den, Meritneith and Djet's overly zealous son, who murdered his mother, Egypt, 2980 BC.

+ Soldier in Athena's army, Isle of Lesbos, 600 BC. He had interest in Athena, although she did not return his interest. He worked the same post as Gregorius on opposite shifts.

+ A friend of Cellen, he was included in the young slave men who attacked and murdered many English soldiers in Bermuda, late 1600s, Hiram getting the blame.

LYNN

+ Dave's younger sister in present life.

+ Illegitimate daughter of Cao Jie's sister with the Emperor
  Xian, China, AD 200. He had his way with both of Cao
  Jei's sisters while he had already decided to marry Cao
  Jie. (She was born to Dave's mother and father in that
  life as well.)

+ Sarah and Robert met her in Liverpool, England, when
  they traveled on Stallion for vacation, purchasing the red
  trim for her new dress. Lynn was the innkeeper's wife
  where they stayed.

+ Maid servant to Henry VI's mother (Dave's former
  present-day wife), England, 1450s. She was present at
  Henry's birth, her present-day brother. She was not willing to care for the queen and her son. Therefore, Henry
  was passed off to Sussan to raise.

+ Sarah Wright, daughter of Jonathon Wright Sr., slain by
  a serial killer, a well-known architect in 1890s Nashville
  who murdered six blond four-year-old girls. She was
  the seventh. Her father killed the murderer (Don) upon
  learning his daughter had been the seventh victim.

MARIE

+ Coworker with Tom in this life; worked as a nurse.

+ Second wife of Fred Myerson, South Dakota early 1700s,
  after Fred kills Julia, his first wife. Julia and Annabelle
  were friends. She and Fred later had three children.

+ She's a slave belonging to Thomas Silversmith, Bermuda,
  late 1600s.

+ Wife of High Priest Terryl, in the Mayan days 700 BC.
  Mother to Brenda then.

+ Mother of King Aethelred the Unready (Dan), who was
  married to Emma of Normandy.

+ Anna Donaldson, second wife of James Donaldson, parents of Ruby Donaldson. She sent her three daughters,

Nancy, Ruby and Bessie, to Chicago for a better life, she thought. She sewed her Aunt Ruby's red ruby ring in the hem of Ruby's dress for an emergency, it being the only thing of value left in the family. She kept it secret from James her husband.

MOTHER

- Cindy in this life and mother to Carla, Paula, Patrice, Cleo, Sharyn and Joan. She acts as our Gatekeeper, keeping any future predicting from us.

- Ms. Mattea Orsini, mother of Katrina Rosetta Carlotta Farnese and consort of Pope Paul III. She was a friend of Giulia Campana, mother of Tullia d'Aragona (our former editor). Katrina taught Tullia to write and paint. Interesting, in this life, she was an editor to us.

- Maid to Cao Jie, in China AD 200. She helped to lift her wedding gown in preparation for marriage consummation. Cao Jie favored her. She removed her wig, makeup and gown the first time Xan and Xu (Cao Jie) made love.

- Mother of Robert Smith of Borough; died working in the fields while he was a child.

- Amaranda, Queen Athena's wiser and older adviser. She arranged Athena and Gregorius's only night together.

- Eden's mother in Bermuda and approved Hiram for marriage after viewing his agility and potential to procreate, along with Eden's grandmother. Her grandmother was Dave's grandmother in this life.

- Ronna and Shanta's aunt in the Mayan life on their mother's side, who was Mother's first cousin Connie in this life.

- She was Paula's Viking daughter, living in Scotland in AD 900. Paula and her husband were in Oadh's troop of Vikings invading other countries.

- Grandmother to Henry VI, mother to Henry V, aunt to Paula then.

NONU (Grandfather in Italian)

- Carla's grandfather in the present life; her name taken from his, Carlo.

- Member of the Counsel. He will speak for Carla and Dave when they pass. He was a beautiful, kind, thoughtful man on Earth and apparently, a very fair one, in Heaven.

- Meritneith's father who raised her to be entitled, Egypt, 2980 BC.

- Athena's father on the Isle of Lesbos, 600 BC. He passed the throne to his daughter much to the dismay of the male politicians. He died early, making her queen at twenty-one.

- Craig, Sarah's father in the Cotswold area of England, early 1600s.

- A lesser, underling priest with Daan in Mayan days, 700 BC and conspired with him to murder Terryl.

- Arthur, Henry's trusted friend, who had been an advisor for Henry V and VI. He carefully watched over Henry VI while his mother was still in the castle. He cared for Sussan as well. The country estate of Henry VI and Sussan, England 1400s, was where they would escape to, to be with their daughter and free themselves of the politics of the royal world.

PAULA

- Dave's medical assistant in his office and Carla's present sister, in the present life.

+ Julia Johansen and Mr. Myerson's neighbor in South Dakota, early 1700s. She attends Julia's wake and brings food for Mr. Myerson. She is married then to her grandson now.

+ Agnes, who lives on the Isle of Lesbos, 600 BC. Her mother is the advisor, Amaranda, to the Queen, Athena. Her father was "Paul, The Breadman" her mother's lover in the present life. Her love is Argos.

+ Priscilla, who played with Hiram and Eden's children as well as Capt. Smith and Caroline's daughter on Bermuda, late 1600s. Gerard was her father then, our step-father now.

+ Prudence, married to a tax collector (her daughter's friend George in this life) in the Cotswold area of England in the early 1600s. She hung around with Bernadette, Dave's former wife. She attended Sarah and Robert's church as well as their wedding. She, along with another church woman, stayed with Sarah while she was ill and dying.

+ Ronna and Shanta's Mayan sister, who was bled and brutalized by Terryl The High Priest as were other young virgin girls in her village.

+ A Viking woman named Gehlda, married to the same man in the present life. They chose to stay with Oahd and Fenella in Scotland to live out their days. Her now-mother was her then-daughter, and her son in her present life was in that life as well.

+ First cousin to Henry VI. Her illegitimate father was her son in this life and the brother of Henry V of Lancaster. Her mother then, was her Aunt Mary in the present life.

+ Bank assistant to J.J. Wright during the 1920s in Chicago, Illinois. Her name was Jane, and she was again married to her present-life husband, a driver for Angelo Genna (Carla's former husband). In the present life, the two men lived together and met Paula and Carla through each other. It is fascinating to learn that her present-life son and Carla's neighbor Don, were together in England and then again as bouncers at D'Andre's in the 1920s.

PATRICE

+ She was sister to Carla, Paula, Cleo, Sharyn and Joan. Patrice passed away in 1992.

+ As a nun, she served under Cardinal Farnese at Basilica di Sant'Eustachio, Rome. Patrice arranged Katrina's gown right before walking down the aisle, saying, "Dear, let's make your dress as beautiful as it can be."

+ The daughter of Caroline and Captain John Smith, Jillian was raised and cared for by Eden until adulthood.

+ The daughter of nobility, (to Cleo and Gerard) she was chastised for playing with the servant's daughter, (Craig and Katherine's daughter), Sarah, in Cotswold, England, early 1600's.

+ Sister to Ronna and Shanta, she was bled and brutalized by Terryl, Mayan life, 700 BC.

+ Neighbor and sister to Aunt Mae, Chicago, Illinois, 1920s; she and her husband eventually alert the authorities to the goings-on at the boarding house.

SHIRLEY ANN

+ She is Carla's very dear, sweet friend in the present life.

+ Meritneith had released her from slavery, in Egypt 2980 BC. Den, her son, reneged on it, burying her alive in his mother's tomb.

+ Rosalind, who worked at the local eatery with Julia Johansen. She attended the wedding to Mr. Fred Myerson. She also attended her wake. She did not approve of their marriage. She was aware of Julia's relationship with Aaron Myerson. She believed Fred to be too old.

- In Egypt, 1250 BC, she was married to one of Dedu's stone carvers working at the site with Tomo. Her husband happened to be her longtime fiancé in this lifetime, Sam. They moved to the Valley of The Kings to work, with Dedu and Carlisse. They were friends in that life too.

- Roseanne, maid to the consort of Henry V kept Sussan from the age of eleven as his consort. She stayed at Windsor Castle most of the time.

- Annie, was the piano player for the flappers at D'Andre's in 1920s Chicago. She played the organ at the wedding of Angelo Genna and Lucille Spingola, accompanying Ruby as she sang.

S.K.

- She is currently Carla and Tom's daughter-in-law, married to Tom's son.

- A slave to Djet and Meritneith, she is freed by Meritneith, even though she is stationed in the palace.

- Xan rescued her as an orphan of war. She was taken to a school started by Cao Jie, (Empress Xian Mu) for other such orphans.

- Slave to Thomas Silversmith, Bermuda late 1600s. She was married to Tom's grandson then, and he was also a slave.

- Daughter of Timothy and Ann Cotswold, England early 1600s. This made her Sarah and Robert's niece. Tom's now son was her brother then.

- Nancy, the two-year-older sister to Ruby, Chicago, Illinois, also sent by train with Bessie to make a new life for themselves. Oddly, she did meet Tom's son in this life as well, but he was an awkward paperboy who never quite approached her in the right manner. Nancy was spared from D'Andre's and the life of gangsters, by Ruby. She made sure of it. Although, she could sew and still can. She died, soon after Ruby when Aunt Mae set the sweat shop on fire.

TOM

- ✦ Carla's husband at the present and for the past twenty-five years. He met Dave and sold his medical practice to him in 1998.

- ✦ Armando, Giovanni's father and owner of the apothecary, in Rome, Italy, in the 1500s.

- ✦ Fred Myerson, in South Dakota in the early 1700s, married and murdered Julia Johansen after learning she had an ongoing relationship with his brother Aaron. He also murdered young Samuel Renner, the stutterer. He also murdered the other neighbor who he accused of stealing one of his cows. It seemed that his second wife, Annabelle, had an affair with that neighbor, from which a son was born. Fred was jealous. He used the excuse of stealing to get rid of him. It just so happens that this supposed cow stealer is the father of Carla's former hairdresser in this life.

- ✦ Thomas Silversmith, slave owner in Bermuda in the late 1600s. He bought the daughter of Hiram and Eden, Moren, despite the fact she was married, took her away from her husband and kept her to himself. They had six children during their lifetime. He was kind to her, although she was still his slave.

- ✦ Tomo, Carlisse's tyrannical father, Egypt, 1250 BC. He sent Dedu off to carve for Rameses II (Don, Carla and Tom's neighbor). He was married to Fauna (Diane).

- ✦ Timothy, Robert's older brother, who later married Ann, Sarah's sister (Diane).

- ✦ Terryl, High Priest, Mayan life 700 BC, married to Marie then. She worked with him, presently as a nurse.

+ Ruby's father, James Donaldson, who died in 1934 shortly before Tom was born in 1935.

TRUDY

+ Mrs. Williamson, Dave's fourth-grade teacher in Nebraska, who left midyear due to cancer, which actually took her life in 1969. She was one of Dave's favorite teachers.

+ Carla's former hair stylist in the present life.

+ Burial specialist for the palace kings in Egypt, 2980 BC. She arranged Djet and Meritneith's burials and their tombs.

+ Her father is shot by Fred Myerson for supposedly stealing his cow. He is their neighbor and she is again her father's daughter as is in the present life. South Dakota early 1700s.

+ Her present-day father was her father in the late 1800s in the South. He was the officer who shot and killed Colonel Robert Gould Shaw at the battle of Fort Wagner, South Carolina.

+ Her father then (her mother now), was an underling priest to Terryl, The High Priest in Mayan life 700 BC. She was never bled and brutalized. She was present at the sacrifice of the young warrior in the opening Mayan story, who was her father in this life.

+ Bessie, Ruby Donaldson's little sister, only five years old when they traveled by train to Chicago to start a better life. She replaced Ruby in D'Andre's at the hand of Aunt Mae, at age thirteen. She was unable to satisfy the customers, and Angelo. He slapped her across the face after scolding her. She slapped him back. He strangled her, right then and there, to death.

- My step-son in the present life. Tom, my husband's favorite son.

- Vatican guard for Pope Paul III, Katrina's father in Rome, Italy AD 1500s.

- An orphan of war, Xan brought him back to attend Cao Jie's school. Her children also attended the school she had started. Therefore, he went to school with his present father who was Empress Cao Jie's son. China, AD 200.

- Hathos, a general for Athena's army in Isle of Lesbos 600 BC. He conspired with Pittacus to be head commander and, indeed, took over the palace post when her army was killed in battle.

- Thomas Silversmith's grandfather, Bermuda, early 1600s, although not a resident of the island.

- Soldier told to discipline a slave by Tomo, but refuses. Tomo struck him in the head, although he wore a helmet, then turned and struck the slave without a helmet, killing him instantly. Egypt 1250 BC.

- Paperboy in a newsstand on Halstead Street, Chicago, Illinois, 1920s. He misses his chance with Nancy, Ruby's sister, due to his awkwardness. Ruby often sees him on her walk to work.

WILLIE

- Dave's good friend in this present life. They share golf, life and a special gift from God.

- As a guard at the Papal Palace at The Vatican, he drove the pope's personal carriage and actually drove Gio and Katrina to their first date at The Sistine Chapel. He was a guard at their wedding in the Basilica di Sant'Eustachio, Rome.

* Soldier for Djet and Meritneith in Egypt 2980 BC.

* Soldier under Cao Jie's Father, Cao Cao, China AD 200.

* Trapper in the same town where Julia Johansen and Samuel Renner lived in South Dakota, early 1700s.

* Chief commander, Demacus, in Athena's army on the Isle of Lesbos, 600 BC.

* The man who doles out the food portions on the boat sailing to America in the early 1600s. He secretly slips Robert extra fruit portions for "Precious" during the journey to keep her well.

* Kehldr, brother of Oahd, (formerly Hdejh), who takes their only valuables, being five silver coins and the red, ruby crystal in lieu of ravishing their land, possessions and women.

* Illegitimate son of Edward I, Longshanks of England who led the English invasion of Scotland in the late 1200s against "Braveheart" William Wallace. He is responsible for confiscating and returning the ruby red crystal during that battle.

* Silas, who shot Colonel Robert Gould Shaw in his Bible, injuring but not killing him. Shaw's bullet took Silas's life, not allowing him to keep his promise to Great Aunt Ruby of marriage which he had done so with a ruby ring from Atlanta.

Authors' Biography

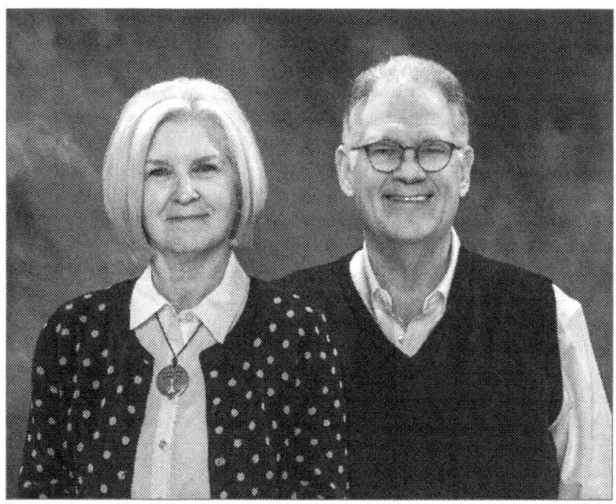

The authors, Dave and Carla, are on a spiritual path, sharing their story with the world.

Dave and Carla teach Meta Meditation classes and The Five Simple Rules for Living; live without conceit, jealousy, selfishness and with forgiveness and love. They trained under Dr. Brian and Mrs. Carole Weiss in Past Life Regression Therapy at The Omega Institute. Dave and Carla have used meditation, self-hypnosis and hypnosis in regression therapy.

Made in the USA
Coppell, TX
26 September 2020